D0065065

I DON'T

BY THE SAME AUTHOR

The Slender Balance
For Better, For Worse

I Don't

A CONTRARIAN HISTORY OF MARRIAGE

Susan Squire

BLOOMSBURY

Copyright © 2008 by Susan Squire

All rights reserved. No part of this book may be used or reproduced in any manner
whatsoever without written permission from the publisher except in the case of brief
quotations embodied in critical articles or reviews. For information address Bloomsbury
USA, 175 Fifth Avenue, New York, NY 10010.

Published by Bloomsbury USA, New York
Distributed to the trade by Macmillan

All papers used by Bloomsbury USA are natural, recyclable products made from wood
grown in well-managed forests. The manufacturing processes conform to the
environmental regulations of the country of origin.

LIBRARY OF CONGRESS CATALOGING-IN-PUBLICATION DATA HAS BEEN APPLIED FOR.

ISBN-10 1-58234-119-2
ISBN-13 978-1-58234-119-4

First U.S. Edition 2008

1   3   5   7   9   10   8   6   4   2

Typeset by Westchester Book Group
Printed in the United States of America by Quebecor World Fairfield

For Namp

"Marriage then . . . is what you call the monster?"

—Henry James, *The Golden Bowl*

Contents

CONTENTS

A Note to the Reader

THIS is a story about the idea of marriage in the West: why it came about, what it was supposed to accomplish, who was behind it, and how it was implanted into the minds of the many—where it remains, whether the many are conscious of it or not. Prepare for an archaeological dig, layer by layer, into the shared subliminal-memory bank.

It's impossible to understand why married life is so confounding, even at the best of times for the most contented of couples, without understanding the historical nature of the beast. It's impossible to distinguish between what can be fixed and what can only be accepted as par for the marital course without some awareness of what that course has been.

Reproduction: That's what marriage is about in the ancient world. When reproduction is the priority, policing the sexual behavior of women becomes essential.

Lust control: That's what marriage is about when the Church—in its singular, pre-Reformation form—writes and imposes the rules of sex.

Love: Marriage as we know it is anchored in the Protestant vision of conjugal life. This book ends when that vision begins to take over the culture in the sixteenth century. You already know what happens after that.

Prologue

To call it "lovemaking" eons before anyone develops the idea of love, let alone links it to sex, would be absurd. In primal time there are no romantic delusions, no secret trysts, no promises, no privacy, no future plans. There's only lust, followed by sex—mindless sex, even for the creatures with minds.

So humans aren't "making love", not yet, but they've already assumed the position without which lovemaking will be virtually unthinkable: belly to belly, length to length, face to face, eye to eye. And in this human proclivity for frontal sex—for "making the beast with two backs," to use the crude Elizabethan phrase—lies the potential for romance, emotional entanglement, erotic passion, and love love love, marital and extramarital.

In the future, who has sex with whom, and when, and where, and in what position will become a very complicated business indeed. What matters in primal time is survival, which depends on rapid reproduction, which depends on copulation unfettered by conscious thought. History will demonstrate ad nauseam that once sex becomes mindful and thereby meaningful—once people figure out, for example, the cause-and-effect relationship between copulation and conception—making the beast with two backs will be subject to impediments. This can't happen too soon, or we wouldn't be here. Evolutionary logic suggests that the endgame of sex escapes awareness until humankind nails survival. There will be plenty of time for impediments later on.

How much later? That question can be answered only speculatively, and loosely, by considering the archaeological timeline. The ability to make tools—a sign of rudimentary intelligence at work—dates back about 2.5 million years. But there's a vast cognitive distance between putting together a spear and putting together something as abstract as, say, a mythological explanation of life's origins, and it takes practically forever to close. Given that distance, and the fact that while maternity is obvious, paternity is not, people probably don't connect sex to reproduction for many hundreds of thousands (if not millions) of years.[1] Until this vital association is made—until men realize that women do not conceive new life all by themselves—there's little reason, in the Darwinian sense, to put the brakes on sexual activity, men's or women's. Notions of morality, propriety, guilt, and sin haven't been formed. Nor has the double standard of fidelity, that future anchor of marital law. And marriage itself—the civilizing agent of sex—hasn't been institutionalized. These developments await a series of external events that begin to converge in prehistory, some time after 12,000 BCE.[2]

By then, modern humans have fully evolved and subdivided into three races. Traveling in groups, or tribes, they're on the move, fanning out from Africa around the globe. Some tribes have already settled around the great river valleys of the Near East, and others inhabit caves farther north in what is now Europe, but most remain nomadic; they follow the food supply wherever it leads.[3]

Tribal members, men and women, pool their skills and their cunning to fend off the recurrent perils of common life. Their united struggle against starvation is waged on two fronts, animal and vegetable—both essential food sources—by two different teams. Innate logic dictates that the labor be split along gender lines. Men's greater strength, higher muscle-to-fat ratio, and unencumbered biology obviously suit them to the rigors of hunting; the breeding cycle limits women's mobility (and when it bears fruit, compounds their tasks), making the job of gathering plants and grains best suited to them.

Crossover is possible. There may be the occasional woman who is rugged enough to haul a spear over treacherous terrain and who's also blessed with the acute vision to spot fast-moving prey, along with the sharp reflexes and sheer raw nerve to kill it—or be killed. There may well be the occasional man who does better in the field than on the trail. Still, it seems safe to say that female hunters and male gatherers are about as representative of the tribal population as female breadwinners and male homemakers are of the average middle-class marriage today: not very.

But while men and women labor daily at different tasks in different places, as they will in the future, it's likely that "women's work" has yet to be downgraded in comparison to men's; women themselves have yet to be downgraded in comparison to men. In the common struggle for survival they are mutually indispensable—each sex contributes something essential that the other isn't equipped to procure or produce on its own—and therefore of relatively equal stature.

Everything is shared: food and water, fire and shelter, the care of children, and the grown-ups' reproductive equipment. Men and women participate in a fluid, inclusive sexual system that anthropologists generally call "group marriage." Its existence can only be assumed (this is prehistory, after all), but the musical-chair-like mating game the term describes is certainly feasible and even probable—simply because such an arrangement would favor survival.[4] Biology alone inhibits mating, although only for women who are already pregnant; as long as there are other ovulating women available, men's work is never done.

Group marriage is plausible while sexual behavior remains un-civilized and instinctive, outside of conscious control. But once the mystery of conception is solved and the idea of ownership is born, it becomes untenable. Organized communal sex will never work again—and not for lack of trying. Both the Marxist-inspired free love movement of the mid-1800s and the open marriage idea

3

spawned by the so-called sexual revolution of the early 1970s, to name two recent incarnations, will be embraced by the outré few and quickly consigned to the dustbin of history's "radical social experiments" without ever attracting more than voyeuristic interest among the majority.[5]

As it happens, the death knell for group marriage (and mindless sex) has already begun to ring. The gender parity that has presumably been the pattern for eons will be reconfigured in relative seconds—a casualty of the civilizing process.[6] What catalyzes that process? It's undocumented by human hand, but there are enough environmental clues to suggest a plausible scenario. Those clues lie in a sequence of interrelated events, precipitated by something that could not sound more mundane: a change in the weather.[7]

Let's say that sometime between 10,000 and 8,000 BCE, in the vicinity of the Mediterranean Sea, a wandering tribe hacks its way through dense underbrush. Upon emerging, these nomads stop dead in amazement. They stand at the edge of a field fertile beyond imagining, a vast edible tableau of golden grains and wheat begging to be harvested, and promising to yield more than enough food to feed everyone for a year. The air is warm, the soil is rich, the sun glitters. Why not stay for the night—and the next, and the next? The gatherers get busy gathering; the hunters, having investigated the verdant forests surrounding the open land and found them full of well-nourished animal life, get busy hunting (and saving time, too, without fruitless hours and days spent tracking elusive prey). Pretty soon the group concurs that chasing the food supply when it's right in front of you, replenishing itself as fast as it's consumed, no longer makes sense. The wandering days are over. The group settles down.

Global warming, of a sort, has made this new phase of human existence possible. The fourth, the longest and (so far) the last, Ice Age has ended. The frozen sheets, hundreds of feet thick, which had turned most of the northern hemisphere into a gigantic skating rink for the past hundred thousand years, have finally returned to their Arctic origins. The newly temperate worldwide climate brings hot, dry summers and cool, moist winters to the Near East, and umpteen generations of European cave dwellers migrating south in search of hospitable temperatures find their way there.

The change in the weather changes everything. It makes settled life possible and sparks the development of farming, which leads directly to an electrifying epiphany—an intellectual eureka moment of incalculable significance. Now that men have become sheperds rather than hunters, they're able to observe animal behavior at close range, day after day. One day the lightbulb goes on.

Here's the scenario: A shepherd watches a ram trot over to a receptive ewe and mount her. When the act is completed, the ram doesn't lie down and go to sleep (as the man, given his druthers, might at such a moment). Instead, he mounts a new partner—sometimes a dozen more before the day's over. Several weeks later, the shepherd notices that the bellies of these same ewes appear to be swelling. The shepherd knows the likely result of this peculiarly female shape-shifting process, but until now has never guessed the cause. In lieu of evidence to the contrary, he assumed that baby making was self-generated by females and wholly unrelated to the sexual act. Suddenly, he gets it.

The shepherd has stumbled upon what will soon be the glaringly obvious truth about male sexuality, human and animal alike: Ejaculation, gratifying though it may be, is not the end of copulation but the midpoint, the indispensable—and heretofore missing—link between copulation and conception. He already knows that his sexual anatomy, which enables him to penetrate a woman's body, is a source of physical pleasure and release. Now he begins to grasp that it is also a source (*the* source, he will soon decide) of life itself. The bellies of women do not swell of their own accord; men must first sow their seeds within. He grasps that his own life-giving power, awe-inspiring in itself, is also—more awe-inspiring still—potentially without limit. While a female is capable of being impregnated only when she's ovulating, and only by one

5

male at a time, allowing the human female to give birth about once a year, a healthy man has the ability to impregnate numerous women—at any time, on any day, of any month, between puberty and death.

In this matter of procreation, men have spent eons upon eons underestimating themselves, and eons upon eons overestimating women. They won't let either happen again anytime soon. On the contrary, now that lightning's struck, they will steadily magnify their reproductive role—until, with a major assist from Aristotle, fatherhood comes to mean nearly everything and motherhood almost nothing. It helps, of course, to be able to document this self-directed progression to stardom. Thanks to the invention of writing, that documentation will be ample indeed.

Exhibit A: The word "seed" is mentioned no less than 222 times in the Old Testament, where it is deemed so precious that to spill it anywhere but inside a reproductively capable woman's reproductive orifice (and none other) is to incite the murderous wrath of God.[8] Exhibit B: In classical Athens, the citizens (all of them, by definition, male) are so enamored of their life-engendering equipment that sculptures of massive erections dominate the cityscape as ubiquitously as crosses later will in Christian Rome.[9] Exhibits C to F: the words incubator, container, receptacle, vessel. To describe the entirety of the maternal role as it will shortly be perceived, pick any one.

Men have always surpassed women in physical strength. The newfound knowledge of paternity helps to anchor in consciousness the idea, or the hope, that men surpass women on the more profound level of *being*—of intrinsic human worth. Over time the notion becomes axiomatic for both men and women and a matter of public policy, whatever the private truth may be. From it, the principle of *patria potestas*, literally "the rule of the father," follows logically.

How curious, then, that men should seem so threatened—so oppressed, especially in marriage—by women, affirming and reaffirming their physical, intellectual, and moral superiority, yet claiming repeatedly to be outmaneuvered and undone by what all presume to be the weaker sex. The intertwined story of women and marriage is largely filtered through a testosterone prism. Because of that, it reveals very little about women's experience, but plenty about what men think or imagine women's experience to be. Which is to say it reveals men's experience of women. Which is to say it reveals men. And men, throughout this story, often seem stymied by women, no matter what measures they take to protect themselves. Western history and literature teem with treacherous females who have their way with men. They have it by stealth, by seduction, by coercion, by dissembling, by their wits; in any case they have it regularly.

More exhibits: Eve hands Adam temptation without disguising it, and he bites. In her wake are Delilah and Jezebel, who somehow force a great warrior and an enthroned king, respectively, to betray or dishonor everything that matters to their society. Elsewhere, in the Mediterranean, Homer constructs an epic poem around the presumption that one woman's beauty will prove toxic enough to start a war and ultimately level an entire society. Recurrent suspicion that women can render men flaccid or tumescent at will, through witchcraft, helps to fuel four hundred years of mass hysteria from Spain to Germany to the American colonies, leading to the ostracization, torture, and execution of alleged evildoers, 80 to 85 percent of whom happen to be female.[10]

What compels the designated stronger sex, whose members produce and preserve the work that defines Western culture, to view itself repeatedly as an easy mark for members of the designated weaker sex? If one side is really convinced of its superiority to the other, why the need to issue ceaseless reminders on that score? How can men have at their disposal an arsenal of weapons, including law and custom weighted heavily in their favor, to be used against women—who have, in any tangible sense, zilch—and yet project themselves as defenseless victims *of* women?

As men's tangled history of their lives with women unfolds through fact and fiction there's a refrain that emerges, a subtextual complaint that the composers may not even recognize, and it reverberates between the lines century after century. In the domestic and sexual union that is unique to married life, there seems to be an inherent contradiction between authority and power. The difference is far from obvious. A husband's authority over his wife is endorsed, accepted, indeed commanded—by God, by law, by social consensus, every which way—from the beginning, without question. It should go without saying that he who has the authority automatically has the power as well, but in marriage this turns out to be not quite true.

In marriage, men cannot help revealing themselves, exposing themselves—physically, emotionally, spiritually, sexually, one way or another—to their wives. This is also true in reverse, of course, but the stakes are so much lower that a wife's exposure can do no worse than to confirm the assumption at the heart of patriarchal marriage: Women are inferior to men as servants are to masters, and no one expects much from inferiors. But masters have a hell of a lot to lose and a hell of a distance to fall. Either way, they're vulnerable.

And here "the rule of the father" comes back to haunt the fathers themselves. That's the source of the power that men unwittingly bestow upon their wives. Whether the women wield it or not is up to them—and if literature mirrors life, sources ranging from the Bible and Roman mythology to Renaissance tragedy, Restoration comedy, and straight through to the modern age teem with women who do. "Men," states one of them in 1993, "exist in a state of perpetual enmity towards women."[11]

But these hellishly complicated feelings men hold toward women across the ages track back to the paternal awakening, to the moment when the rapture fades and the anxiety creeps in. The heightened sense of potency has a flip side: heightened vulnerability. Against it men try to armor themselves. Instituting "the rule of the father" provides a semi-safe harbor along the shoals of daily life. It means that wives enjoy the same legal status as children and slaves, which is to say none. They're deprived of civic voice, property rights, and all the rest. But the buffer systems men devise are no more than that. Awareness of paternity afflicts them with apparently permanent insecurity. They often seem stumped by their need for women, starting with the undeniable reality that women possess the only suitable containers in which seed can thrive. And that's the heart of the dilemma: How can a man be sure that it is his seed alone she breeds, not his brother's or cousin's or neighbor's? The answer, until the advent of DNA technology in the 1980s: He can't.

"It's he who has no wife who is no cuckold," Chaucer writes in the latter half of the fourteenth century,[12] crisply distilling one of the most persistent themes in Western culture since the start of history. The belief spans ancient, medieval, Renaissance, and even Victorian eras: women are sexually rapacious, indeed insatiable. A catch-22 arises out of the prehistoric paternal euphoria, eventually becoming a historical constant: Women must be controlled, but women can't be controlled.

When civilization finally stirs in its Near Eastern cradle, men have just begun to feel uneasy. How can they safeguard the precious paternity they've just discovered? They've awoken to a problem that they identify as Woman, and now they set about solving it. At the outset there's no reason to think that success might elude them. After all, if goats and dogs and cows can be domesticated and possessed, why not women?

So the civilizers make the control of sex their first priority. It's the right move at the right time: To control sex is to control reproduction, and to control reproduction is (theoretically) to control women, by controlling their access to sexual partners—and to control women is to ease or even eliminate entirely the threat to men. They devise numerous strategies to achieve this goal, and though their successors adjust the mix, tailoring the details to fit the times, at all times men reach for the same end, and fall short.

Of those strategies, three eclipse all others: patriarchal marriage ("the rule of the father"); the double standard of sexual fidelity

9

(loose for husbands, rigid for wives); and confinement at home ("woman's place"). Men put these tactics in play at the start and keep them in play throughout history.

We'll see how well they work.

ONE

Paradise Lost, Just Because He Listened to His Wife

H ERE's the heart of the matter, the belly of the beast, the big slam dunk: the first, and until modern times the only, template for marriage in the West. With the consistent backing of Church, state, and society, this becomes the one-size-fits-all standard of behavior to which husbands and wives must conform (or else), dictates their respective roles, and defines their mutual obligations. It governs the development of Jewish and Christian doctrine as well as secular law. Its impact on marriage and family life has been, to put it mildly, significant. It's the idea that will not die. And it's a marvel of concision, to boot.

One line. Six words. Eight syllables. The book of Genesis, chapter 3, verse 16: *Your husband . . . shall rule over you.*[1] So God commands Eve when he returns to the garden after his seventh-day rest to find her and Adam skulking around, covered in fig leaves and shame. As long as religion holds sway over the West, so will the belief that the Bible is a literal transcription of God's words, and so will the belief that God's commands are final, subject to neither challenge, revision, nor dismissal by humans. So too, then, the belief that when God commands Eve to be ruled by her husband, he commands all wives to be ruled by their husbands—and, by implication, commands all husbands to rule their wives, which will not go unnoticed. And there things stand for umpteen centuries.

The idea of husbands ruling their wives would not be news to most people living in the biblical era. Work on the book of Genesis—a collaboration between several writers/editors plucking themes and variations from a vast oral network of source narratives—is thought to span most of the final millennium BCE (c. 1200–1000 to c. 200 BCE). For contemporary Israelites as well as their pagan neighbors, Genesis 3:16 restates the obvious. Hierarchy is common protocol. Subjects must obey their kings, servants their masters, children their fathers, wives their husbands. Nothing else makes sense, for now. People don't possess the leisure, the life span, the social permission, and God knows what else to mess around with horizontal power-sharing arrangements, or even to imagine them. This world order is vertical; it's all about chains of command, and the rough justice that awaits those who break the chain. Break it they do, of course, men and women both—and if they're discreet, they might just get away with it. Otherwise, they'll be pilloried by their communities.

The distance between what is supposed to be and what is can be immense, as these men and women already know from experience. Some husbands don't, won't, or can't rule their wives; some wives don't, won't, or can't obey their husbands, no matter what. And that's the beauty of Genesis 3:16. Cast as a direct order from God himself and delivered with the infinite force of his certitude, the writers transform secular consensus into divine imperative. God-fearing men and women take divine imperatives very seriously indeed—more seriously, perhaps, than secular ones. Considering that God-fearing men and women will be the rule and not the exception until, let's say, the nineteenth century, this is an excellent move. In addition to social pressure, spouses have another reason—a sacred duty—to play their prescribed roles, something that the religious establishment will pointedly remind them at every opportunity. And if further inducement is needed, there's the biblical God himself. His attitude toward humans who fail to take him or his orders seriously will soon become apparent.

This God is unlike all other gods worshipped in the ancient world, and not just because they are plural. He doesn't belong to or even lead a pantheon of immortals, nor does he incarnate some element of nature (heaven, earth, sun, sea) or of human experience (love, war, wine, fertility). He *is* the pantheon; he incarnates nothing, yet is everything; he is indivisible. He is also, most uniquely, invisible. Awestruck biblical characters testify to their personal encounters with God, who seems to be everywhere at once—atop a mountain, emanating from a shrub, gliding through a garden in the cool of the day. They tremble and swoon when he approaches; they swear that his presence is palpable, terrifyingly so. Yet they cannot see him. In the Israelite conception, God does not, in any material sense, exist. Any suggestion to the contrary, any attempt to anthropomorphize God, to carve or paint or engrave his image as other cultures depict their idols, is anathema. (The mere idea that he would assume human form to wander barefoot through the Galilee as a Jewish rabbi named Jesus of Nazareth, preaching to crowds and sharing meals with disciples—much less bleeding while nailed upright to a cross—will be reason enough for the Jews to reject Christianity out of hand.)

If God is sui generis, so must be his creative process. Accordingly, the primal saga that plays out in the first three chapters of the Bible distinguishes itself from the start. Typically, these ancient myths ascribe the birth of heaven and earth and so forth to the divine performance of a familiar human activity. Both the Babylonian and Assyrian myths, for instance, begin with an act of copulation between god and goddess (solid evidence, surely long after the fact, that men's reproductive role is no mystery). The Egyptian rendering makes it hard not to infer that men there must really be on a roll: The great sun god Atun stands on a precipice, masturbating, and at the climactic moment he aims his semen into the watery depths far below.[2] Who needs to make the beast with two backs when all you need is your hand? But the God of Genesis works in no way that humans can discern or comprehend; the writers don't even try to do either. Biblical creation, like the creator himself, is inscrutable and abstract, a manifestation of divine intellect. Let's just say that God thinks, and therefore we are.

Although we're not anywhere, yet. Genesis takes its sweet

time, twenty-six verses in all, getting to the human arrival. "In the beginning," as the Bible famously begins, all is nothing, vast and unformed and empty, with darkness shrouding the water (as in other ancient traditions, water is present before heaven or earth or anything else, signaling its primary importance to life), sometimes rendered in English as "the deep." But there is also, in verse 2, "a wind from God sweeping over the water," for God is already rolling up his metaphorical sleeves. In verse 3 he pounces. "Let there be light," he says, and light there is. He calls it Day, separating it from the darkness he now labels Night; he summons dry land, and dry land appears, which he calls "Earth"; he tells it to produce plants and herbs and fruit-bearing trees, each "containing its seed after its kind," and Earth complies. He summons the sun, "the greater light to dominate the day," and the moon, "the lesser light to dominate the night," and the two lights perform as instructed. Having spent the first four "days," as the Bible reckons, arranging the inanimate universe to his liking (step by step he revels in his work, "sees" that it is "good"), God begins to populate it. He conjures living creatures out of nowhere, it seems, other than his mind, and sets them aloft in the sky or swimming in the sea or crawling across the earth, exuberantly and flawlessly orchestrating their movements. Whatever God says—or thinks, or wills—into existence, there it is, just like that; and whatever he commands is done. With this track record established in chapter 1, the biblical audience has every reason to assume that when God tells Eve, "Your husband . . . shall rule over you," in chapter 3, this too will be done.

With each life-form, God makes a point of differentiating male from female, equipping them all with whatever they need to comply with his directive to "be fertile and increase" (also rendered, in the more poetic but also more antiquated parsing, "be fruitful, and multiply"). God himself, you may recall, has no body and is therefore neither male nor female. Yet whenever the writers substitute a pronoun for "God" or the alternatives (Yahweh, Elohim, et al.), as writers must sometimes do in reference to major characters, for variety's sake, they invariably use "he"; whenever they substitute a nonspecific noun, they invariably use male-identified ones such as "Lord" or "Father." How can they do otherwise? They're unfurling a novel theology, centered on a novel God, for a society that could not be more conventional at this time and in this place. Under these circumstances, novelty can go only so far. The rule of the biblical God is the rule of the Father writ very large indeed: God is the immortal patriarch all mortal patriarchs serve. Besides, God is omnipotent—and that's as male as it gets. He can't be "she" or, God help us, "Goddess," and as for the linguistic contortions that English translators of the past few decades have willingly performed for the sake of gender neutrality, sacrificing authenticity on the altar of political correctness . . . but let's not go there. He has to be, and should remain, "he."

On to Day 6, or in literary terms, verse 26, and the long-awaited human moment, which is confusing as hell. For there are in fact two moments, occurring on two different Day 6s, Genesis 1 containing the first, and what happens here corresponds not at all to what happens next. Both accounts, thought to be composed by two different authors working generations apart, make it into the finalized text of Genesis and into the biblical canon, to be copied over and over in Greek and Latin and later printed en masse in countless languages. To this day, in the gazillion Hebrew and Christian editions of the Bible available all over the world, both remain in place, with the discrepancy often footnoted and occasionally analyzed at length. But only the story of Adam and Eve, which begins in Genesis 2, becomes a thematic touchstone for the philosophers, theologians, social commentators, artists, and literary lions whose work receives continued public exposure over the centuries, with the effect of cementing it into cultural memory.

The Genesis 1 account, however, leaves a mark as enduring as a snowflake's. It's there in the text, yet effectively out of sight, invisible to the mind's eye. This is the case even after the fifteenth-century convergence of widespread literacy and mass printing ensures the Bible's ubiquity across Christian Europe, and it's still the case as I write. (Try asking ten reasonably well educated people how human creation unfolds in Genesis, and consider it astonishing if more than one of them parries with "which version?") And here's the gist of the first account: "male and female He created them."

Simultaneous creation: male and female, together, at once. As if God intends them to be equal in stature, a notion so alien to so many people for so long that the collective mind fails to absorb it. Having created male and female in unison, God addresses them in unison, though his initial statement would be fully acceptable to this society—in fact, Jewish tradition regards it as the first of the Torah's 613 commandments: "Be fertile and increase." The directive is assumed to include marriage. (Biblical scholars have spent thousands of years debating whether it extends to women, but the majority thinks not; men alone are so obliged, once they turn eighteen.) After that perfectly reasonable utterance comes a mindblower: God appears to grant the man and the women, together, joint dominion over the earth. Again he speaks to them in unison. "Fill the earth and master it; and rule the fish of the sea, the birds of the sky, and all the living things that creep on earth."

Master? Rule? Of all the traditionally male-specific words in the English language, of all the sturdy semantic barricades erected to separate the men from the girls, these two tower above the rest. Yet the text implies something extraordinary: Here is God, the patriarch of patriarchs, nimbly breaching those barricades, placing the ruler's scepter between the man and the woman for them to share in their divinely designated roles as co-masters of the universe. None of this is made explicit; all of it is, in the premodern context, unthinkable. In any case, thinking about it has yet to occur to ordinary people.

Genesis 1 tells the story that no one remembers, but then there's no story here to tell. There's no action, no conflict, no characters to love or hate, zero emotional content, nothing to inspire middling works of art, let alone great ones—in short, nothing to compel remembrance. Once God tells the humans to fill the earth and so on, that's it; he doesn't make rules that can be broken or set limits that can be exceeded, not here. The human event boils down to "male and female He created them": a single statement, a summary of what happens after it happens. Which is probably just as well, because that statement appears to undermine the sexual status quo. Combine a politically untenable message with lack of narrative punch (lack of narrative, period), and no wonder this account induces historical blindness. Without a hook, you can't even hang a Sunday sermon on it—a major issue in the medieval world to come.

From the fall of Rome to the Reformation, daily life operates on a religious rather than a secular schedule; for the vast majority, exposure to the Bible is virtually unavoidable. But since illiteracy is widespread among the laity for most of that period, exposure to the Bible is largely aural—and controlled by the Church, through local priests. If people don't hear it, they won't know it's there. You can bet that the average priest won't waste much if any breath on the simultaneous-creation nonsense of Genesis 1. Why bother even mentioning an idea that is not only subversive but has no moral traction, nothing useful to say about—just for starters—the sin of disobedience or the tricky nature of women, when he can skip right over it and go straight to the story that has everything?

What Genesis 1 covers in twenty-six leisurely verses, Genesis 2 crunches into six. Having thus summarily dispatched with God's first five days of labor in what amounts to less than two paragraphs, the writers roll out, frame by riveting frame, what is arguably the most influential narrative in Western literature. It starts in verse 5, when God notes the need for a "man to till the soil." He shapes "the dust of the earth" into the form he deems appropriate and blows the "breath of life" into its nostrils. The result, in Hebrew, is "*adham*," a gender-neutral word meaning "humankind" or "human," which in conventional English translations loses its neutrality to become "man," or in Christian editions, "Adam." (As a rule, the Hebrew Bible uses "man" exclusively.) Since the man has been made expressly to till the soil, God places him in the garden "east of Eden" to do just that. The man will need sustenance, so God causes the ground "to grow every tree that was pleasing to the sight and good for food," placing in the middle "the tree of knowledge of good and bad" (or as it is sometimes translated, "evil"). This time he limits human access: "Of every tree of the garden you are free to eat," God instructs, "but of the tree of knowledge of good and bad you must not eat . . . for as soon as you eat of it, you shall die." What God means isn't that the man will drop dead on the spot, only that he will become mortal.

Having dropped that bomb, God surveys the human environment. The man has food, shelter, a job, and the first of many rules to live by; still, the Omniscient One knows that his work is not yet done. "It is not good for man to be alone," he muses. What will relieve man's solitude? That depends upon the Bible at hand: whether it's aimed at Jews or Christians, where on the spectrum between rigidly orthodox and implacably secular those Jews or Christians fall, what the particular sensibility of the translators and editors involved happens to be, and when the translation is done. The possibilities can range from the "helpmate" of several centuries ago to the profoundly anachronistic, highly current "partner suited to him," and splitting the difference, "a helper as his partner."[3] In my Hebrew Bible, God says this: "I will make a fitting helper for him." It's Groundhog Day, apparently, for now God proceeds to make—again—"all the wild beasts and all the birds of the sky." Only this time he forms them as he formed man, "out of the earth," and it takes less than a sentence. Does God really hope to find a "fitting helper" for a human among wild beasts and flying birds? There's nothing in the text to suggest otherwise.

Like an eager kindergartner at show-and-tell—God is at his most endearing in this sequence—he parades the potential candidates before the man "to see what he would call them," as God himself called out the names of earth and sun and so forth in Genesis 1. Dutifully the man comes up with names; as a human, he is capable of recognizing the nature of other creatures, which makes him capable of labeling them. But he also recognizes his own nature, and sees that he shares it with none of the birds or beasts on display. By the end of this exercise, the man is still alone, and God will not rest until he solves the problem. Which he does, right away, by performing a surgical procedure that will yield a "fitting helper" for the man, and that's not all. The monolithic Church of the future, command center for social as well as religious life, will take from this operation exactly what it needs to promote and enforce its vividly convoluted teachings on marriage, sex, and women. What the Church takes—or so it will claim, to great effect—is unassailable evidence that women are inferior to men, which nicely coincides with evolving Christian theology. The religious establishment could not dream of a more fitting helper to promote its agenda.

The surgery begins, sensibly enough, with anesthesia. In verse 21, God casts a "deep sleep" upon Adam in order to open him up and extract one of his ribs. (The rib idea may have been lifted from Sumerian lore, already an ancient source in biblical times, about a goddess or other being known as "Nin-ti," translated as "Lady of the Rib"—or, alternatively, "Lady of Life," from which "Eve" derives.)[4] Then God closes up the patient's flesh by undisclosed means and proceeds to fashion the rib into a living being, human like the man yet distinctly other than a man. With this second—but, notably, sequential—act of human creation, God's primal work is done. When he shows the result to Adam, who is by now wide awake, there's no doubt that this being suits the man as none of the skyborne or earthbound creatures could. Adam is joyful: "This one at last is bone of my bones and flesh of my flesh," he exults. In the next verse, 23, the man does for the woman as he has done for the other living beings—he names her. "This one shall be called Woman, for from man she was taken." (Why "woman"? The Hebrew *adham*, "man," is used generically for "human being" in Jewish bibles; the Old English prefix "*wer*" or "*wyf*" is added to distinguish between, respectively, male and female. But Middle English drops "*wer*" entirely in favor of "man," which from this point forward is used to specify "male human be-ing," while "*wyf*man"—now updated to "woman"—is retained to indicate the female variety.)

Sequential creation: man first and primary, woman second and secondary, point taken. A further point: God might have cho-sen to make the woman of "dust from the ground," just as he made the man (and in the Genesis 2 rendition the birds and beasts, too). She'd still be secondary, yet of independent origin. But God makes her *of* man, *from* man, a literal subsidiary; even her name, in He-brew and English, derives from man's. God's chosen method proves his intent: Women are inferior to men not because society says so (although it does), not because men need to feel superior (although some do), but because *that is God's plan*. So the Christian tradition will have it—and that's the one that counts. (Not a few Jewish thinkers will argue the opposite, that by making woman of man's rib, God signals their equality. Others say it means that a man without a woman is incomplete, literally missing a part of himself. And there's been strong support for the hermaphrodite theory—that the original human was literally bisexual, both male and female, until God physically separated one from the other. Go figure.) The making and naming of woman in Genesis 2:22–23 becomes the indispensable corollary to Genesis 3:16, and vice versa, in an end-less loop encircling domestic life. Women are inferior to men, ergo wives are inferior to husbands; inferior creatures must be led by and defer to their superiors, for reasons too obvious to mention; wives must obey their husbands, husbands must master their wives. And so forth.

Through verse 23 the story's pace has steadily accelerated—and then, at what seems to be the wrong moment, or at least an odd moment, it slows to a crawl. Apparently this program is being in-terrupted for a brief word from the sponsors. Yet these are uncom-monly skilled storytellers, too skilled not to know that they're toying with literary suicide by freezing the action like this, just when things are heating up; the message they need to convey must be urgent. And now that they've got the reader's attention, they may as well deliver it.

"Hence a man leaves his father and mother and clings to his wife, so that they become one flesh." With that, the primal setting recedes, time accelerates forward to what may be the writers' own era, and the human population has clearly multiplied. Since when does Adam have a father and mother, and how could the newborn woman already be his wife? He doesn't, and she's not. The "man" who is to leave his parents isn't the guy God just built from dust, and the "wife" isn't the woman God just built from Adam's rib. These are generic terms meant to represent the men and women of ancient Israel.

Verse 24 is pivotal, for didactic rather than narrative reasons—and its placement here, immediately following Adam's release from splendid isolation, has to be deliberate. It testifies to the primacy of marriage in Jewish life, one of many statements of this fact in the Bible, and in so doing it adds meat to the bones of the last two verses. The converse of "it is not good for man to be alone" isn't merely "it is good for man to have a companion, or fitting helper," and the solution to his solitude goes beyond placing a woman by his side. (Traditionally, the Hebrew Bible uses "side" instead of "rib.") Given verse 24's placement and content, the ideal converse of "it is not good to be alone" is "it is good to be married"—and the companion man needs is not only a woman, but a wife. Marriage won't be mentioned by name in Genesis until long after the human idyll in Eden comes to its inevitable end, but nonetheless, it's pretty clear that this verse is about a man's duty to leave his parents and make his own family with his own wife. Marriage is presented as God's mandate; it is not a matter of personal choice.

There's new information here, too, about what marriage means—for men, at least. "Clings to his wife" (sometimes translated as "cleaves," among other variations) sounds like it's about sex, but in the context of "leave his father and mother" actually refers to this patriarchal culture's seemingly unpatriarchal custom that calls for a man, upon marriage, to become part of his wife's family and household rather than the other way around. "Become one flesh," on the other hand, is all about sex—the penetration that connects a man and a woman literally as "one flesh." (Some recent translations delete the word "flesh," standard in English Bibles since the sixteenth century, which seems unnecessarily prudish.) But the phrase also carries symbolic meaning. To "become one flesh" with the woman makes the man whole again—joins him with that extracted rib—and if you buy the hermaphrodite theory, returns humanity to its original, bisexual, conjoined male-and-female state.

The next verse is the last for Genesis 2, and there's a lot going on: "The two of them were naked, the man and his wife, yet they felt no shame." But they will, and soon. Verse 25 sets up the primal drama's climactic third chapter, and when it's over, shame will be the least of what humans must learn to live with. In their current state—cast as idyllic, but it sounds pretty boring—Adam and Eve are still babes in paradise. Their nakedness means as much to them as it would to any newborn infant, which is exactly nothing. The labels "man" and "wife" leave no doubt that they are sexually mature, but they don't know what their nakedness exposes; their lack of shame shows that they're sexually unconscious. (Why is that a good thing?) It's as if God has equipped them to "be fertile and increase" but hasn't flipped the switch on desire, so it's still in the off position—where it will stay until the humans sample forbidden fruit.

But he hasn't told the humans of Genesis 2, as he did in Genesis 1, to "be fertile and increase." Not yet. And the bit about becoming one flesh isn't directed at them, either. It seems we're meant to think that these two haven't consummated their union, but it also seems that a union already exists between them. The key word is "wife." In the preceding verse that word is used generically, but not here. This time it refers unmistakably to Eve. No less significantly, verse 25 adds a possessive pronoun. When last seen just before the commercial break, Adam has just named her "woman." What has caused this sudden transformation from "woman" to "wife," specifically "*his* wife"? In the Bible it usually means that sex has occurred. (Without the urge, would there be an act?) In this literary world, and in the actual world it presumably reflects, a sexually awakened woman is or should be a wife (unless she's a prostitute, but God hasn't made any of those yet), and her carnal experience is or should be with just one man—the man stipulated by the "his" that precedes "wife." The reverse doesn't apply as rigorously. It'll be another seven verses before Adam is referred to as "her husband." He remains "the man," because he is one. A man's sexual activity, current or impending, doesn't sound the alarm that a woman's would; the text doesn't get around to wedlocking Adam until the sixth verse of the next chapter. In the real world he wouldn't be tied to one woman exclusively, and while she would become "his" in the legal sense as well, he would not become "hers."

Inside and outside the text, a man owns his wife in the same sense that he owns his cattle and crops. Human, animal, or vegetable, they are his and his alone. The tenth commandment that Moses will bring down from the mountain in the book of Exodus, following Genesis, puts it all in perspective: "You shall not covet your neighbor's house; you shall not covet your neighbor's wife, or his male or female slave, or his ox or his ass, or anything that is your neighbor's." A man possesses a woman through sex or he possesses her through marriage, and if one is true, so is (or should be) the other. The imperative "be fertile and increase" has already established a man's duty to marry and have children, which of course is the same as saying that a man's duty is to have sex with his wife, although in the case of ancient Israel, make that "wives."

This is a male-centered society that places a premium on reproduction, a premium so high that their central religious text turns it into a sacred command in the very first chapter. Not surprisingly, the Israelite marriage system is polygynous.[5] Here a man can have sex with as many women as he can manage and afford, increasing his odds of breeding as many children as possible; thus he fulfills God's mandate while demonstrating to one and all his sexual potency as well as his fertility. But the Israelites also take the paternity-protection business very seriously indeed. The default security system here as elsewhere is, for lack of a better word, marriage. Not marriage in the mutual-exchange-of-vows-and-rings sense (by definition, a polygynous system precludes mutuality between husband and wife); it's about marriage in the "his wife" sense. The point is this: If you fuck 'em, you own 'em, and vice versa. And if you fuck your neighbor's women, breaking the tenth commandment and possibly provoking a paternal-identity crisis, you'll invoke the death penalty. The Bible spells out the method: public stoning, executed by your friends and neighbors. The Israelites cherish the fruit of men's loins and show no mercy to those who tamper with it.

Nonetheless, the architects of Judaism take a sublimely hardheaded approach to human behavior. To cope with its vicissitudes they design coping strategies for everything from sex to grief that testify to the triumph of practical experience over wishful thinking. They're fully cognizant that even the ultimate penalty won't deter some men from sleeping with other men's women, that such unions might well produce children, and that the mothers of these children might be less than honest about who the fathers are. Averting confusion about paternity is a major concern that will eventually lead the Jews to make a patriarchally counterintuitive choice. Unlike their Christian or Muslim brethren, they'll trace their ancestry through the maternal line.

In the garden east of Eden, none of this matters. Even if sex has occurred, Adam needn't worry about Eve's fidelity. After all, he's still the only man in town. But there's also a serpent in town, his presence noted at the start of Genesis 3, and that's worth worrying about. When a serpent slithers into a Near Eastern creation story—and serpents are always slithering into these stories, to battle gods, beguile humans, and wreak general havoc—it's not a good sign. (In the Babylonian epic of Gilgamesh, to name one of the more famous examples, the serpent steals the plant of life, costing the hero his immortality.)[6] Serpents make useful villains for mythmakers, who must explain as best they can not only the genesis of life but also the genesis of human suffering and death. The biblical writers accomplish more than that, whether they intend to or not. The final act of this drama is set in motion through contact between serpent and human, but the human in question is the female, not the male. In using Eve to catalyze the powerful sequence of events that follow, these writers both explain and justify, in primal terms, why men should be wary of women. Standing at the heart of the creation story that outlasts them all, the one that appears in every translation of every edition of the best-selling book on the planet for the last million centuries—a million centuries of preachers and teachers and parents passing the word about Eve down the generational corridor, a million centuries of art made and words written about those people in that garden, a million centuries of playing telephone—well, everyone knows what happens there, even if they've never opened the Bible.

The problem is that the word about Eve and the words in the text do not, in one critical respect, correspond. By chance or by design, her criminal role in what is called "the Fall" has been exaggerated—she's guilty, but not *that* guilty—and this has been to the benefit of no one, male or female, up and down that generational corridor. The locus of the problem is Genesis 3:6, in which Eve offers Adam a taste of forbidden fruit. (Whatever fruit the writers have in mind is almost certainly not, as tradition will have it, an apple, which happens to be a familiar product in Christian-centered Europe but is alien to the Near East; think fig, grape, or some sort of citrus.) Check your memory: Does Eve dupe Adam? Does she say, or imply, that the fruit comes from a permissible tree? When Adam asks if the source is the tree of good and evil, does Eve deny it, change the subject, evade the question, or pretend she doesn't know? And if there's no outright deception, evasion, or misrepresentation of the fruit's origin, does she pressure, cajole, seduce, or in some other way talk him into this?

The answer is: none of the above. Not in any of the eleven English-language Bibles, seven of them Christian and four Hebrew, that I've checked, and sampled below. (That leaves many hundreds unchecked, in English alone, so feel free.)

Authorized King James Version (1611, Christian classic): "She took of the fruit thereof, and did eat, and gave also unto her husband with her; and he did eat." The Torah, Stone edition (1993, aimed at relatively rigorous Jews): "she took of its fruit and ate; and she gave also to her husband with her and he ate." Revised English Bible (1992, Christian, fashionably gender-neutral): "She also gave some to her husband, and he ate it."

Adam (finally debuting as "her husband," in case you missed it) is "with her" every time, and at no time since this chapter began, five verses earlier, has there been reason to think he is anywhere other than "with her." This means that Adam and Eve must be together while the serpent shrewdly works her over—for it's Eve who balks, and the serpent who pressures, cajoles, and seduces— starting small, with what appears to be an innocuous question: "Did God really say: You shall not eat of any tree of the garden?" Adam must be well within earshot when Eve responds, as if the serpent doesn't already know, that he is mistaken; God allows them to eat the fruit of every tree except for one. "It is only about fruit of the tree in the middle of the garden that God said: You shall not eat of it or touch it, lest you die."

By the way, how does Eve know all of this? When God points out the tree of good and evil in the center of the garden and says that it bears lethal fruit, Adam is his sole audience; God has just anointed him soil-tiller, and Eve doesn't exist. God has yet to utter, "It is not good for man to be alone." She must have been informed off-camera, probably by Adam—why would the omnipotent creator bother repeating himself? Hierarchy again: The CEO tells his senior officer, who passes the word to his own assistant. Shouldn't this buck stop with the senior officer, not the assistant?

Meanwhile, the serpent nimbly assuages Eve's anxiety by impugning God. Au contraire, the wily one says, "You are not going to die." (Why doesn't it occur to these people that someone is lying to them, and the odds are one in two that it's the serpent?) God wants them to think the fruit is lethal because—and here's the clincher—"God knows that as soon as you eat of it your eyes will be opened and you will be like divine beings who know good and bad." If Adam is "with her," which we must continue to assume, he's heard everything that Eve has. And now, as she reconsiders the fruit on that tree without fear darkening her vision, Adam sees as she does that it is, after all, "good for eating and a delight to the eyes," not to mention "desirable as a source of wisdom." Besides, what's the downside? The fruit's gorgeous, looks delicious, confers godlike knowledge, and does not cause death. No downside for them—only for God.

There's nothing left to think about. Eve takes the fruit, eats, hands it to her husband, who is with her, and he eats. That's it. No hesitation on Adam's part, no need for persuasion—only Eve shows signs of inner conflict before the serpent allays them—but there's no indication that Adam struggles with his conscience or with Eve. There's no indication that he gives in to her in any way, or that she tricks him, because in fact Adam never does ask where the fruit comes from; if he's been "with her" the whole time, he already knows. Yet the word on Eve is that she's an operator, that she manipulates or misleads or somehow makes Adam become her partner in crime. The word travels through time, rolling from one place to the next, repeated from one person to the next, a juicy bit of celebrity gossip that is eventually converted to cultural fact. Take the association of Eve with "temptress," lodging in popular consciousness early on. How, exactly, does Eve tempt Adam?[7] The alignment of Eve with "temptress" speaks to some kind of truth—so do catchphrases like "there's a little bit of Eve in every woman"—but whatever that truth is, it's not in the text.

Until a few hundred years ago, men are the ones who tell us about the past. Women speak only rarely, and their numbers are too few to convey a sense of their common experience, let alone what they think of Eve, or whether they see themselves in her. But there are plenty of men who can't shut up about the third chapter of Genesis; they use Eve's performance to shed light, and not a flattering one, on the murky nature of women. For those men who pontificate about the hell awaiting other men who put their trust in women—and none do it better than the fathers of the Church—Eve is the gift that keeps on giving. Here are a few examples out of many, starting with Ambrose, bishop of Milan in the late fourth century and St. Augustine's mentor: Eve "was responsible for deceiving the man . . . [she] instigated her husband to sin."[8] The good bishop may be echoing his influential predecessor Tertullian, a second-century writer whose intellectual impact on this developing theology is so large that Catholic historians call him "the Founder of Latin Christianity" as well as a "Father of the Church." In a polemic directed at Christian women, Tertullian asks rhetorically, "And do you not know that you are each an Eve? The sentence of God on this sex of yours lives in this age; the guilt must of necessity live too . . . *you* are the unsealer of that tree: *you* are the first deserter of the divine law: *you* persuaded [persuaded?] him whom the devil was not valiant enough to attack." Bottom line, and you'll hear it again: "*You* are the devil's gateway."[9] The Protestant reformers will put an end to the Church's captial-C status, but they don't do much reforming when it comes to Eve's image. As no less an eminence than John Calvin writes in the mid-sixteenth century, "women must needs stoop and understand that the ruin and confusion of all mankind came in on their side, and that through them we be all forlorn and accursed and banished [from] the kingdom of heaven . . . there is none other way but for them to stoop and to bear patiently the subjection that God hath laid upon them . . . to keep themselves lowly and mild."[10]

While Eve is pilloried repeatedly, especially in the Middle Ages, Adam's performance is overlooked. This is no accident: If Eve makes women look bad, Adam makes men look worse. Why would men, who will have the field of biblical scholarship all to themselves for many centuries, expose their own shortcomings when they can avoid doing so? And then there's the sequence. The long habit of vilifying Eve and failing to mention Adam can also be attributed to the timing on which the story turns. Eve—as Tertullian has already noted—goes first, and that makes all the difference.

After Adam takes the fruit from Eve and samples it, "the eyes of both of them" are opened, and they become aware of their nakedness. By the time they hear "the sound of the Lord God moving about in the garden at the breezy time of day" (what sound does a deity without a body make as he moves around a breezy garden?) they're wearing the fig leaves they've sewn into loincloths. They try to hide from God, clearly a waste of energy; God simply calls out, the text specifies, to the man. "Where are you?" God says ("to him"). The man responds, lamely, "I heard the sound of you in the garden, and I was afraid because I was naked, so I hid." Adam, if he personifies men as Eve personifies women, does them no favors as this sequence proceeds.

"Who told you that you were naked?" asks God, although this must be a rhetorical question, like the one that follows: "Did you eat of the tree from which I had forbidden you to eat?"

Does Adam do the manly thing? Does the buck stop with him? No way. He blames Eve. He even blames God. He blames everyone but himself. "The woman you put at my side—she gave me of the tree, and I ate."

Does God, whose instructions regarding that tree have been, as far as we know, directed only at Adam, allow these lame excuses to slide by without comment? Yup. He leaves Adam alone, for the moment, and zeros in on "the woman," saying, "What is this that you have done?" It's clear that "you" is not meant to be plural. "You" is Eve, and only Eve. On the timing the story turns; the crime turns; and also the punishment.

Eve doesn't win any points for grace under pressure, either. She joins in on the blame game: "The serpent duped me, and I ate."

God lets that slide, too, for the moment. He turns to the serpent in verse 14, opening the penalty phase of this trial. God says the serpent will be "cursed," forced to crawl on his belly and eat dirt for eternity. Plus, God promises to "put enmity between you and the woman and between your offspring and hers," meaning that humans ("they shall strike at your head") and snakes ("you shall strike at their heel") will be engaged for all time in attempted mutual murder. So much for the serpent; now it's Eve's turn to be cursed. We've come full circle.

Verse 16—all of it this time. "I will make most severe your pangs in childbearing; in pain shall you bear children," God says (some scholars suggest that the use of "the curse" for menstrual cramps derives from this very scene), "yet your urge shall be for your husband." Hard to tell if this "urge," obviously for sex (also rendered as "desire" or "craving"), is supposed to compensate women for the agony of labor by letting them enjoy the act that causes it, or to maximize the torture by getting them pregnant as often as possible; still, that "yet" suggests the latter. "Yet your urge shall be for your husband," and we already know how that sentence ends: "and he shall rule over you."

On the face of it, taking into account only the characters and what they've done to get us to this point (as if the story has unfolded in a historical vacuum in which the positions of wives in relation to their husbands, or women in relation to men, have to be determined) the idea that Adam shall rule over Eve seems either psychologically obtuse or an extreme example of divine cruelty. Once God makes Eve and Adam names her "woman," he yields the spotlight to her, and she takes over. She powwows with the serpent; she decides to trust him all on her own, without input from Adam, the passive player in the drama. She evaluates the fruit on the tree and sees that it will make good eating, but what she likes most is the wisdom it will confer; curiosity seems to be part of her nature (which hardly seems worth vilifying). But all we know of Adam so far—and only eight verses remain before the creation saga spins out—is that he's good at naming things and not a very standup guy. Eve's the one who plucks the fruit and takes the first bite. Adam waits, as he has been waiting all along, until she hands it to him, and he eats.

In short, she leads and he follows. She initiates the crime; he's the accessory, the accomplice, the sidekick, the—could it be?—

helper. What is God thinking when he commands Eve to be ruled by her husband, which amounts to commanding them both to play against what we know of their respective natures? One of the major benefits of hierarchical marriage, according to its proponents through history, is that it's highly conducive to domestic peace and harmony, if practiced diligently by both spouses. But if Eve's sisters are anything like her, and Adam's brothers anything like him (which, of course, is a ridiculous thought, but that doesn't stop the Eve-equals-women theorists), God's rule would lead to domestic warfare. If he intends to guarantee every couple a daily diet of marital friction from this day forward, making Voltaire's crack about divorce being invented a few weeks after marriage seem like a matter of fact, it's a brilliant plan, and so deeply perverse that you have to wonder if it's meant to be a cosmic joke.

Now that the serpent and the woman have been judged, the penalty phase of the man's trial begins—and it seems that in the eyes of God and the Bible, his crime is not the same as his wife's. A few verses back, when Adam told God that he hid because of his nakedness, God wheeled on Eve and said, rhetorically, "What is it that you have done?" What she did is clear: She took forbidden fruit from that one forbidden tree and tasted it. The crime she committed is the crime of disobedience. Adam didn't take the fruit from the tree, he took it from Eve, but by tasting it he, too, disobeyed. That, however, is not what has enraged God, who clarifies the precise nature of the transgression for which Adam is about to be sentenced: *"Because you have listened to your wife."*

This is another theme destined to become a cultural tradition. A man who listens to his wife will be portrayed as either a disaster waiting to happen or a fool waiting to be ridiculed, often both at the same time, and efforts will be made to keep vulnerable men from falling into this particular marital trap—the most elemental being to minimize, if not eliminate, women's use of their vocal cords. (The New Testament alone commands silence from women, not once but three times.)[11] The implicit corollary to "your husband shall rule over you" isn't just "you shall rule over your wife," but also "if you don't rule over your wife, she shall rule over you," essentially the meaning of "Because you have listened to your wife."

Because Adam has listened to his wife, God promises, his labor in the fields will be as excruciating as hers in the birthing room—a punishment that will be passed down to future generations. "Cursed be the ground because of you; by toil shall you eat of it . . . thorns and thistles shall it sprout for you . . . By the sweat of your brow shall you get bread to eat." The final curse is mortality: "For dust you are," proclaims God, "and to dust you shall return." Maybe this is another blessing in disguise. (No one would want to endure that daily torment for eternity.)

God is kind enough to dress the feckless humans in "garments of skins," surely better suited than fig-leaf loincloths to the harsh conditions and far more finicky dress code of their new lives in exile, which begin immediately. There's nothing more for God to do but kick them out of Eden, bringing this story to its bitter end. Paradise is over; welcome to paradise lost.

Out there in the real world, people see what they want to see, unconsciously twisting the story to fit their needs. Adam becomes the elemental symbol of manhood undone by womanhood—not an admirable role, but not an especially culpable one, either—the worst-case scenario of what can happen to men who let down their guard around women. Eve puts men on notice that woman, bone of man's bone and flesh of man's flesh, can be his worst enemy if he gives her the chance. More than that, she takes the heat for human misery; she deflects the bullet that might otherwise hit God, a boon to the religious establishment, while also giving both men and women someone to blame for the vale of tears in which everyone is forced to live. Let the Bible—Ecclesiastes 25:24—cast the first stone: "From a woman sin had its beginning, and because of her we all die."

Eve is just one of many fictional females who will establish and reinforce the ever-present theme that women endanger men. But as the one and only primal wife, she will be an exceptionally useful vehicle for men seeking to advance their theories about marriage, and in the process to vent the anger, anxiety, and desire that women (some of whom surely deserve at least a portion of the vitriol) evoke in them. Yet there's an unforeseen consequence to all of this. In order to become a villain, Eve takes on a significance unwarranted by the events on the page. Adam, meanwhile, becomes the victim, and his role is diminished. As a result, denigrating women through Eve also invests them, imaginatively, with a degree of power over men that is denied them in reality. No one can win this game, and it's only just started.

Call that game *caveat femina*: Beware the woman. And let John Milton, the miserably married seventeenth-century poet who advocated divorce three hundred years before its time (much to the fury of his own contemporaries), supply the ad copy. Fittingly, it's from *Paradise Lost*, and the speaker is—who else?—Adam.

> *Thus it shall befall*
> *Him who to worth in women overtrusting*
> *Lets her will rule.*

TWO

Struck Dead, Just Because He Spilled the Fruit of His Loins

I N ancient Egypt, Babylon, Athens, and Rome, it's customary for a man to believe in multiple gods and sleep with multiple women but have just one wife to bear his children. In ancient Israel the reverse applies: a man believes in only one god, sleeps with multiple women, and has as many wives to bear his children as he can handle. Chances are he can't indulge in as many as King Solomon—seven hundred, by the biblical count, plus three hundred concubines—but two or three might be manageable.[1] For the culture that considers "be fertile and increase" a sacrament at a time when marital fidelity is neither required nor expected of men, this marriage system makes sense.

Naturally, it has a pecking order. The top spot could go to the third or fifth (or four hundredth) wife as easily as to the first, because stature is determined by fecundity. What matters most to the Israelites isn't that marriage precede sex, but that reproduction follow marriage: To cleave is to beget. To cleave but not to beget, a dysfunction typically ascribed to the woman, is doubly loaded—not only has she failed to perform her natural role, but that failure is seen as a sign of God's displeasure with her.[2] A husband can easily divorce his wife for barrenness, and if he'd rather not, the court can force him to change his mind. God help the Israelite woman who bears the curse of barrenness.

And God does help a few, starting with Sarah in Genesis 16.

Of course he starts with Sarah: Her husband is the unflinchingly devout Abraham, whose seed will generate the chosen people, and Sarah is to play founding matriarch to his patriarch, a tricky feat for a woman who is barren. She needs God's special brand of infertility medicine. More than once God promises Abraham, who broods in private about having no heir, that his offspring will be as numerous as the stars in the sky—although Sarah, brooding in private about the same thing and blaming herself, is left out of this loop. She takes matters into her own hands, ordering her Egyptian slave girl, Hagar, to receive the fruit of Abraham's loins. And wouldn't you know it, Hagar conceives on the first try. Apparently she's absorbed the native values all too well; having proven her own fertility, Hagar looks upon her barren mistress "with contempt," even though carrying Abraham's child doesn't change Hagar's household position. (Israelites during the biblical era live under the civil law code of Hammurabi, which explicitly states that a slave girl whose mistress assigns her to concubine duty cannot claim equal status if she conceives the master's child—she does not become a wife.)[3]

The last thing Sarah needs at this juncture is to endure the smug disdain of the servant who has become pregnant at her own command. Cornering Abraham, she lets him have it. "The wrong done me is your fault! I myself put my maid in your bosom; now that she sees that she is pregnant, I am lowered in her esteem. The Lord decide between you and me!" But Abraham leaves Hagar to Sarah: "Deal with her as you think right." Although pregnancy doesn't make Hagar a wife, it does mean that she can't be sold or thrown out of the house against her will,[4] so Sarah's only option is to treat her "harshly." Although no details are provided, Sarah's disciplinary methods apparently work: Hagar runs away of her own accord. But Hagar is slated to bear Abraham a son, a "wild ass of a man"—call him Ishmael—who will seed the Arabic nation, so God can't let her go far. Long story; the upshot is that Hagar returns without her attitude problem, and all is well and good aside from Sarah's continuing barrenness. By the time God gets around to fixing her up, Sarah is ninety. You can't blame her for laughing out loud at God when he tells her she'll conceive a son within the year. (Sarah appears to be the only biblical character to laugh at God. This is as witty as he gets.)

Clearly, the Israelite marriage system can wreak a special brand of domestic havoc—and not just for women. If managing one wife is a challenge, as men have been reporting from day one, the Torah (as the first five books of the Bible are collectively known) testifies to the complicated business of managing them in multiple. The Torah focuses intensely on married life, anticipating what seems to be every conceivable scenario and prescribing procedures and remedies for each with clinical thoroughness. Married life, after all, is reproductive life—and the Torah is all about protecting and promoting the latter, even at the expense of the former. According to Deuteronomy, "If two men get into a fight with each other, and the wife of one comes up to save her husband from his antagonist and puts out her hand and seizes him by his genitals, you shall cut off her hand; show no pity." And if a man should voluntarily separate himself from his genitals, presumably to gain the respect and influence that the surrounding pagan society accords to eunuchs, there will be consequences: "No one whose testes are crushed or whose member is cut off shall be admitted into the congregation of the Lord."[5]

Another form of protection is embedded in the tenth commandment, which distills the laws of ownership, clarifying the essential nature of a wife's relationship to her husband: "You shall not covet your neighbor's house: you shall not covet your neighbor's wife, or his male or female slave, or his ox or his ass, or anything that is your neighbor's."[6] House, wife, slave, ox—legally, they are equivalent: All are chattel, the lawful property of the man who possesses them. (For nearly a thousand years, an Englishman sick of his wife could slip a halter around her neck, lead her to market—the cattle market—and sell her to the highest bidder, often with her willing participation. This informal route to divorce for the lower classes lasted, amazingly, until at least 1887.)[7] Keeping that in mind, the seventh commandment—"You shall not commit adultery"—has to mean one thing for women and another for men. And it does: A woman is guilty of adultery if she sleeps with any man other than her husband, while a man is guilty of adultery only if he sleeps with another man's wife or betrothed. (In either case, the "bride-price" has been paid to the woman's family.) He's broken the property law, but that's just a starting point. Since the item of property he has plundered is a woman, he is guilty of compromising reproductive integrity—as, of course, has she—at a time when the Jews still trace lineage through the father.[8] Even more seriously, he has disobeyed two of the ten divine laws that form the covenant between God and the Jews, while she has defied both God and husband. In Israel's view, no crime is more deserving of the death penalty than adultery, which merits public execution, usually by stoning and sometimes by fire. (Unless you're King David, who is hailed as a hero, even though he surely should have been stoned to death for his crimes: lusting after one of his loyal soldiers' wives, Bathsheba; making her his mistress; getting her pregnant; trying to persuade her unsuspecting husband, Uriah, to leave the battlefield for a brief conjugal visit so that he and not David will appear to be the father; arranging for Uriah's death in combat when he's too honorable to desert his troops just to have sex with his wife; marrying the grieving widow. But David shows such extreme contrition—and with Uriah dead there's no paternity issue—that God forgives him. Some people have all the luck.)[9]

Still, provisions are made for gray areas. Suppose a woman becomes pregnant, and her husband is convinced—based on nothing more concrete than his imagination—that she bears some other man's child? The book of Numbers has the answer: "If any man's wife has gone astray and broken faith with him, in that a man has had carnal relations with her unbeknown to her husband, and she keeps secret the fact that she has defiled herself without being forced, and there is no witness against her" but her husband suspects she's been fooling around—"a fit of jealousy comes over him," even if in fact she has not gone astray at all—he must bring his wife to "the priest." He also has to bring seven pints of barley flour: "No oil shall be poured upon it and no frankincense shall be laid on it, for it is a meal offering of jealousy, a meal offering of remembrance which recalls wrongdoing." The priest concocts "the water of bitterness that induces the spell" (sometimes translated simply as "the ordeal-water") by filling a vessel with sacral water and mixing it with equally sacral earth. Then he bares the woman's head, places the jealousy-laced flour in her hands, holds the bitter-water vessel in his own, and finally tells her what's going on. The priest is going to write down a curse (dictated by God, obviously), only to rub the writing off (don't ask) into the water. The woman is to say "Amen, amen!," by way of acknowledging that she accepts the terms of the test. Then the test proceeds: The wife drinks the water, and if she's guilty, the curse will kick in, "causing the belly to distend and the thigh to sag." The word "thigh" may be a euphemism for "vagina" or refer to dysfunctional ovaries, possibly both, but what it seems to come down to is the biblical woman's worst nightmare, infertility. But if she's innocent, "she shall be unharmed and able to retain seed."[10] Well, God help her.

Israelite men can divorce their wives for reasons far more vague than infertility. (Wives can't divorce their husbands for any reason.) If, for instance, "She fails to please him because he finds something obnoxious about her," there's no need to hire a pricey lawyer. He simply "writes her a bill of divorcement, hands it to her, and sends her away from his house."[11] He'd better be sure this is what he wants, because he can't get her back again. Some biblical commentators say that this law is intended to prevent wife swapping, and since a woman who is not a slave becomes a "wife" as soon as a man possesses her sexually (unless she is someone else's wife, in which case they're both dead), such a law would probably be useful.[12]

On both sides of the aisle, the biblical laws police those who shirk or abuse their marital responsibilities. As usual, the text lays out the scenario in exhaustive detail: "A man marries a woman and cohabits with her. Then he takes an aversion to her and makes up charges against her and defames her, saying, 'I married this woman; but when I approached her, I found that she was not a virgin.' In such a case, the girl's father and mother shall produce the evidence of

the girl's virginity before the elders of the town at the gate"—someone
has to be responsible for the female, and if not the husband, it will be
the father. "And the girl's father shall say to the elders, 'I gave this
man my daughter to wife, but he has taken an aversion to her; so he
has made up charges, saying, "I did not find your daughter a virgin."
But here is the evidence of my daughter's virginity!'"

The traditional evidence is a bloodstained sheet—examining
postnuptial sheets for signs of the bride's virginity is still customary
in parts of Eastern Europe, North Africa, and wherever the honor of
men remains a matter of life or death—and if the father can produce
one, his son-in-law will suffer. But not too much: The elders are to
"take the man and flog him, and they shall fine him a hundred
shekels of silver and give it to the girl's father; for the man has defamed a virgin in Israel." (With no high-tech crime labs around,
who's to say that the blood doesn't come from an ox?) After the
flogging and the fine comes the real piece of rough justice: The
woman "shall remain his wife; he shall never have the right to divorce her." What a moron. If he'd simply said she was obnoxious in
the first place, he'd be divorced already instead of stuck for life.

In the event that no bloody sheet or other proof of premarital
purity materializes and the husband wins his case, "the girl shall be
brought out to the entrance of her father's house, and the men of
the town shall stone her to death; for she did a shameful thing in
Israel." This is the penalty for adultery, yet she hasn't committed
adultery. She's committed premarital sex with one man, and married another. In itself, premarital sex doesn't merit death, or even
flogging. If a virgin not yet purchased from her father is deflowered, she'll escape punishment, while the man involved will be
compelled to "make her his wife." (Her father can refuse, but he
gets paid the market value for a virgin either way.) But to protect
paternity as well as morality, a woman who sleeps with two men in
any sequence is judged an adulteress and punished without mercy.

Deflowering a virgin possessed by another man in the financial, if not yet sexual, sense means death for the man, but
the virgin's fate depends on geography. If the deed occurs "in

town," then both parties must be taken outside the gates of that town and stoned to death by the community, "the girl because she did not cry for help in the town, and the man because he violated his neighbor's wife." But if the encounter takes place "in the open country," where, it is assumed, her cries would be unheard, only the man will be executed—"you shall do nothing to the girl," the text explains, because "this case is like that of a man attacking another and murdering him. He came upon her in the open; though the engaged girl cried for help, there was no one to save her." Maybe, and maybe not. She could just as easily have come upon him in the open and not cried for help because she didn't want to be saved—the romp was consensual. But in lieu of evidence to the contrary, the law assumes that she tried to resist or had reason to fear that resistance might be fatal, and confers upon her the protection due the weaker sex—the benefit of the doubt.[13]

Protecting members of the weaker sex against one another requires a more intricate calculus, especially where childbearing is concerned. With more than one woman carrying the fruit of the same man's loins, the paramount concern isn't protecting the women or even the man, it's protecting the fruit—specifically the fruit that yields the firstborn son. The rule of primogeniture is observed in many cultures, but the Israelites, consistent with their general approach to the matter of generation and regeneration, seem inordinately preoccupied by it. (Or so the Bible suggests, starting with the interminable lists in Genesis that follow the creation story—lists of begettings of firstborn sons, one lineage after another, with names and ages recorded meticulously—but since everyone seems to live until the age of nine hundred or so, probably not so accurately).

Biblical laws governing inheritance (and also trying to avert domestic war) compel the man to separate his feelings for the mothers of his children from his obligation to the firstborn son, regardless of the mother's identity.

If a man has two wives, one loved and the other unloved, and both the loved and the unloved have borne him sons, but the first-born is the son of the unloved one—when he wills his property to his sons, he may not treat as first-born the son of the loved one in disregard of the son of the unloved one who is older. Instead, he must accept the first-born, the son of the unloved one, and allot to him a double portion of all he possesses; since he is the first fruit of his vigor, the birthright is his due.[14]

The first fruit of his vigor—the first son produced by his sperm. The health, welfare, and distribution of this commodity is of paramount importance to the Israelite nation, chosen but fragile, a lonely dot of monotheism in a pagan sea. The sex and marriage laws coalesce around the topic of sperm: who it spawns and in what order, which wife is barren and which is fertile. The Bible's rigorous policing of sexual behavior seems less about morality than about following the sperm trail, which, of course, manifests itself in the maternity trail.

The Bible grants women no legal rights, marital rights, divorce rights, or sexual rights. But it does grant them the right to maternity. In claiming those rights, women are allowed a startling amount of leeway in their behavior, which cannot be mere coincidence. Take levirate marriage (from *levir*, "husband's brother"): If a man dies before his wife can bear him a son, his unmarried brother is obligated to take over. And there is no ambiguity about what is expected. The widow "shall not be married to a stranger, outside the family. Her husband's brother shall unite with her: take her as his wife and perform the levir's duty. The first son that she bears shall be accounted to the dead brother, that his name may not be blotted out in Israel." The levir may find the prospect of sleeping with his sister-in-law repellent, or of his dead brother's name being blotted out in Israel delightful; resistance to this law must be common enough to require close attention from the Torah, which supplies step-by-step countermeasures. First, the widow must tattle on her brother-in-law, specifically to the ominous "elders." They summon the sacrilegious fellow and work him over verbally. If they can't persuade or pressure him into doing the right thing, public humiliation follows: The widow "shall go up to him in the presence of the elders, pull the sandal off his foot, spit in his face, and make this declaration: Thus shall be done to the man who will not build up his brother's house! And he shall go in Israel by the name of 'the family of the unsandaled one.'"[15] Spitting, obviously, is meant to degrade him; the loss of the shoe symbolizes the widow's freedom from duty to her husband's family.[16]

Not so terrible, compared to the fate of that famous coitus-interrupter, Onan. This levir fulfills half of his obligation—he's all for having sex with his dead brother's wife, on multiple occasions—which is worse than fulfilling none of it. "But Onan, knowing that the seed would not count as his, let it go to waste whenever he joined with his brother's wife." Onan breaks the levirate law, but more important, he breaks the sperm trail, and for that, God strikes him dead. But there remains the widow, Tamar, who now becomes the problem of Judah, her father-in-law—he is legally bound to give Tamar his one surviving son, still too young for marriage. Judah doesn't intend to do so, now or in the future, but pretends otherwise; he sends Tamar back to her father's house, promising that when the boy is old enough the two will marry.[17]

Time passes—enough time for Tamar to figure out she's been duped—and she goes after her maternal rights with vengeance. Posing as a temple prostitute (as opposed to a common whore), she veils her face, dresses in whatever temple prostitutes wear, and sits by the roadside, waiting for Judah to pass by. When he does, all he sees is a fetching prostitute; he doesn't recognize Tamar. And he falls into the trap, propositioning her. She wants something in return—a goat, or so she says. Judah agrees and promises to deliver one, but Tamar insists on collateral. She asks for Judah's seal, its cord, and the staff he holds to be returned when he makes good on the goat. Sex follows, as does pregnancy, unbeknownst to Judah. But when Judah sends the promised goat by messenger to the roadside spot where the tryst occurred, the messenger comes back with the goat—and no seal, cord, or staff.

A few months later Judah hears the gossip: Tamar "has played the harlot; in fact she is with child by harlotry." Society holds Judah accountable, as her father-in-law, for Tamar's behavior, and society expects her to be put to death. The method this time is burning, not stoning. Just before Tamar is to be escorted to her death, she sends a package to Judah containing the staff, cord, and seal, along with a message: "I am with child by the man to whom these belong." Faced with undeniable proof, Judah admits that his deception justifies her deception: "She is more in the right than I," Judah says, "inasmuch as I did not give her to my son Shelah." Tamar goes home, vindicated, and eventually gives birth to twins. They're considered her dead husband's children, spawned by her father-in-law—levirate principle honored, sperm trail unbroken, maternal rights invoked.

Two sisters pull off a similar scam with their own father, Lot, after the family flees Sodom on a tip from some messengers from God that the town will be destroyed. Mom doesn't make it—she's the one who turns into a pillar of salt for disobeying God's order not to look back on the city—but Lot and his two virgin daughters find a cave in the hills and hide out. The older sister must believe that their exile will be permanent, since she comes up with the idea to take turns being impregnated by their unwitting father. "[T]here is not a man on earth to consort with us in the way of all the world . . . Let us make our father drink wine, and let us lie with him, so that we may maintain life through our father." Two nights in a row they get him drunk; big sis sleeps with him on night one, little sis follows. We are meant to assume that Lot is so drunk that he doesn't know what he's doing, much less who he's doing it with, yet can still perform. But never mind, the important thing is that both daughters end up bearing the sons of their father. No word on whether they ever got out of the cave, or if Lot was overjoyed at the news of impending fatherhood/grandfatherhood.[18]

So obsessed is this society with making babies that it bars new husbands from making war. "When a man has taken a bride, he shall not go out with the army or be assigned to it for any purpose; he shall be exempt one year . . . to give happiness to the woman he has married"[19]—the Israelite perspective on what constitutes female "happiness" surely needs no further explication—and after he's seeded his wife, he can spread it elsewhere. On the battlefield, for instance. The Bible, leaving nothing to chance, provides soldiers with a lesson on the fine art of taking enemy women to wife after the enemy has been vanquished—all's fair in love and reproduction—which extends the protective impulse even to captive females. You don't just throw her on the ground and have your way with her then and there. You don't throw her on the ground at all. And you don't have your way with her for an entire month. No, "you shall bring her into your house, and she shall trim her hair, pare her nails, and discard her captive's garb. She shall spend a month's time in your house lamenting her father and mother; after that you may come to her and possess her, and she shall be your wife." The lesson includes instruction on how to get rid of her, too. No bill of divorcement is required, but restrictions do apply: "Then, should you no longer want her, you must release her outright. You must not sell her for money; since you had your will of her, you must not enslave her."[20]

The only reproductive avenue that the Bible sternly forbids men to take, aside from the one populated by women who belong to other men, is the one lined with "strangers." This is code for pagans, who vastly outnumber the monotheists in the ancient Near East. Paganism threatens the Israelites because it allures them as they struggle to heed the rigorous demands of a God unknown to the freewheeling polytheists; the biblical writers try to counter the threat with some shrill fearmongering. As God leads his people out of servitude in Egypt and brings them to the edge of Canaan, the promised land, he vows that they will occupy that land by defeating the "seven nations much larger than you." But even in victory they'll be living among the idol-worshipping remnants of those nations, unless the Israelites massacre them all—not a bad idea, it seems.

God addresses his people: "You shall not intermarry with them: do not give your daughters to their sons or take their daughters for your sons. For they will turn your children away from me to worship other gods, and the Lord's anger will blaze forth against you and He will promptly wipe you out." To avoid that disaster, God recommends some nasty measures: "[Y]ou shall tear down their altars, smash their pillars, cut down their sacred posts," although none are as merciless as this: "You shall destroy all the peoples that the Lord your God delivers to you, showing them no pity." And how will God reward the invaders for their brutality at his behest? His people will "multiply," he'll "bless the issue" of their wombs—and best of all, he'll wipe out barrenness: "There shall be no sterile male or female among you."[21]

If God's threats and promises don't work to turn his chosen people against outsiders, the biblical portraits of wicked foreign females bent on seducing and destroying Israelite men might do it. Delilah the Philistine cuts off the mighty Samson's secret power source, performing castration by haircut (he also has his eyes gouged out, but who remembers that?), and King Solomon takes so many foreign wives that God swears he'll "tear the kingdom" from the lustful king's heir.[22] But of all the exotic idol-worshipping females who undulate their way through these pages and spell catastrophe for the men of Israel, Jezebel is the most reviled, and the most fascinating. She's a royal Phoenician who marries the king of Israel, Ahab, and has him completely in her thrall. Using his power to satisfy her sadistic impulses, Jezebel takes delight in having one hundred prophets executed in a single day. Because she belongs to the cult of Baal, the Canaanite storm god, Ahab endorses Baal worship in Israel—the ultimate betrayal of God's law, sure to provoke divine retribution of the first order. All of this is buildup to the final outrage.[23]

The feckless Ahab covets (yes, it's tenth commandment time again) the vineyard adjacent to the royal palace and offers the owner, Naboth, all kinds of money, even a better vineyard. But Naboth won't sell; the Lord, he says, forbids him to surrender his family's ancestral land. Ahab reacts with all the regal dignity of a spoiled three-year-old. He goes home "sullen and angry . . . he took to his bed, covered his face, and refused to eat." Jezebel wants to know what's bothering him, and when Ahab explains, she says, "Are you or are you not king in Israel? . . . Come, eat and take heart; I shall make you a gift of the vineyard of Naboth of Jezreel." On the face of it, Jezebel is modeling one of the traditional qualities of the Good Wife—furthering her husband's interests, whatever they may be—but then, so was Lady Macbeth.

Jezebel composes letters in Ahab's name, marks them with his seal, and sends them off to the elders of Naboth's city. The elders follow what they assume to be the king's instructions: Invite Naboth as the guest of honor to an official gathering, include among the guests two unscrupulous men who will accuse him of cursing his God and his earthly monarch—good old King Ahab—exposing Naboth as a traitor. As such, the elders must "take him out and stone him to death." When Jezebel receives confirmation, she tells Ahab: "Get up and take possession of the vineyard which Naboth refused to sell to you, for he is no longer alive; Naboth of Jezreel is dead." Ahab does as told, asking no questions.

God has apparently been biding his time with these two, but now he takes action. He sends his messenger, Elijah, to deliver Ahab's sentence: "I shall bring disaster on you; I shall sweep you away and destroy every mother's son of the house of Ahab . . . because you have provoked my anger and led Israel into sin." But that's not all Ahab has done. The writers break the narrative to announce: "Indeed, there was no one like Ahab, who sold himself to do what was evil in the sight of the LORD, urged on by his wife Jezebel." Déjà vu, anyone? "Because you listened to your wife." It's Adam, all over again. This husband does not rule. But Ahab puts on such a good show of humbling himself in sackcloth and ashes and prayer in front of Elijah that God whispers in Elijah's ear that "Because he has humbled himself before me, I will not bring the disaster in his days." Instead, the sins of the father will be visited upon the next generation: Ahab's seventy sons (presumably not all by Jezebel) will be massacred. As to Jezebel, not about to humble herself before any god but Baal (and maybe not even him), Elijah quotes the Lord: "The dogs shall eat Jezebel within the bounds of Jezreel."

Many verses pass before Jezebel meets her destiny. After a long narrative absence, she reappears in Jezreel on the day of her death, fully made up with her head regally adorned, standing at the window on an upper floor of her house—as if she's about to favor her adoring subjects with a glimpse of their noble queen. In fact, she awaits her prophesied killer, Jehu. (Jehu will also be the one to dispatch Ahab's seventy sons, destroy the remnants of the cult of Baal, and eventually rule Israel.) As he enters the gate, she taunts him, hurling insults from the window, until Jehu turns to three eunuchs and tells them, "Throw her down." Out the window she goes, to be trampled by horses, her blood splashing all around. "See to that accursed woman," Jehu instructs his lackeys, "and bury her; for she is a king's daughter." Then he goes off to the nearest tavern, apparently ravenous, but not quite as ravenous as the dogs who fulfill Elijah's prophecy. When the dogs have had their fill, the eunuchs enter the tavern and tell Jehu that when they went to bury the queen's remains, "they found no more of her than the skull and the feet and the palms of her hands." To which Jehu responds, "This is the word of the Lord . . . the dogs shall eat the flesh of Jezebel; and the corpse of Jezebel shall be like dung on the field in the territory of Jezreel, so that no one can say: 'This is Jezebel.'"

She's guilty of treachery, deceit, and murder, but for all the many, many acts of treachery, deceit, and murder in the Bible, no one else is shredded to oblivion. It's not just Jezebel's identity as an outsider and Baal worshipper that compounds her crimes; pagans abound in the Bible and meet brutal ends, but none get the Jezebel treatment. There's some other, unstated reason for making dog food out of Jezebel. As a wife, she is the ultimate patriarchal nightmare, and her marriage the ultimate subversion of the rule of Genesis 3:16. She represents something deeply disturbing to men at this time—something they fear about themselves in relation to women—and they don't want to be reminded of it. Jehu suggests that the near-total annihilation of her flesh means they won't be: "No one can say, 'This is Jezebel.'" She wears the pants in a royal marriage, making a mockery of manhood by showing off the mockery of a man who is her husband. This diminishes men in their own eyes and reminds them of the dangers that can accrue to he who blindly follows his wife's lead—Adam's big mistake. It doesn't further a husband's interests to expose him for the less-than-masterful creature he sometimes suspects he is. Jezebel exposes both husband and king. She is the biblical wife from hell.

The biblical wife from heaven has no name, but then she doesn't need one—she's not a character in any story. She's a paradigm. The Good Wife makes her debut in the book of Proverbs and will be hard to shake after that. Century after century and with truly striking consistency, the Good Wife glides serenely through the minds and works of men who seem content to leave her just as she is: More than the good wife, she's the perfect wife. (Too perfect to be fun, not to mention real, but you can't have everything.) Her polar opposite also appears century after century, blasting her way through many more works of many more men, sometimes cast as a wife, sometimes not. Her attributes are consistent in the sense of being consistently tormenting; the possibilities are endless, as are the portraits—she's wildly entertaining on paper almost regardless of the winter. Proverbs 12 sums up both paradigms: "A good wife is the crown of her husband, but she who brings shame is like rottenness in his bones." And Proverbs 31, verses 10 to 31, explains what "the crown" of a husband means in fastidious detail.

The book of Proverbs is a nonreligious compendium of poems and aphorisms based on folk wisdom from Egyptian and other sources, the kind of wisdom parents feel compelled to impart to their children. In the case of Proverbs 31, make that teachers to their students. It's written in the form of an acrostic, each line beginning with a successive symbol of the Hebrew alphabet—ideal for making a lesson seem like a game. (This final entry in Proverbs is inexplicably cobbled together with the shorter, unrelated prose poem that precedes and was once independent of it.)

Of the poem's opening verses, the first has bacome a pop-culture classic:

> *Who can find a virtuous woman? For her price is far above rubies.*[24]
> *The heart of her husband doth safely trust in her, so that he shall have no need of spoil.*
> *She will do him good and not evil all the days of her life.*

This dream wife doesn't do much dreaming, as she doesn't do much sleeping; her "lamp does not go out at night." She "works with willing hands . . . rises while it is still night and provides food for her household." Notably, she has some financial autonomy—"she considers a field and buys it"—but this adds to her workload: "With the fruit of her hands she plants a vineyard." She spins wool, weaves it into fabric, and makes clothing for everyone in her household, including herself, even though she could go naked if it wouldn't shame her husband: "Strength and dignity are her clothing." Somehow there's still time to run a "profitable" wholesale business, selling linen garments to merchants, and to care for the poor. Needless to say, she "does not eat the bread of idleness." Her husband may be slaving away as well, but like the shepherd under the shady tree, it doesn't look that way. He's vaguely important, "known in the city gates, taking his seat among the elders of the land." What the seated elders do isn't mentioned, but you can bet they're not spinning wool.

The Good Wife needs to have more than a strong work ethic and the right attitude—those "willing hands"—if she's going to compete with her evil twin as a model for other women. She also needs to know how to keep her mouth shut. From Aristotle and St. Paul to Jonathan Swift to Norman Mailer and beyond, men can't stop talking about women who can't stop talking, or describing the maddening forms their talking takes. Mindless ramblings, worthless chitchat, malicious slander, whining, nagging, repetition, unreasonable demands, baseless accusations, and downright lies. The undeniable fact is that women do go on, mindlessly and otherwise—there's truth to men's complaints. Not that any man would complain about Mrs. Proverbs 31, whose verbal rectitude is a relief: "She opens her mouth with wisdom, and the teaching of kindness is on her tongue." Once again we're reminded of her even temperament. No barking, beleaguered, martyred Supermom is she: "Her children rise up and call her happy; her husband too, and he praises her." What does he say? "Many women have done excellently, but you surpass them all."

Yawn.

Throughout this homage, there is not even an oblique reference to her physical attributes, although elsewhere in the Bible such references are common. Genesis describes Sarah, wife of Abraham, as "very beautiful." Rachel, wife of Jacob, is "graceful and beautiful"; even the unloved Leah, Rachel's sister and co-wife, has "lovely" eyes. But they are all recognizably human characters, while the woman of Proverbs 31 is meant to be a composite of ideal wifely qualities. She is sober, modest, charitable, maternal, industrious, thrifty, prudent, discreet, selflessly supportive of her husband, "homely" in the ideal sixteenth-century-Protestant sense—a type celebrated by one writer of that far-off era as "constantly with her house, like the snail that carries its little home with it wherever it goes."[25] She is also, by implication, asexual, not the sort of woman other men covet. Thus her husband can saunter through those city gates and take his place among the elders of the land without brooding about what she's up to. Proverbs 31 has done double cultural duty for the better part of two thousand years as the inaugural, and definitive, model of the Good Wife for not-so-good wives—and also an escapist fantasy for their beleaguered husbands.

Meanwhile, off to the west, the husbands of Athens appear to be living this fantasy for real.

THREE

Do Athenian Husbands Have It All?

COOL heads, fit physiques, clean lines, calibrated pleasures: The textbook rendering of Athens in its heyday, circa 500–300 BCE, seems improbably serene. In the foreground, older men swan around in pristine white togas, trading lofty insights about the nature of the soul whenever they're not inventing democracy. Because these men strive for a happy medium in all things, they put their cerebral concerns on hold every so often to feast their senses on the eye candy arrayed before them: teenaged boys playing competitive sports in the nude, every lissome inch of flesh on delectable display. The structural clarity and grace of their strong young bodies in motion is echoed in the civic architecture visible in the background, which serves to enhance rather than clutter the scene. Clutter has no place in the Athenian aesthetic, which may explain why there are no women in this picture. "What's outside is men's business, and let no woman give it thought," says a character in Aeschylus's *Seven Against Thebes*. "Let her stay inside and do no mischief."

Men's business in Athens is conducted by a privileged citizen-elite that applies this patriarchal truism with special rigor. Its members believe in keeping their wives sequestered in an all-female wing of the household, allowing them out once or maybe twice a year to attend a women-only festival and the occasional family funeral.[1] Aside from the performance of his procreative duty, the upstanding Athenian husband rarely associates with his wife, even at home, and never in public. He spends his days with men like himself, engaged in political or cultural matters, and his nights with some of the same. But at night men's business is pursued in the company of the hetaera, the forerunner of the European courtesan—a trophy without being a wife. Hetaerae are well-educated, culturally literate, and socially as well as sexually sophisticated: everything a wife is not.

In addition to having a mistress, the Athenian husband might also keep a young boy on the side. And for a quick fix with the added advantage of anonymity, male and female slaves are always available for hire—thanks to the system of organized prostitution that Athens bestows upon Western culture, along with everything else. Solon, the aristocratic leader and lawmaker who develops that system in the early sixth century BCE,[2] is most closely associated with the founding of democracy, although it's the carnal activity of other people that seems to be his particular interest.

Solon has a strong moralistic streak, and since he holds the levers of power he can and does manage to impose his personal standards on everyone else. He makes the preservation of female chastity a priority; thus men are granted the legal right to sell their unwed but no-longer-virgin daughters or female dependents into slavery. Solon shares his sexual preference for young boys with many other prominent citizens, but unlike some of them, he thinks there's such a thing as too young. He also thinks that adult men who seduce prepubescent boys deserve the death penalty—and what Solon thinks has a way of becoming law.

At some point during his career, Solon perceives that too many married men are plunging heedlessly into too many adulterous liaisons with questionable characters of either sex—it's not the adultery that bothers him, it's the heedlessness—which seems to be causing family chaos. The antidote to chaos is order, and that's just what Solon creates in the extramarital universe. Deciding that domestic life would improve if men's needs for casual sex could be met cleanly, safely, efficiently, and without fuss, he develops a network of whorehouses stocked with male and female slaves, known as concubines. Although Solon's brainstorm may or may not improve Athenian family life, the brothel business soon becomes an indispensable accessory to sexual life. It suits the Athenian government, which profits from men's patronage. It suits the patrons, who can be good citizens and please themselves at the same time. And because it simplifies—clarifies—men's relations with women, it suits the prevailing aesthetic. What is current practice for the Israelites would be anathema for the Athenians, with their apparent distaste for emotional and domestic sturm und drang. Multiple bedmates, definitely; multiple wives, no way.

Since this is Athens, the marriage code is as crisply delineated as the architecture—even the bedmates are organized by function, with no blurring of boundaries allowed. If it works half as well as it sounds, the Athenians win the gold medal for wife control in the Western Olympics, twenty-five centuries running. Among the champions is Demosthenes, the orator who famously summarizes the code about two hundred years after Solon establishes prostitution: "We keep *hetaera* for our delight, concubines for the daily needs of our bodies, wives so that we may breed legitimate children and have faithful housekeepers."[3]

Maybe this is why the men of Athens are so productive. With their sexual needs identified, compartmentalized, and fulfilled by a dedicated service team assigned to each one, they can be laser-focused on the work that turns the classical age into a golden one. That triangulated system is itself an unsung Athenian legacy that continues to affect the male psyche, although Demosthenes's three-part harmony has long since become two. Some call it the Madonna-whore complex. Freud calls it "the most prevalent form of degradation in erotic life." In an essay by that title, he defines the form as a man's inability to desire the woman he loves, or to love the woman he desires—a conflict vividly on display in late-Victorian England, where Freud resides. This is the era when the mothers of the ruling middle class allegedly advise their virgin daughters that on the wedding night they should just close their eyes and think of England. Their reward for enduring sexual inter-course is motherhood, and once married, their respectability de-pends on their apparent or actual frigidity. Not coincidentally, this is also the era when middle-class husbands are notorious for lead-ing sexual double lives. They sit in church with their families every Sunday, spending their off hours secretly exploring the wonderful worlds of pornography and (praise be to Solon) prostitution.

There's no need for secrecy or pretense back in Athens, where even the decorative arts attest frankly to the sexual system in place, and to just how far this society's mania for order extends. The im-ages painted on vases and other artifacts suggest a correspondence between sexual position and sexual stature—the more demeaning the position, the more demeaned the class of worker—that pre-sumably operates in real life. Position distinguishes not only be-tween categories, but within them. Over-the-hill hetaerae rank as low as if not lower than prostitutes; both are subjected to rear-entry, likely anal, penetration, among other indelicate acts. In a typically graphic scene, a woman performs fellatio on one man while a sec-ond, gripping her hair at the base of her neck, thrusts into her from behind. She is depicted as dumpy, aging, and—another sign of her lowly stature—stark naked.[4]

By contrast, the young and beautiful courtesan is dressed ele-gantly, if flimsily, and appears in one-on-one scenes that convey eroticism and even affection, with men who behave like lovers, kissing and embracing her, stroking her hair or cheek. No brutality or anal sex for her; respect for pulchritude and desirability is con-veyed by the frontal position. Her real-life model might find these paintings instructive, especially the ones that feature female de-crepitude, because she ought to know what's coming. At the top of her game, the Athenian hetaera has all the fun a wife does not. But she's not allowed to marry, and once she loses her looks (or be-comes pregnant, despite her knowledge and practice of contracep-tion) she's on her own, without the social security and respect that cushions the Athenian wife.[5]

Athens takes very good care of its wives in exchange for

producing new soldiers for the army and officials for the government, providing them with various protections and benefits—and respect. When a husband calls on his wife for a round of presumably unerotic, presumably procreative sex, the presumable position will be frontal—because it conveys the esteem to which she is entitled as a mother, legitimized by marriage.

For breeding purposes, and there is no other purpose to marriage in Athens, men try to refrain from selecting extremely youthful mates. In the animal world, notes Aristotle, "generally the products of very young unions are defective, usually female and diminutive, so the same kind of results are bound to follow in human beings." Besides, a little age on a bride is "more conducive to faithfulness" later on. Aristotle recommends eighteen for the woman and thirty-seven or thereabouts for the man, because "intercourse will then take place when they are both physically in their prime." (Once conception occurs, Aristotle warns men not to let their wives get lazy, going so far as to suggest that pregnant women be required by law to take a daily walk.)[6]

Biological considerations aside, the prospective husband goes prospecting for a bride among his peers. She should be the daughter of a similarly well-regarded citizen; raised in the women's quarters of her father's house, promising an easy transition to the women's quarters of her husband's house; and schooled in the womanly arts of spinning, household management—and nothing else. If all goes well, his wife-to-be will eventually personify the Athenian ideal, as articulated by that most golden of golden-age statesmen, Pericles: "The greatest glory of a woman is to be least talked about by men."[7] But for all to go that well, there must be a postnuptial training period. Xenophon, an associate of Socrates, offers some tips in the *Oeconomicus*, his guide to household management. During a pretend dialogue between Socrates and "Ischomachus," who is really Xenophon himself, the author describes how he handled his own fourteen-year-old bride. So young was she, explains Ischomachus, that in the realm of housework she knew no more than "how to turn out a cloak."

55

Before the lessons can start, Ischomachus and his bride pray to the gods—he "that I might really teach," while she concentrates on "earnestly promising before heaven to behave as she ought to do." Her earnestness convinces Ischomachus that she'll be a good pupil, "docile and sufficiently domesticated to carry on a conversation," although what he then recounts to Socrates is hardly a conversation—it's a ponderous monologue about his domestic philosophy, with barely a peep from the girl. As soon as she asks what she "can possibly do to help in the improvement of our property," Ischomachus plunges into his lecture. The gods have coupled together male and female, first of all, for the production of children, who will support the parents in old age. Beyond that primary reason, there's the fact that humans need shelter—they don't live in the open air, like animals. "[A]nd since both the indoor and outdoor tasks demand labor and attention, God from the first adapted the woman's nature, I think, to the indoor and man's to the outdoor tasks and cares." A woman's body and mind are less capable of enduring harsh weather, long travel, and so forth; her disposition is "fearful" while the man's is courageous, so he'd be the one to defend the household against "any wrong-doer" lurking outside. But both have "the power to practice due self-control." During his speech, Ischomachus says something about a queen bee, prompting a reasonable question from the long-suffering bride as to how the tasks of a queen bee resemble the tasks expected of her. The answer is, "she stays in the hive."[8]

For all the respect that Athenian society allegedly accords its wives, the terms commonly used to describe them suggest that what's respected is less the breeder than the breeding. One of two generic nouns are commonly used to identify their reproductive status: "childbearer" (*gyne*) before menopause, "old woman" (*graus*) afterward. The Greek legal term for "wife," *damar*, comes from the verb root *damazo*, to subdue, as in taming animals, working metals, or "of maidens, to make subject to a husband."[9] In fact, a new bride endures the same ritual as a newly bought slave: Both get a basketful of nuts dumped on their heads for good luck.[10] A man's wife is his legal property, in Athens as elsewhere, like—but not exactly like—his slaves. The difference, to one twenty-first-century historian, is subtle, but psychologically loaded: "Slaves and their agonies could be excluded from one's consciousness, like the sufferings of animals, but women are men's mothers, wives, sisters and daughters, and the battle of the sexes had to be fought over again in the mind of every male Athenian."[11]

In the hierarchy of human relationships reportedly codified by Plato, cerebral love between men (women are incapable of achieving it) is considered the highest form; sexual love between men, though not as exalted as the "platonic" variety, is still superior to heterosexual passion (for a courtesan, of course, not a wife), which should be fleeting. This culture idealizes masculinity and frowns upon men who get carried away by hetaerae. To fixate on a woman, no matter how delectable, she may be, is seen as a waste of a man's intellect and reason. A women, it is assumed, possesses neither— although that's the least of her problems, in Aristotle's view.

What defines a man and distinguishes him from a woman, according to Aristotle, is his "particular ability" to produce sperm; he is the "generating" parent, the one who makes life happen. What defines a woman and distinguishes her from a man is her "particular inability" to produce the same; she receives, he gives, and everything follows from there. Men go bald because both their brains and their output of seminal fluid are the largest of all animals. Women don't go bald, because "their nature is similar to that of children," incapable of producing semen. Eunuchs don't go bald, because they have made a transition from male to female, and "the female state" is, by its very nature, "a deformity," given that the female is nothing more or less than "a deformed male." The clitoris is essentially a penis interrupted. Menstrual fluid is analogous to seminal fluid in that it must be present for conception to occur—that idea won't be discredited until 1651[12]—but is, by nature, "impure" and enfeebled. It lacks "the principle of Soul," the vital force that powers the creation of new life and is, of course, exclusively contained in semen. Females are generative accidents, conceived by mistake when sperm is "thwarted, either because of the unsuitability

57

of the receiving matter itself" (that would be the feckless menstrual fluid) or because—see if this makes sense—"the wind is in the south."[13] Don't blame the sperm; blame the weather.

Aristotle lays out this one-sex model in *Generation of Animals*, his masterwork on human physiology. Galen, the Roman physician whose eminence will equal Aristotle's own, comes along six hundred years later to verify it all: Vaginas are would-be penises, labia correspond to foreskin, uteruses to scrotums, ovaries to testicles—citing the anatomical evidence gleaned from dissections of cadavers. Only around 1800 does the combined influence of these men wane and the concept of two separate, biologically distinct sexes emerge.[14]

Aristotle's work casts an aura of scientific truth over a pattern of thought already established in fiction. Long before the classical age, men have been steadily elevating their reproductive role and reducing women's in the process. Those stories include the Greek myths, which ascribe staggering generative feats to Zeus, the god of gods. He swallows the mother of his daughter, Athena, when Athena is still a fetus. She emerges from his head, full-grown and dressed for battle, while her brother, Dionysus, springs from Zeus's thigh. The castrated genitals of Uranus, the sky god, engender Aphrodite; she rises from the foam of the sea to her place in the pantheon, presiding over beauty and erotic love.[15] Aeschylus, the stellar Athenian dramatist, moves the idea that men generate life and women merely incubate it from the realm of popular storytelling onto the literary heights. A century or so before Aristotle's time, Aeschylus feeds this line to a character in his play *Eumenides*: "It is not the mother who is the parent of the child . . . she is merely nursemaid to the newly planted fetus. He who mounts is the one who gives birth . . . she, a stranger to a stranger, merely preserves the seed."

All of this is to be expected from a society that exalts manhood, a job made easier by denigrating womanhood. It's all about potency, and not just in Athens; such is the way of the ancient world. But even in context, these men celebrate the fact of being male so relentlessly, so ostentatiously, and sometimes so gratuitously, in pictures and in words, that you have to wonder if they're protesting too much. Maybe all the blathering about their great friendships with one another and the great sex with their boy toys, the humongous size of their brains and the amazing properties of their semen, is still not enough to persuade them of their own supremacy. They need to see the evidence, and there's no such thing as too much of it. They need visuals—graphic reminders that they are men and men are powerful. Or so it seems.

Whatever the reason, the men who preach moderation harbor an immoderate obsession with immoderately inflated penises as objets d'art, styled to look menacing rather than playful or erotic. Enormous, rock-hard organs dominate the vase paintings, attached to figures who brandish them like weapons (which is surely the point) in scenes with prostitutes. Illustrations of mythic battles between male warriors and female Amazons often show the enemy aiming her spear at the warrior's phallus, while he targets her nipple. Don't bother asking who wins the battle. Sculpted in marble or painted on clay, always colossal and always erect, displayed in public squares and private homes, the phallus is to Athens what the cross will be to medieval European towns: all over the place. Citizens can attend to men's business in town without losing sight of men's pride and joy, due to the fully engorged marble phalluses sculpted on statues of the gods.

And then they go missing. One summer morning in 415 BCE, the men of Athens wake up, throw on their togas, and head out of the house to powwow with their peers, expecting as usual to pass one, two, twenty, who knows how many priapic statues. Except that the statues have been castrated. Imagine the horror. These men control civic life; if tumescent-penis sculpture doesn't make them happy, there wouldn't be so many around. And suddenly there aren't any around. (The perpetrator's identity remains unknown, despite the best efforts of historians, not to mention the Athenians.)[16]

Maybe the sexual-triangulation routine doesn't work as well as Demosthenes makes it sound. He is, after all, a star orator; words are his business. In his apparently smug description, the system sounds like a man's dream come true, but in all probability it's no better than any other system designed to keep women at bay. The phallic excess doesn't exactly confirm that the supremacy of Athenian men goes unchallenged by women—that the hetaerae, the concubines, and the wives (especially the wives) do what they're told and stay where they're told—but it doesn't prove that the system has failed, either. The evidence says only that Athenians like to look at oversize erections and perhaps fantasize about using them against certain types of women. It suggests that men in Athens worry about their own erections, brood about being manly enough, and need to be reassured that they are. Too bad they've set things up so that they can't get reassurance from their wives, for obvious reasons; they can't get it from concubines, for equally obvious reasons; and they can't get very much of it from hetaerae, or their peers will look down on them.

If the women of Athens are so easily categorized and controlled, why is Greek literature filled with murderous Amazons, adulterous and shrewish goddesses (Aphrodite and Hera, respectively), wives withholding sex to stop their men from going to war (Lysistrata), and other troublemakers—such as Pandora, the Greek version of Eve? (The two characters are more or less contemporary, and probably derive from the same oral tradition.)

Pandora brings pain and misery to humanity because Zeus creates her for that express purpose. Still, she gets all the blame, and Western culture gets another legendary woman to kick around. Hesiod, the poor man's Homer, is responsible. This curmudgeonly farmer-poet records the first Greek creation saga in the eighth century BCE: "From her [Pandora] has sprung the race of womankind. / The deadly race and tribes of womankind. / Great pain to mortal men with whom they live . . . women are a curse to mortal men— / As Zeus ordained."[17]

Zeus, the pantheon's top dog, is a ruthless control freak who rises to power by staging a coup d'état against his father,

Cronus, orchestrated with the help of Zeus's mother. (The apple doesn't fall far from the tree in this family: Cronus uses a sickle—and the help of his mother— to castrate his own father, clearing his path to the same throne, presumably because the god of gods must be in possession of a penis.)[18] Zeus wants Prometheus punished for stealing fire, so he conjures Pandora to do the dirty work. He gives her a vessel (call it a box, if you must), then tells her that it will be her wedding gift to the man she marries, whoever he may be, without telling her what the vessel holds, or that opening it will unleash woe upon the world. Pandora finds the man to marry, who turns out to be the dim-witted brother of Prometheus (Zeus, of course, steers her in the right direction), and gives him the vessel. She doesn't know what's inside and hasn't tried to find out. There's been no disobedience; if that's the measure, Pandora is already a better woman than Eve. In any case, it isn't clear that Pandora actually opens the thing. The groom might be the one who lets woe into the world.[19] Woe passes from man to man, Zeus to the unnamed brother of Prometheus; Pandora is just the mule. But who wants to hear that story?

As for the perfect wife, she is Alcestis, eponymous star of a play by Euripides that has been called "perhaps the most beautiful celebration of conjugal love in all literature."[20] Not that there's much competition in this area. Celebrations of conjugal love in literature, even unbeautiful ones, are rare—possibly because reading (or writing) about conjugal love, as opposed to experiencing it in life, can be tedious. There's the duc de Saint-Simon's will, late seventeenth century, with its request for his-and-her coffins to be chained together so that he and his wife can enjoy eternal union. There's the Old Testament analogy of human marriage to the mystical union of God and Israel and the New Testament analogy of same to Christ and church, the latter expanded upon ad nauseam in epics by Milton and Spenser. There's the occasional tender scene in Shakespeare, though the bard doesn't often fall into this trap. There are saccharine sermons by sixteenth-century Anglican preachers (marriage, says one, is "an earthly paradise of happiness"),[21] poems by the Puritan housewife Anne Bradstreet, Elizabeth Browning's love letters—but generally speaking, conjugal love makes bad narrative.

In any case, the conjugal love most prominently on display in Euripides's drama flows in one direction, from wife to husband. (It may be mutual, but that is not the play's concern.) Alcestis is the queen of King Admetus, whose life is about to be snatched from him by the Fates. Apollo intervenes, brokering a deal; the Fates agree to accept a surrogate in the king's place. But surrogates, it seems, are hard to come by. As Apollo tells it, the king approached "all his kinsfolk, sounding them out, but only in his wife did he find a willingness . . . to die for him." The play opens on the day when Alcestis will die, praised by the chorus as "the noblest wife a husband ever had" and by her maidservant as "this paragon among women." Alcestis prepares herself by praying at various altars to various gods, pale but dry-eyed. Only when she enters the marital chamber does she break down: "O my bed of marriage, where once I gave myself, a virgin, to the husband for whom I now die, farewell! I do not hate you. Yet you and you alone have caused my death; for it is my reluctance to betray you and my husband that brings about my death." She throws herself on the bed, kissing it, soaking the coverlet with her tears. Many times she tries to pull herself away, stumbling out of the bedchamber, only to turn around and throw herself back on the bed. Her children show up (there seem to be two, a boy and a girl), crying and clinging to her dress, but by now Alcestis has composed herself. She hugs them, bidding farewell to each in turn as she tells them she has to die.

After that heartbreaking scene, Admetus begs his wife not to abandon him—whatever he felt about her in the past, the fact that she has volunteered her life for his has deepened his love for her a zillionfold—but she senses the winged figure of Hades, leading her to death, and knows that time is short. She must convey her last wishes to her husband, although all she asks in exchange for her sacrifice is this: "Do not marry again and give them a stepmother to ill-treat them, your children and mine, someone who will love them less than I and eye them with jealousy . . . a viper would show them more affection." Admetus agrees, obviously, and makes some additional promises: to loathe his parents, either one of whom could and should have volunteered in Alcestis's place, since they've already lived their lives; to end all merrymaking at the palace; to order a sculptured image of Alcestis to "lie outstretched" on the conjugal bed, which he will "clasp and fold in my arms; I will call your name and imagine it is my darling wife I hold in my embrace." Finally, he'll instruct their children to entomb him in her coffin, because "I have no wish to be parted ever from you, the only one who was true to me, not even in death."

After Alcestis's death and burial, Admetus descends into grief. He berates himself for being a coward; he should have answered death's call when it came, and spared his wife. His anguish is terrible, but it won't last long. Unbeknownst to Admetus, his friend Heracles ambushes Death himself near Alcestis's tomb, and fights him until Death cries uncle and returns Alcestis to the living. No matter, she still passes the Athenian perfect-wife test with an A -triple plus for expressing the ultimate in conjugal devotion. Variants of the test will reappear in story and verse until the perfect-wife model is revised (don't hold your breath, the modern age is a long way off). And while some characters will equal Alcestis's performance—her Roman counterpart, Lucretia, for one, and the medieval Griselda, for another—virtually none will surpass it. To the ancient (and medieval, and Renaissance) mind, nothing is more valuable to a man than his honor, and nothing is more virtuous than a wife who behaves in a manner that brings him honor. Thus Alcestis is the ultimate in virtuous wifehood, as her maidservant points out: "How would a woman give greater proof of honoring her husband than by freely giving her life for his?" She even makes it into Plato's *Symposium*, written in the same time period. Phaedrus, one of the participants, gushes on about her, "for she was willing to lay down her life on behalf of her husband, when no one else would," an act of such nobility that it impressed not only mortals but also the gods, who so deeply admired her noble act that they returned her to life.

It doesn't work that way in reverse. A man who gives his life for other men in battle is honorable; a man who gives his life for God (or, in the biblical case of Abraham, is willing to murder his only son for love of God) is honorable, but a man who gives his life for his wife is a disgrace. In the *Symposium,* which is, after all, a discussion about love, Phaedrus begins his discourse by saying, "Love will make men dare to die for their beloved—love alone; and women as well as men." He duly provides examples: Alcestis first, then Achilles. Who does Achilles die for? Another man, "his lover Patroclus." For that, "the gods honored him even above Alcestis, and sent him to the Islands of the Blest." As long as people subscribe to the notion that men are superior to women, it goes without saying that they'll also subscribe to the notion that men's lives are more precious than women's. This will change when the mantra of manliness switches to "women and children first," sometime between the age of chivalry and the sinking of the *Titanic.* The Athenian mantra goes something like this, as parsed by Euripides: "Better a thousand women should perish than that one man cease to see the light."[22]

It's difficult to imagine those breeder-wives acquitting themselves as nobly as Alcestis, but chances are good that they're not quite as compliant as their citizen husbands might wish. Plutarch argues as much, has an arsenal of choice anecdotes to support his thesis, and also has the advantage of hindsight; living a few centuries after the time of Aristotle, Plato, et al., he has nothing to fear from those earlier masters of the universe. In "On the Avoidance of Anger," Plutarch paints a scene involving Socrates and his famously un-docile wife, Xanthippe, who is furious at her husband for bringing a buddy home for dinner without warning her. "Xanthippe laid into them angrily, hurled insults at them and eventually overturned the table," Plutarch recounts. Insulted, the guest springs to his feet and heads for the door. Socrates has to save face—and comes up with a zinger. "When we were at your house the other day," he reasons with his friend, "a hen flew in and did exactly the same, but we didn't get cross, did we?" The metaphor is apt and purposeful. Socrates is telling his friend that to storm out would be to lower himself to Xanthippe's level—the inferior female level—and as Plutarch notes, "The most infirm minds are most liable to pain, and consequently their anger is greater because their weakness is greater. This is also why women are more irascible than men."

So tickled is Plutarch by Xanthippe's table-flipping that he recycles the anecdote in another essay, "On Contentment," with different characters playing the roles of Socrates and his wife. This time the victimized husband is Pittacus, a man who is "outstandingly famous for courage, wisdom and morality." After his wife tips the table (Pittacus has committed the same crime as Socrates), Pittacus says to his shocked friends, "No one's life is perfect; anyone with only my troubles is very well off." Since he's ostensibly not talking about the heroic Socrates, Plutarch is free to editorialize: "In public this man is an object of envy, but as soon as he opens the door of his home, he's in a pitiful state: his wife is in complete control, she bosses him about and argues all the time. He's got rather a lot of reasons to be miserable, whereas I've got none."[23]

Plutarch's own marriage, if his report is trustworthy, appears to be both placid and mutually faithful. And his wife, Timoxena, is no ignoramus; she's as literate and cultured as a hetaera, capable of grasping the philosophical allusions Plutarch makes in letters to her. One of these, "In Consolation of His Wife," written upon the death of their beloved two-year-old daughter, reveals a loving and respectful husband who regards his wife as an equal—in the domestic sphere, at least. He calls her "my partner in bringing up so many children—all brought up with no one else's help in our own home." Like other well-off Athenians, Timoxena could employ full-time childcare but apparently chooses not to, which Plutarch clearly admires. He appreciates her for all the paradigmatic qualities, such as her handling of their daughter's funeral "with discretion and in silence." While other, lesser wives might "wallow in empty, indecent grief,"

Timoxena manages to project "unaffectedness and frugality in sad circumstances." She's been through this before—the couple lost a son or two before the daughter—and has already proved to her husband "that you can remain stable under these circumstances" without becoming bitter or withdrawn, and still perform "noble acts stemming from motherly love." Beyond her stellar maternal performance, Timoxena has impressed Plutarch's friends with "the inextravagance of your clothing and makeup, and with the modesty of your lifestyle."

Then again, Plutarch is probably no slouch in the wife-training department himself. He may be half a millennium removed from his cultural forebears, but that's nowhere near long enough for the marital ideal to change. "A wife should have no feelings of her own, but share her husband's . . . a wife ought not to have friends of her own, but use her husband's," Plutarch writes in his "Precepts of Marriage," composed as a wedding gift for a young couple of his acquaintance. "You are her 'father' and her 'mother' and her 'brother,'" he tells the groom, "but it is just as honorable to hear a wife say, 'Husband, you are my guide and philosopher, my teacher of the noblest and divinest lessons.'" Is this self-styled conjugal sage really doing the groom a service by inflating the bride's expectations about what a husband can be and do for her? Maybe Plutarch doesn't have a hetaera, but this young man ought to keep that option open. There's no reason not to; this is ancient Athens, where it's perfectly normal for respectable men to enjoy multiple bedmates. What Freud described as "the most prevalent form of degradation" in the Victorian's erotic life is certainly prevalent here—but it's not perceived as degradation.

"In a wife I would desire / What in whores is always found— / The lineaments of Gratified desire." So writes William Blake in the century before Freud's, voicing the unsung classical legacy: There is one kind of woman you marry, and another kind of woman you fuck.

FOUR

Do Roman Wives Have It All?

A T the end of the year 218 BCE, the Iberian general Hannibal pulls off one of the most stunning maneuvers in military history. Evading hostile Gallic natives as well as Roman forces, Hannibal leads some thirty-eight thousand foot soldiers, eight thousand cavalry, and fifty or sixty elephants over the Alps—in wintertime, yet—and enters northern Italy, to the unpleasant surprise of Rome's republican government. Despite heavy losses sustained during the Alpine crossing, Hannibal manages to demolish the Roman army in battle after battle over the next two years of this second Punic War. By 215, Rome's panicked political leaders, desperate to conserve resources for military use, consider austerity measures. One is imposed on the people—or on half of them, anyway. Known as the Oppian law, after its author, the tribune Oppius, it forbids Roman women to carry more than a half ounce of gold, to wear colored clothes (saving on dyes), or to ride in carriages on public streets unless they are priestesses engaged in sacred business.[1]

The war goes on for another fourteen years, but in the end Rome prevails. Peace and prosperity follow—yet the Oppian law remains in force. The senate doesn't take up the issue of repeal until 195, six years after the defeat of Hannibal, and the ensuing debate quickly descends into a prolonged shouting match between the conservatives opposed to repeal and the progressives in favor.

When word gets out that the conservative faction is gaining ground, women launch what may be the first women's rights demonstration in history. They march through the streets of Rome in expanding numbers. Ladies pour into the city from the provinces to join the locals; they ring the Forum; they even storm the senate and conduct a sit-in, occupying the offices of the bad guys.

Needless to say, their actions put some of the politicians on edge. The conservatives come into the debate already alarmed by women's increasing assertiveness—they see it as symptomatic of a society in moral freefall—and this outrageous protest only justifies their fears. It also hardens their position: The Oppian law restrains women from making men's lives even more hellish than they already are. If nothing else, it keeps wives from the most egregious displays of extravagance, and from hounding their husbands for the money that mounting such displays requires.

The consul, the highest elected official in the republican government, is Cato, and he is disgusted by the outrageous behavior of the women who have breached the very walls of the senate. (Historians identify him as Cato the Elder or the Censor to distinguish him from his great-grandson of the same name.) He holds men themselves responsible for the widespread breakdown in patriarchal control.

"If every married man had been concerned to ensure that his own wife looked up to him and respected his rightful position as her husband, we should not have half this trouble with women en masse," Cato thunders before the senate. "Instead, women have become so powerful that our independence has been lost in our own homes and is now being trampled and stamped underfoot in public. We have failed to restrain them as individuals, and now they have combined to reduce us to our present panic." Furthermore, he notes, "If women were modest enough to restrict their interests to what concerns them, they should properly be completely uninterested in knowing what laws were being passed or rescinded in this House." Why don't the Romans, never shy about appropriating elements of Athenian culture, do the same with their approach to conjugal life? Even at its most rigid, Roman society has never denied married women freedom of movement outside the home. Maybe it's time to reconsider that position.

Then Cato moves in for the kill: "Woman is a violent and uncontrolled animal, and it is no good giving her the reins . . . you have got to keep the reins firmly in your own hands[2] . . . What they want is complete freedom—or, not to mince words, complete license. If they carry this present issue by storm, what will they not try next?" If the senate votes for repeal, he warns, the dominoes will continue to fall one by one until every man endures the fate worse than death, and it will be every man's fault: "Suppose you allow them to acquire or to extort one right after another, and in the end to achieve complete equality with men, do you think that you will find them bearable? Nonsense. Once they have achieved equality, they will be your masters."

Anchoring the debate for the progressive side is Valerius, the tribune, an office reserved for plebeians. As such, his view can be assumed to reflect popular opinion more closely than Cato's. And Valerius is quick to point out the hypocrisy of the conservatives' position:

Our wives alone, it seems, are to receive no benefits from the restoration of peacetime conditions. Men, of course, will have purple on their togas if they are magistrates or priests; so will our sons; so will the bigwigs of the country towns and, here in Rome, even the district officials . . . even to the extent of their being cremated in their purple when they are dead. But women, if you please, are to be forbidden to wear purple. You, being a man, can have a purple saddle-cloth; the lady who presides over your household will be forbidden to wear a purple cloak; and so [Valerian moves, in for the kill] your horse will be better turned out than your wife.

Against Cato's argument that as long as "the regulations about dress apply universally," no woman needs to feel "ashamed or angry" to be denied some possession that another is allowed, Valerius scoffs,

> in a state where nobody possesses gold, no jealous rivalry exists between one woman or another. And what is the present state of affairs? One in which every single woman feels distressed and angry. They look at the wives of our Latin allies, and what do they see? These women are allowed the ornaments which Roman women are forbidden; these women are a striking sight in their gold and purple; these women drive through Rome, while [our wives] have to walk, as if it was the Latin allies, not Rome, that ruled the Empire.

This, says Valerius, ought to distress men no less than women. And besides, women can't enjoy the privileges of men. They can't be magistrates or priests, they can't acquire "the gifts and spoils of war." For women the prizes are "elegance, jewelry, and beauty-culture." Purple and gold is what they go without when in mourning; is that supposed to be their permanent state?[3]

In the end, the idea of men's horses being better dressed than their wives disturbs the majority more than the threat of men being under the thumb of their wives. The senate strikes down the Oppian law, and the defeated conservatives slink home to their wives.

Whether the Catonians need be alarmed by the restiveness of women is a matter of opinion, but they're correct on at least one score: The Oppian protest is no isolated incident. For much of the last century, the chorus of women clamoring for release from men's iron grip has risen in volume, and the demand to wear purple and gold is the least of it. What women really want is emancipation from the rigorous conventions of the marriage code in place since the early days of the Republic, and by the time of the senate showdown, their efforts have already begun to pay off. The code grants men absolute authority over their wives as well as any property they bring to the marriage or may inherit later on. It also allows husbands sole discretion over when, whether, and how to punish errant wives, up to and including murder in cases of adultery, with no questions asked by the state.[4]

At first the men who settle Rome (they arrive from Alba around 750 BCE, some five hundred years before Cato) don't need a marriage code. They need women—they've got a settlement to populate.[5] But the locals resist handing over their daughters outright to foreign interlopers they consider barbarians, so the interlopers try a more oblique approach. They throw a festival for their neighbors, the Sabines, and more to the point, for their nubile offspring. At a prearranged signal, the settlers (who may or may not have lured the male population out of the area on some pretext) seize the best-looking girls in reach and spirit them away. From this comes the supposedly factual story of "the rape of the Sabine women," promulgated most notably by Livy, the patriotic Roman historian-cum-mythmaker. In his account it hardly sounds like rape; the kidnappers treat their captives with all due respect that night, leaving them to sleep with their alleged virginity intact. The next day the girls listen to a sales pitch delivered by the settlers' leader, Romulus, about the glorious conjugal life that lies ahead for those who elect it, each to her own abductor—and no further persuasion is necessary. When the settlers return to town with the newly deflowered girls, now their de facto wives, the Sabine elders go nuts, and war ensues.

At some point, perhaps when each side has proven its manliness to the other, a truce is called. After that, the Sabines stop thinking of the men from Alba as barbarians and start thinking of them as sons-in-law; the men from Alba accept the Sabines as co-settlers. Together they build the city and determine that it will be ruled by kings, the first of whom is Romulus, who gives Rome its name.[6]

Livy's saga is intended to illuminate the otherwise obscure ancestry of the Roman people, accomplished to great effect. Whether intentionally or not, the Sabine legend also explains the origin of a deeply primitive wedding rite—perhaps in order to justify its continuing presence in Roman life long after society moves on to a more progressive form of marriage. This nuptial custom derives from an ancient cross-cultural practice known as "marriage by capture," precisely what the Sabine scenario depicts.[7]

It takes place in the evening, after the negotiations over dowry, bride price, and other business matters have concluded, and the couple has been joined before witnesses. Tradition calls for the bride, putting on a show of maidenly fear, to be snatched from her mother's arms by friends or relations. They veil her in flame-colored fabric and drag her outside where others are waiting. With two young boys holding the bride's hands and a third leading the procession, the crowd marches her through the streets to her new home, singing ribald songs. The leader carries a lit torch, and upon reaching the groom's residence, he tosses the torch into the crowd, provoking mayhem. The mayhem has nothing to do with fear of self-immolation—people aren't trying to escape the flaming object, they're trying to catch it. (From this comes the tradition of tossing the bridal bouquet, though he or she who catches the torch wins a long life rather than the next walk down the aisle.) After the bride is carried over the threshold and pays her respects to the household gods, she's deposited in the marital bedchamber. There she is undressed by *univirae*—Roman women who've been married only once, which confers high stature—and otherwise made ready for the imminent defloration-consummation-"rape" that seals the deal.[8]

Once the deal is sealed, this bride has to become a wife, preferably a good one; she'll need a model. Cue the story of Lucretia, a Roman original destined to enchant Chaucer and Dante and Shakespeare, Rembrandt and Botticelli, St. Augustine and Alexander Pope, Benjamin Britten and the BBC, to name a few.

Livy is again the essential source of the story that both explains the collapse of the Roman monarchy (circa 510 BCE) and recasts the iconic Good Wife in three dimensions.[9] The tale begins in an army camp, where officers of high rank and two sons of the king huddle in the quarters of Sextus Tarquinius, one of the princes. The topic under discussion is not military strategy—the men, including the royal brothers, are far too drunk for that—but women, specifically their wives. They take turns bragging about their wives' virtue, and as the drinking continues, the bragging escalates. Finally one of them breaks in to suggest that they settle the matter once and for all: "Let us mount our horses and see for ourselves the disposition of our wives." This man is confident, as he should be; his wife is the virtuous Lucretia. Off they go, "heated with wine," to catch their wives doing whatever they do when their husbands aren't expected home anytime soon.

One by one the men have to eat their words as they find their wives engaged in various frivolous pursuits—the king's daughters-in-law loll around at a luxurious banquet trading gossip with their airhead friends, to the princes' shame—and then they get to the home of the man who suggested this test. He is clearly the winner, for even though the hour is late, Lucretia toils away spinning wool in the lamplight in the company of her maid-servants. She rises to greet the men with consummate grace, and her victorious husband invites them to dinner. At this point Sextus Tarquinius is "seized with a wicked desire to debauch Lucretia by force," but he bides his time. After the men return to the camp, Sextus sneaks back to Rome and to Lucretia, asking if he might be accommodated for the night. Naturally she shows him to a guest room—she has no idea of his purpose, and besides, he's the king's son—and there Sextus waits, "burning with passion," until the house is quiet.

Now he's on the move. He draws his sword and enters Lucretia's room, where she is asleep in bed. Sextus, "holding the woman down with his left hand on her breast," tells her that he'll kill her if she makes a sound, then attempts to sweet-talk her into consensual sex, but gets nowhere. So he goes further: If she doesn't comply, he'll stab her to death, do the same to the servant he brought from camp, and dump the servant's naked body into bed with hers. That does it—what could more dishonor her husband (and his name, his

73

family, and his descendants) than to discover his wife "put to death in adultery with a man of base condition"? She lets the lustful Sextus have his way with her. When it's over, he leaves, "exulting in his conquest of a woman's honour."

Lucretia, overcome with grief, dispatches messengers to her father in Rome and her husband at the camp, asking them to come at once with trusted friends. When they arrive, Lucretia tells them that her heart is guiltless but her body has been violated, and asks for their promise that Sextus will be punished. The father, the husband, and the trusted friends so pledge; then Lucretia pulls out a knife she's hidden in her dress and plunges it into her heart.

The men carry Lucretia's corpse to the marketplace and tell the gathering crowd what has happened. People already hate the violent Sextus, his equally brutal brothers—there are at least three—and their father, who has tyrannized his subjects for the twenty-five years of his reign. But the men of this family are nothing compared to the evil queen, Tullia, whose crimes include orchestrating the murder of her own sister—formerly the wife of the king—so that she could marry her erstwhile brother-in-law and become queen. The news of Lucretia's rape and suicide seals the fate of these wicked royals; everyone wants to rid Rome of the entire clan. The plot goes forward immediately. The king is exiled, along with his sons—save for Sextus, who is murdered before he can get away—and his charming queen. The monarchy is dead: Long live the Republic.[10]

Livy, writing two hundred years after Cato, was less concerned with the historical accuracy of his work than with its ability to restore moral order to Roman society, and if turning fact into fiction or fiction into fact allows him to convey his message more effectively, so be it.[11] Predictably enough, most of the women who parade through Livy's works are either impossibly good or impossibly evil, the usual symbols employed for the usual purposes of inspiration or deterrence. Lucretia's his baby; Livy puts her on the cultural map, and he does an artful job. He presents her as a real person in real time, a player on the stage of real life—and also as a fantasy, a flawless jewel, the quintessence of the perfect wife. The one belies the other—either she's real or she's perfect; she can't be both. But she becomes both and remains so, long after the Roman monarchy, the Roman Republic, and the Roman Empire fade to black.

The locus of what Livy sees as moral decay and what Cato rightly perceives as the overarching demand of the Oppian protestors is the relaxation of male authority in marriage.[12] From the third century BCE, the people who disagree—they see it as social progress—begin to multiply and ultimately to prevail over the conservatives. Until then, marriage for women means a change of masters; literally the handoff (the custom is known as *in manum* "into his hand") of the bride directly from father to husband, with no break in the chain of her dependence or her servitude. (When a father takes the arm of his daughter and walks her down a twenty-first-century aisle, he doesn't release her until they reach the groom and she takes her place by his side at the altar. That's a symbolic reminder of *in manum*.) Marital union occurs in one of two socially acceptable forms in these days. The first and most ancient is *coemptio*, a simple civil procedure before witnesses with little fuss or expense, preferred by those lacking in money or patience or both. The second appeals to the patricians; called *confarreatio* ("sharing of spelt"), it's as elaborate as *coemptio* is simple, replete with complicated rituals, animal sacrifice, special foods—including spelt bread—and precise choreography. *In manum* follows both.

But then suddenly the matrimonial winds shift: between the fifth and third centuries BCE, a new, "free" form replaces *in manum*. Almost no historical record survives of the age during which this shift occurs—nothing to explain exactly how and why it occurs—but presumably a majority wants it, or it wouldn't have happened.[13] *Usus*, or free marriage, resembles trial marriage, common-law style. It requires neither ceremony nor consummation; there is no immediate transfer of authority, and until there is, the father holds on to the property or other assets he has promised as a dowry. A man and a woman become husband and wife simply by setting up house together and remaining in "continuous association" for a year.[14]

Usus gives women (make that girls, for it's still customary for fathers to marry off adolescent daughters to middle-aged men) an amount of freedom that is remarkable in the ancient world. For the first year she can escape male control entirely, since the man who has control is not the man she's living with. And if she's very clever, she can avoid her husband's control forever. According to the principle of "continuous association," a couple can spend no more than two consecutive days and nights apart during the course of that first year, or the countdown starts all over again. The father profits as well as his daughter, for as long as he controls her, he also controls her dowry. And if the marriage goes through but later falls apart, he gets a good chunk of his investment back. As *usus* becomes an entrenched custom and the transfer of power (over daughters or dowries) becomes increasingly rare, some of the legal restrictions placed on married women begin to loosen. Wives gain a measure of economic independence—due to revised property laws allowing them to keep and manage family inheritances instead of automatically relinquishing everything to their husbands. They're also allowed to divorce their husbands at will. Under *usus*, dissolving a union is as easy as forming one, for either spouse: One or the other simply moves out of the shared residence. That's all it takes. And there's nothing to stop either of them from embarking on a sequence of these unions, which amounts to unbridled sexual license for wives, compared to the old days.

Still, the male autocracy remains firmly in place. *Usus* doesn't free women to initiate legal action, sit on juries, legislate, vote, run for office, or even to become the legal guardians of their own children[15]; they play no public role. As for the domestic sphere, things haven't changed all that much. Roman society has never maintained a policy of domestic confinement for wives; even during *in manum* they were allowed considerable mobility. In theory, mobility would open the door to infidelity—exactly why Athens does confine its wives—but in practice, the old Roman approach to unchaste wives served as a powerful deterrent. The husband who caught his wife in flagrante delicto could do as he wished: divorce her, banish her, beat her, kill her, even forgive her. He still can. As Cato explains, just after the transition to *usus*: "If you should take your wife in adultery, you may with impunity put her to death without trial. If you commit adultery or indecency yourself, she dare not lay a finger on you, and she has no legal right to do so."[16]

But *usus* is revolutionary enough to agitate conservatives, growing ever more voluble as Rome undergoes its third and last political restructuring, from republic to empire. They may be in the minority, but since they tend to be prominent men of letters or state, they make a disproportionate amount of noise. In essays and poems, on the public stage and in private huddles, these men bemoan the loss of the good old days when men reigned supreme and women knew their place. "Wives were different then," writes Juvenal, the second-century satirical poet. En route to trashing the women of his day, he pays homage to the fictional Athenian character who epitomizes that difference: "Our wives sit and watch / Alcestis undertaking to die in her husband's stead: / If they had a similar chance, *they'd* gladly sacrifice / Their husbands' life for their lapdogs."[17]

The naysayers who blame all of Rome's monstrous social problems on the laissez-faire attitude embedded in *usus* go too far, but that's not to say their hysteria has no basis in reality. For starters, all this freedom has not done wonders for marital harmony. This is troublesome because lack of marital harmony tends to cut down on marital sex, and without marital sex the underpopulation problem can only get worse. If the trend continues, the consequences for the Roman state will be disastrous—no babies, no soldiers. The specter of an impotent military has haunted the Republic's leaders since the reproductive slowdown became apparent in the second century BCE. If ancient Rome was in the habit of conducting surveys on the frequency of marital sex, they have yet to turn up. But it seems reasonable to assume a connection between the rise of *usus* by the third century BCE and a birth rate plummeting precipitously enough to alarm politicians just one hundred years later—around the time that the public conversation begins to center on marital strife. That conversation, revolving around the well-fed and well-bred population, will only intensify with time.

It makes sense that well-fed and well-bred couples would be prone to more than the usual allotment of conjugal discontent. On the one hand, affluent wives have the money, the leisure, and now the autonomy to do as they please. On the other hand, money combined with leisure can mean frivolity and extravagance, something for which the men of Rome will criticize the women of Rome with mounting passion until Rome is no more. One writer will even refer back to the repeal of the Oppian law, two hundred years earlier, as the catalyst of it all, attributing the disaster to the men who made such a wrongheaded decision. The senators "had no conception of . . . the extremes to which [women's] brazenness would go, once it had succeeded in trampling on the laws." If only these dolts had foreseen the havoc they would unleash in the future, "they would have set their faces firmly against the devastating spread of extravagance at the moment of its introduction. But why speak of women?" this first-century CE writer asks. "Lacking strong mental powers and being denied the opportunity of more serious interests, they are naturally driven to concentrate their attention" on mindless matters. "What of men?"[18]

What of men, indeed? While the wives idle away their time grooming themselves for assignations with their lovers or picking fights with their husbands out of boredom—or pondering divorce, now that *usus* has made it so easy—their husbands' behavior is far from exemplary. They seem to have as little to do as their wives, spending their days and nights schmoozing with other men in resentful avoidance of their overly emancipated and therefore overly aggressive spouses, issuing pompous judgments to each other on women's moral lapses. They dump their wives as easily as their wives dump them, citing such trivial reasons as vanity, shrillness, or developing too many wrinkles.[19] Unless these couples regard mutual hostility as erotic, they're not likely to be having much sex with each other, especially given the reports of rampant adultery on both sides.

When Augustus assumes power of the new Roman empire in 27 BCE, the population problem has become a looming catastrophe. Desperate to reverse the trend, the emperor comes up with a two-part plan designed to encourage reproduction. Part one passes into law in 18 BCE, part two in 9 CE; they are known collectively as the Lex Julia et Papia. The legislation bars bachelors from high positions, such as the governorship of a province, and restricts the ability of single men between twenty-five and sixty and single women twenty to fifty to receive inheritances. Childless widows or divorcees are given, respectively, twelve and six months to remarry or face penalties. (In the year 9, when the second part of the legislation is instituted, those intervals will be extended to two years for widows and eighteen months for divorcees.)[20]

In what seems to be a realistic nod to the high rate of infant mortality that parents are forced to accept throughout the West until modern times, the Lex J & P allows couples whose childlessness is due not to lack of breeding but to the early death of offspring a free ride if they meet one of three conditions: they produce three children who live until their first birthdays, or two who survive to age three, or one who reaches the age of marriage (twelve for girls, fourteen for boys). Meanwhile, the practice of deliberate infanticide, otherwise known as exposure, goes on.[21]

The Lex J & P offers rewards for good reproductive behavior as well as penalties for noncompliance. It's not uncommon for men—outside of the patricians—to remain unmarried because they already live with women who once were slaves. They'd be happy to wed these mistresses and raise children with them if it was legally possible, but the status of such alliances have never been clarified; now Augustus's legislation specifically endorses them. It also rewards wives for bearing a minimum of three children. For this they are granted full legal autonomy over themselves as well as any assets they brought to the marriage; if their husbands hold civil office, they'll be promoted. (In the Roman suburbs these benefits don't kick in until a fourth child is produced, and in the provinces it's a fifth.)[22]

Affluent couples have the most to gain through these incentives. Both spouses may be candidates for inheritance, the wives probably have substantial dowries, and the husbands are the likely holders of civic office. But the target audience pays no attention; neither the rewards nor the penalties induce couples to conceive. The Lex J & P has had time to prove its effectiveness for more than a century when Tacitus offers this terse assessment in 116 CE: "Childlessness prevailed."[23] There are so many factors contributing to the prevalence of childlessness in Rome, the majority of them endemic to everyday life, it's hard to see how that situation could be reversed. Even if married couples live in harmony and have sex every night, they probably use contraception. If that fails, there's always abortion. Romans have a long history of practicing both. And the shared conviction now held by the monied classes that too many children spoil the marriage doesn't help.

The Roman way of life is laden with inducements to infertility that would be invisible to the Roman lawmaker.[24] First of all, lead poisoning is virtually unavoidable. There's lead in the pipes from which Romans draw their water, lead in the powder women use to whiten their faces, and lead in the pots that are used to cook food and to boil down the grape syrup used to sweeten the wine that is drunk in copious amounts by men and women. Men consume it by the gallon while they're at the baths, and they're at the baths nearly every day, arriving in the late afternoon and sometimes staying until dawn, drinking away with other men. Of course, excessive drinking, even without lead exposure, can cause sterility, not to mention impotence. And spending many hours in the baths, almost always in warm to hot water (only at the end of the ritual would a man plunge into cold water, and only briefly) inhibits sperm production. And, of course, sexual promiscuity spreads disease. Romans may not be having much marital sex, but they're far from chaste.

As befits the first ruler of the newly created empire of almighty Rome, Augustus possesses an acute sense of self-importance and a knack for pious observations, which he generously shares with his people during frequent public appearances. Both qualities are apparent in his private life as well. A decade before he becomes emperor—an ascendance largely due to being Julius Caesar's adoptive son and heir—Augustus he divorces his first wife, citing the "moral perversity" of her negative attitude toward one of his concubines. That is more than enough justification for divorce in Rome, but it's not his only reason; he's passionately in love with a teenager named Livia, who is six months pregnant with her own husband's child. They move in together, Livia obtains a divorce, and three days after her baby is born, she and Augustus marry. (At the wedding, Livia's ex-husband is nice enough to give her away.) The marriage lasts for fifty-one years, until the emperor's death. Unlike the first wife, Livia gives Augustus no flak over his numerous extramarital involvements, and even more endearingly, she indulges his taste for deflowering virgins by helping to procure them.[25] Through it all, Augustus proselytizes "family values" as tirelessly as any Republican politician in America today, with the same old goal in mind: to encourage reproduction.[26]

Brothels, the keeping of concubines, and sexual congress with slaves remain lawful (for men) during the reign of Augustus, but he of all people is responsible for Rome's first adultery laws—ostensibly to raise the moral IQ of society by protecting the institution of marriage. Adultery is still, as ever, something that only a wife can commit. But now that jurisdiction has been transferred from the family to the state, uroxide for infidelity is officially outlawed.[27] The state prefers banishment for both wife and lover—to different islands, naturally—but first the case must be tried in court. If found guilty, the lover also loses half his property, the married woman a third of hers and half of her dowry. Her husband gets a portion of the remainder, more if there are children; and if the woman remarries on her lonely island, it can't be to a freeborn Roman. The husband must initiate prosecution within sixty days of divorcing his unfaithful wife; the law is designed to shame him into doing both, even if he'd rather forgive and forget. If he goes through with the divorce but fails to prosecute, anyone over the age of twenty-five can take action against her instead. If the cuckold doesn't divorce her, she can't be prosecuted, she's immune—but anyone else can prosecute him for moral failure. Anyone male, that is—legal action is still the exclusive domain of men.

When Plutarch turns his quizzical eye on Rome late in the first century, he's astonished by its marriage customs. One of the things that astonishes him has been routine in Rome since the days when *in manum* structured conjugal life. At a glitzy dinner party in the not-yet-eternal city, Plutarch finds himself in uncharted social waters. It's not that men and women are mingling, common enough back in Athens; it's that husbands and wives are mingling—with each other.[28] Here in Rome respectable wives can trot around town without their husbands, talking freely with men not married to them, even with men who are strangers—and still be considered respectable. Do Roman women have it all?

Plutarch finds so many aspects of Roman life mystifying, marriage included, that he addresses them one by one in an interrogatory essay called "Roman Questions," supplying no answers. (The questions say it all.)[29] Why do these women kiss their male relatives on the lips? Could it a leftover custom from the days when drinking wine was off-limits to women, and their menfolk wanted to catch the scofflaws? Why is it acceptable for husbands and wives to receive gifts from anyone but each other? Plutarch wonders if it has something to do with Solon's old law of inheritance that rendered marital bequests suspect, or with some misguided attempt to elevate the conjugal relationship above all others, depriving the couple of pleasure. And what compels Roman men away from home to alert their wives of their imminent arrival? Are they so certain of their wives' good behavior that surprising them, and possibly finding them up to no good, seems unnecessarily vigilant? Are the men giving the women time to calm a fractious household, ensuring their own "undisturbed and pleasant" homecoming? Or possibly the husbands assume—as the smugly married Plutarch himself might assume—that their wives have been longing for them, and will be ecstatic to hear that the wait is over.

While Plutach mulls away, Juvenal rips into Roman marriage and Roman wives with copious amounts of venom. It must be said that Juvenal, whose "Satire VI" is described by one twenty-first-century writer as "the locus classicus of ancient misogynism,"[30] is an equal-opportunity satirist of Roman life—really a verbal carica-turist, to whom nothing and no one is sacred. His artful wife-bashing, rendered in verse, suggests an author taking dark delight in the literary mounting of a personal vendetta. There is no record of his marital status. He might be a resolute bachelor like Colonel Pickering, minus the gentility; he might be the epitome of the henpecked husband; he might be a sharp-eyed homosexual, or a very witty eunuch, or just another Roman husband pinioned by a tongue-lashing wife, who saves his retorts for the page.

"Satire VI" is a litany of wicked female behavior in the form of a prose poem, addressed to a soon-to-be-married friend named Postumus. Marriage is a foolish endeavor, Juvenal warns. He ex-presses astonishment that Postumus, "once the randiest hot-rod-about-town," could be the same man now "sticking his silly neck out for the matrimonial halter." Juvenal mocks his friend for imag-ining that his bride, Hiberina, possesses "old-fashioned moral vir-tues" just because she was brought up in seclusion, in the country. The "chaste and modest bride" is an extinct breed. "Tell me, will Hiberina / Think one man enough? You'd find it much less trouble / To make her agree to being blinded in one eye."

> *Postumus, are you* really
> *Taking a wife? You used to be sane enough—what*
> *Fury's got into you, what snake has stung you up?*

Why endure such bitch-tyranny when rope's available
By the fathom, when all those dizzying top-floor windows
Are open for you, when there are bridges handy
To jump from? Supposing none of these exits catches
Your fancy, isn't it better to sleep with a pretty boy?
Boys don't quarrel all night, or nag you for little presents . . .
. . . or complain that you don't come
Up to their expectations, or demand more grasping passion.[31]

Poor Postumus can also expect Hiberina to exhibit some or perhaps all of the following traits: an uncontrollable bladder, nymphomania, a talent for cuckoldry (Postumus will hang laurel wreaths on his front door, thinking he is about to welcome his own child into the world—until he sees its face, which "recalls some armoured thug"), priggish condescension, a "gold-digging itch," and "sadistic urges." She will destroy his boyhood friendships, insist that he include her lovers in his will, sic her mother on him, bribe her servants, pretend sickness in order to entertain her doctor/lover under the sheets, corrupt her daughters, and shed crocodile tears to get what she wants. And even if Postumus continues to desire her, he should not forget that "The bed that contains a wife is always hot with quarrels / And mutual bickering; sleep's the last thing you get there. This is her battleground, her station for husband-baiting."

Juvenal's an entertainer, an observer, and a writer, not a Roman senator or a self-styled guardian of public morality (often one and the same, neither of them immune to Juvenal's stiletto pen). But he definitely has a thing for the materfamilias of yore, and a thing against the loose-living wives of his time.

In the old days poverty
Kept Latin women chaste; hard work, too little sleep . . .
Hands horny from carding fleeces, Hannibal at the gates
Their menfolk standing to arms. Now we are suffering
The evils of too-long peace. Luxury, deadlier

Than any armed invader, lies like an incubus
Upon us still.[32]

Still, but not forever. Juvenal's life begins a generation after Jesus's ends; the movement spawned by the rabbi from Nazareth will be outlawed for nearly three more centuries. When its status changes, the sensibility that so agitates Juvenal will go underground.

A perfect society operates with liberty and restraint in perfect balance, while real societies can and do remain stable despite continual fluctuation between those extremes if the degree of fluctuation in either direction is temperate. But there are times when the swing has been drastic enough to provoke a counterreaction of similar or greater force. So it happens in Rome. And since Rome has been the dominant Western society, what happens there happens—eventually—everywhere. First the binge, then the purge.

The corrective to Roman excess assumes a form aptly described in the nineteenth century by the German philosopher Heinrich Heine. He calls it "the starvation diet of Christianity."

FIVE

The Cure for Lust

Jesus. The man still leaves every other history maker deeply in the dust, even though he's onstage for just three years before he dies at thirty-three; plus, he writes nothing down. Officially, no one else does, either; news of Jesus spreads by word of mouth during his lifetime and for a few decades afterward. Then Paul initiates the process of documentation that will yield the New Testament, the most direct and, since the fourth century, the only Church-validated source of biographical information about Jesus. Whether that information is reliable is anyone's guess, but for now let's just assume that it is—and that he, the rabbi from Nazareth, actually exists in history.

On his background before he goes public, the pickings are slim indeed. But we do learn that Joseph, though a lowly carpenter, is "of the house of David." Therefore Jesus is, too. The Gospel writers are clear about this; they painstakingly trace his stellar paternal lineage, which extends beyond King David to the biblical patriarchs—from Jacob to Isaac to Abraham—and from there all the way back to Adam, "son of God."[1] (These writers make almost as much of Jesus's ancestry as they do of his mother's virginity, without explaining how Jesus could inherit Joseph's genealogy without being the product of Joseph's loins.) Jesus grows up in the rural village of Nazareth, far north of the throbbing heart of Jewish life in Jerusalem. For a working-class family like his, traveling

86

to Jerusalem from the Galilee Valley in the first century would involve considerable discomfort and a couple of days on the road. Still, Joseph and Mary are observant Jews who consider the rituals of faith—and the religious education of their son—important enough to make the trip south with him every year for the Passover festival. The Gospel of Luke describes what happens in Jerusalem at the conclusion of one year's festival, although the choice of year is far from random. Jesus is twelve and approaching bar mitzvah age, his initiation into Jewish manhood.

The festivities are over, the family's belongings have been packed, and the parents are ready to begin the long journey home to Nazareth, but their son is missing. Joseph and Mary ask friends and kin if they've seen the boy. They search for him everywhere, but for three days of mounting terror Jesus is not to be found. Finally the kid turns up at, of all places, the temple, official Judaism's power center. He has spent those three days huddled with the rabbis, amazing them all with "his understanding and his answers." Mary, seeing that her son is alive and well, reacts as any mother would under the circumstances: She is furious. "Child," she cries, "why have you treated us like this? Look, your father and I have been searching for you in great anxiety." Jesus, astonished, wonders why they didn't realize where he was: "Did you not know that I must be in my Father's house?" Good point; his true identity was explained well before his birth, to relieve Joseph and Mary's understandable confusion about how she, a virgin, could conceive a child. Oddly, his parents don't get the point. They have no idea what he's telling them, but whatever. The family returns to Nazareth, and the window of information shuts on the twelve-year-old Jesus, to be reopened when he's thirty.[2]

That mini-bio, sketchy though it is, offers two telling details. First, Joseph and Mary have given their son a traditional Jewish upbringing, and Jesus has learned his lessons supremely well. He would know the first and most basic of the Bible's 613 commandments, "Be fertile and increase"; he would know that "it is not good for man to be alone." He would, in other words, be deeply aware that young Jewish males are expected—obliged—to marry and reproduce. Second, bloodlines matter to the Jews, as we already know, and Jesus has inherited one spectacular bloodline. To sever it deliberately would be, given his background, something close to heresy. But that, of course, is just what he does. Jesus embarks upon his brief but stunning career as a rabbi—a rabbi so radical that he leads a rigorously chaste, openly celibate life, and who, postmortem, is taken by his acolytes to be the long-awaited messiah (the "Christ" from the Greek *Khristos*).

The acolytes fan out beyond their native land to the gentile communities of the Mediterranean, founding churches and spreading the Gospel (the "good news") of Christ's ascension in the face of vehement persecution by the heathen Roman Empire. But no matter how many believers are captured, tortured, and executed, the empire can't keep up with the pace of conversion; for every new martyr there are seemingly thousands of replacements. It's only a matter of time before Rome yields to the inevitable. When the emperor Constantine legalizes the Christian faith in 316, the celibate ideal exemplified by Jesus will have been percolating across the length and breadth of the empire for nearly three centuries. In that time the stature of marriage has plummeted from divine command in the Old Testament to a necessary evil preferable to fornication in the New Testament—and the New Testament is just the beginning.

That text comes together in about eight decades, as quick as an eyeblink compared to the Torah's twelve to fifteen centuries. There are the four pseudonymous Gospels, centered (with considerable overlap) on the life and work of Jesus, followed by material on the life and work of the nascent church: the Acts of the Apostles, a semi-historical, semi-theological, semi-riveting narrative; the Epistles (Letters), most importantly Paul's; and finally, the freakish and unnerving Revelation. The Greek word for revelation is *apokalypsis*, which says it all.

Apocalypse nigh is the theme of the first century, spawning cults at the fringes of Judaism even before Jesus forms his own. The Bible has predicted the coming of a savior who will bring on the end of days,[3] and once Jesus is seen by his fervent band of associates to be that long-awaited figure, they get the word out: The prophecy has been fulfilled. The word has been circulating expansively for a generation when the New Testament writers get to work. Some of them, notably Paul, are leading the missionary charge. All of them, as fervent believers in Jesus as Christ, are certain that in the next five minutes, hours, days, weeks (soon, anyway), earthly life will end. Urging people to conceive more of it is not going to be part of their game plan. In an apocalyptic frame of mind, the value of marriage and children would be approximately nil.[4]

Fueling the endgame fervor is Stoicism, the first-century philosophical system developed by pagan ascetics.[5] Stoic ideas about lust (disgusting; control it), sexual pleasure (irrational; avoid it), passion in marriage overall (suspicious), husband's passion for wife specifically (shameful; equivalent to adultery), sex in marriage (for reproductive purposes only), love in marriage (offensive; not to be trusted), and sex as an expression of love (huh?) permeate the foundational Christian texts down to the marrow for four hundred years, starting with the New Testament. Emperor Constantine—an early defender of Christianity and an eventual convert—even goes so far as to revoke part of the Lex Julia et Papia, the laws put in place by Augustus to stimulate reproduction. Marriage, in his view, is defined not in the traditional way, by consummation, but in the Christian way, by consent, a view he maintains even as the Roman population plummets.[6] Season the Stoic influence with a little eau d'apocalypse, and there you have it: the New Marriage, aka the dumping ground for sex. What would Jesus make of it all?

The Gospel writers don't portray him as an enemy of cleaving and begetting. He tells his disciples to abandon wives, children, livestock, and all desire for money or sex or a place to call home. If they want to join his inner circle, he tells them to do as he does. But he doesn't preach chastity or celibacy or virginity to the listening crowds. Jesus himself seems neither disdainful of conjugal life in general nor agitated by its physical component in particular. But there's still plenty of time for that kind of thinking to develop. Leave it to the men who build the Church founded in the name of Christ and are known as its "fathers."

Paul is the early bird in that flock, writing for the New Testament twenty to thirty years post-crucifixion. He'll feather the theological nest with many supremely useful passages, including that perpetual fatherly favorite, "it is better to marry than to burn." Paul used to be Saul, a Jewish native of Tarsus (then the capital of Cilicia, a Roman province in Asia Minor) working as a professional bounty hunter for the Romans. He tracks down and arrests secret converts to Christianity—then called the Way—among his fellow Jews, and by all accounts he does his job zealously and effectively.[7] The New Testament reviles Saul for "ravaging the Church by entering house after house; dragging off both men and women," and throwing them in jail en route to martyrdom, and claims that he does so on the authority of Jerusalem's high priests. Wicked Saul becomes Good Paul in the course of a business trip to Damascus, where he plans to ferret out undercover members of the Way in the city's synagogues. When he and his cohorts hit the road, Saul is psyched, "breathing threats and murder." But as they approach the city, "a light from heaven" sends him crashing to the ground, suddenly blind. Then he hears the voice of Jesus telling him to proceed to Damascus and wait for further instructions. Saul's companions lead him there, as he is still unable to see—he'll be blind for three days, refusing food and drink—but after that he is Paul, destined for martyrdom and eventual sainthood.[8]

Saul belonged to the most rigorously orthodox sect in Judaism; he was "a Pharisee, son of Pharisees,"[9] who adhere to the letter of biblical law. That detail, combined with the fact that he was well into adulthood before assuming the identity of Paul, makes it almost certain that Saul was a married man. Paul is not only celibate and chaste, but he also wishes that "all were as I myself am," telling his congregants, "It is well for a man not to touch [have sex with] a woman."[10] But he isn't delusional. The sexual urge exists, alas, and Paul knows that only the lucky few are capable of "practicing self-control," as he does. Everyone else should marry, says Paul, "for it is better to marry than to be aflame with passion."[11] (The premodern translation, "it is better to marry than to burn," still sounds better.) Here he sets up the hierarchy of sexual life that will persist until Luther breaks it down in about fifteen centuries. Single and sexless, celibate and chaste—that's the coming gold standard, the ideal human state. Marriage is inferior to celibacy by a long shot, but superior to fornication. Since fornication is defined as any form of sex outside of marriage, and most people can't muzzle their libidos, marriage must be allowed "by way of concession, not"—definitely not—"of command."[12] In Paul's view, marriage is not a sin. It's a lust-containment facility. And for the facility to function properly, mutual sexual service must be provided.

In the Christian marriage bed, if not outside it, husband and wife are equal. "The husband should give to his wife her conjugal rights, and likewise the wife to her husband," Paul explains to his congregants. "For the wife does not have authority over her own body, but the husband does; likewise the husband does not have authority over his own body, but the wife does." Paul is articulating what will be known as the "conjugal debt" that each spouse owes the other—the flip side of their mutual rights. If the debt is not paid (how often it can be claimed is never specified) and the flames are not quenched, fornication is the next step. Paul doesn't want anyone getting to that point: "Do not deprive one another except perhaps by agreement for a set time, to devote yourselves to prayer, and then come together again, so that Satan may not tempt you because of your lack of self-control."[13] These are pivotal passages, in which Paul affirms the importance of physical intimacy in marriage (which protects against adultery) and of mutual fidelity (a major break with the traditional double standard). In the Middle Ages the Church leaders will conveniently ignore the former and the aristocracy will ignore the latter, but eventually Paul's conjugal principles are reborn by the Protestant reformers, who loudly reassert them.

In the moral universe inhabited by Paul, lust is an unfortunate reality that must be tolerated, and satisfied within the limits of marriage. Compared to the fearful malevolence that will be directed at marriage (and sex) later on, Paul's attitude is blessedly sane, if a bit disdainful. Bertrand Russell describes it to perfection: "I remember once being advised by a doctor to abandon the practice of smoking, and he said that I should find it easier if, whenever the desire came upon me, I proceeded to suck an acid drop. It is in this spirit that St. Paul recommends marriage."[14]

Still, Paul giveth with one hand and taketh away with another: He tells people to marry rather than burn, but can't stop trying to dissuade them from both. His successors will make this a pattern. "Those who marry will experience distress in this life," says Paul to his unmarried listeners, "and I would spare you that." By "distress" he doesn't mean bickering: "The appointed time has grown short; from now on, let even those who have wives be as though they had none, for the present form of this world is passing away." When it does, single people (assuming they are chaste) will have the best shot at salvation's short list, because they've been able to give their full attention to God. They have the further advantage of traveling light, enabling them to zoom up to heaven— while all the married couples, encumbered by each other, are left behind.

"I want you to be free of anxieties," Paul goes on, pointing out that some anxieties are more helpful than others: "The unmarried man is anxious about the affairs of the Lord, how to please the Lord; but the married man is anxious about the affairs of the world, how to please his wife, and his interests are divided." A wife is in the same situation. But the "impending crisis" of Judgment Day doesn't mean that spouses should divest themselves of each other, only that singles should avoid marriage. "Are you bound to a wife? Do not seek to be free. Are you free of a wife? Do not seek a wife."[15] Just practice self-control at all times—no sex—and the good news is, there's not much time left.

What married people actually do in bed is less interesting to

Paul than how they relate to each other outside of it. He does such a masterful job of Christianizing the principle of Genesis 3:16 that his successors keep chanting it verbatim for many, many centuries to come. "Wives, be subject to your husbands as you are to the Lord. For the husband is the head of the wife just as Christ is the head of the Church . . . Just as the Church is subject to Christ, so also wives ought to be, in everything, to their husbands."[16] Paul instructs husbands to love their wives "as they do their own bodies . . . For no one ever hates his own body, but he nourishes and tenderly cares for it, just as Christ does for the Church." His message to wives is succinct: "A wife should respect her husband."[17] Apparently the reverse doesn't apply or doesn't matter; he says nothing about wives loving their husbands or husbands respecting their wives.

Laying down yet another thematic track for the future, Paul reminds married women that their behavior must be beyond reproach, lest they show something other than respect for their husbands. For instance, "Women should be silent in the churches. For they are not permitted to speak, but should be subordinate . . . If there is anything they desire to know, let them ask their husbands at home."[18] Wives must veil their heads at all times, in and out of church. To leave their hair loose and uncovered is to mimic pagan priestesses and prostitutes, and worse, disgraces their husbands.[19] "For a man ought not to have his head veiled, since he is the image and reflection of God; but woman is the reflection of man. Indeed, man was not made from woman but woman from man. Neither was man created for the sake of woman, but woman for the sake of man."[20]

It looks like Genesis 2's account has already knocked Genesis 1's off the map, and this is only the inaugural Christian text. Consider the Epistle of Timothy (another pen name): "Let the woman learn in silence with full submission. I permit no woman to teach or have authority over a man; she is to keep silent." And what does Timothy base this directive on? "For Adam was formed first, then Eve; and Adam was not deceived, but the woman was deceived and became a transgressor."[21] Yet another Epistle, by Peter, hammers the theme of wifely subjection, saying that women should not braid their hair or wear "gold ornaments or fine clothing"; they should "adorn themselves by accepting the authority of their husbands." Peter crafts what will become one of the most familiar phrases—and one of the most useful, well into the modern age—when telling husbands to "show consideration for your wives . . . paying honor to the woman as the weaker sex,"[22] or, as some will prefer, "the weaker vessel." Either way, this one's a keeper.

The Gospels convey no message that wives must submit to their husbands, but then the Gospels concern the teachings of Jesus, not to be confused with the teachings of the Church. Jesus is opposed to hierarchy in any form. He seems to regard men and women as equals without qualification—equally capable of sin and equally worthy of salvation. Paul and the anonymous authors of the Epistles go halfway. They impose a single sexual standard that is no less rigid for husbands than for wives, allow spouses mutual rights in bed, and indicate no break with the sinful-salvageable equation. Men and women are equal—equally superior if they're single, equally inferior if they're married—on the spiritual level, in itself a radical departure from the social norm. And that's quite enough for now. In the Christian household, as in the heathen household, husbands are still supposed to rule their wives. The men who make up the brain trust of post–New Testament, premedieval theologians—the fathers of the Church—aren't about to disagree.

Tertullian is one of them. Born in the middle of the second century, he's a visionary whose theological contributions are vast enough for Catholic historians to single him out for the title "Founder of Latin Christianity."[23] Tertullian is also the man behind the genius phrase "devil's gateway," coined to describe Eve and her sisters. But in this truncated form, it can't be fully savored. The longer version contains the key image, wrapped in an irresistible sexual double entendre: "Woman is the gateway through which the devil comes."

As the son of a Roman centurion, he's born a heathen and converts to Christianity in adulthood. Tertullian, who lives with his Christian wife in the North African city of Carthage, is a married man whose view of marriage—or rather of the evil force that marriage is designed to corral—grows darker, and his reverence for chastity and celibacy correspondingly deeper, over his long lifetime. (Tertullian dies at the probable age of eighty.) In this he both mirrors the increasingly ascetic bent of his adoptive, still-illegal religion and foreshadows its future, which, as a gifted polemicist, he helps to create.

Tertullian's asceticism is exacerbated by the bad example set by Rome's pagan upper class, whose members—men and women—continue to pursue the outer limits of pleasure with exhibitionistic zeal. In his day the ban on female adornment so heatedly debated by members of the Roman senate is long forgotten; a man's horse cannot outdress his wife unless the wife insists on it. Such a wife would be much appreciated by Father T, who stretches Paul's counsel about veiling their heads into an entire treatise, "On the Apparel of Women," which also happens to be home base for "devil's gateway."

Therein, he exhorts Christian wives to distinguish themselves from their gentile counterparts, whom he deplores. They flaunt their jewels, paint their faces, and blithely show off their paramours—in public, no less, where in his opinion no Christian woman belongs except for "serious" reasons, such as visiting the sick or spreading the word of God. "What causes have you [women] for appearing in public in excessive grandeur?" he pontificates, reminding his audience of the biblical character Tamar, who decked herself out as a harlot to deceive her own father. Instead, he urges them to "paint your eyes with bashfulness, and your mouth with silence." He commands, "Submit your head to your husbands and you will be enough adorned. Busy your hands with spinning; keep your feet at home." The men of Athens said as much six hundred years earlier. But unlike the men of Athens, Tertullian is an ardent Christian convert and theologian, translating tried-and-true ideas into a new spiritual language.

Tertullian urges women to stay home, and out of men's sight unless a death in the family, Christian missionary or charity work, and so on; demands their public presence. On these hopefully rare occasions, he reiterates, they must veil themselves, dress "modestly," disdain "adornment," and keep their mouths shut. You know why: So as not to provoke lust in men's hearts and subsequently the humiliation of their husbands. The faces of women are "perilous," Tertullian lectures, and for that reason they "ought to be shaded." He warns "you . . . who have fallen into wedlock"—nice attitude for a married man—"not to outgrow . . . the discipline of the veil, not even in a moment of an hour . . . Let them know that the whole head constitutes 'the *woman*.'" In case any of the women who have fallen into wedlock wonder where the head ends and the body begins, he explains: The head reaches "as far as the place where the robe begins." Which means, naturally, that every millimeter of neck must also be covered, for "the veil is their yoke." As role models, Tertullian suggests that Christian women ignore the harlotlike gentile wives in their own backyard and look further afield to "Arabia's heathen females" instead, who "cover not only the head, but the face also, so entirely, that they are content, with one eye free, to enjoy rather half the light than to prostitute the entire face."

Mrs. T (whatever her name may be goes unmentioned) rates her own essay, as the title makes explicit: *Ad Uxorem.* "To His Wife." Here Tertullian's purpose is to convince her, and any other potential women who might be listening, to avoid remarriage in the event of widowhood. (This essay also covers his opposition to mixed marriage between Christians and gentiles.) His negative attitude isn't based on anything so petty as wanting Mrs. T. to remain chaste for his sake—to be like a virgin when they enjoy their next nuptial union in heaven—because, what a relief, there won't be one. "When the future time arrives, we shall not resume the gratification of unseemly passion," he assures Mrs. T; only on earth do "such worthless, filthy things" happen. Good Christians like themselves can look forward to death, because they will be resurrected as "holy angels . . . undisturbed by feelings of carnal jealousy."

Mr. T reminds his wife that since marriage was invented by God, he—Tertullian—doesn't "reject" it. But he accepts it even less wholeheartedly than Paul did, little more than a century before. (Or maybe he's a tell-it-like-it-is type, not one to shade the truth as he sees it.) Tertullian says, "What sort of good, I ask you" (as if he hasn't already made up his mind), "can that be which is such only when it is compared to what is bad? Marriage . . . is better because burning is worse! How much better it is neither to marry nor to burn!"

Continuing his diatribe against remarriage, Tertullian points out that there are only two reasons to do so, and both are bad. The first is obvious: sexual lust. The second: lust for everything else. Women, he opines, want "to queen it over another man's household; to gloat over another man's wealth; to wheedle the price of a wardrobe out of another man's pocket." Better, far better, for Mrs. T to muster "all the self-control of which you are capable" and conquer these despicable urges for her own sake, if for no other reason than that on Judgment Day she will "leap forth lightly," free of the "heaving baggage of marriage." As for those despicable women who do remarry, Tertullian has this to say: "Let them harvest the fruit of their repeated nuptials—right seasonable fruits they are for the latter days—swollen breasts and nauseating wombs and whimpering infants." All that hectoring for nothing; in the end, Tertullian outlives his wife.

"To His Wife" is the first and mildest of his essays on marriage (which is also to say sex and lust). In "On Monogamy," written less than a decade later, Tertullian's attitude has hardened quite a bit. Now he thinks that a widow—he's addressing women but says his comments apply to men as well—commits "a grievous sin" by remarrying, because she would have "one husband in the flesh and another in the spirit." This, he insists, "is adultery— joint knowledge of one woman by two men . . . To which of them will you play the adulteress?" Tertullian claims to derive his view from Paul, and here's what Paul says: "A wife is bound as long as her husband lives. But if the husband dies, she is free to marry anyone she wishes, only in the Lord."[24]

Funny, it doesn't sound like Paul considers remarriage a sin, grievous or otherwise, but Tertullian knows better; he insists that Paul doesn't mean what it sounds like he means. Paul's phrase "only in the Lord" signals that he refers only to heathens who convert to Christianity after being widowed (by other heathens). This is the one situation, Tertullian says, in which Paul permits remarriage—assuming, of course, that the convert marries a Christian, "in the Lord." Because heathen marriages don't count? As further "proof," Tertullian throws in various tidbits from both testaments. They seem just as dubious: Jesus attends only one wedding, "no more frequently than he wished [marriage] to be celebrated"; Christ has only one spouse, the Church; Christians recognize but one God; God took only one rib from Adam; God told Noah to bring one male and one female of each species onto the ark. Tertullian is an early father working out the rules of the Scripture game: Take from the text whatever you can bend, twist, massage, or exaggerate to fit the argument. Ignore or deny the rest.

His successors will outplay him. They'll use the game against Tertullian, because of one sentence he writes. By the time this happens, the sentence will be nearly two hundred years old. The contretemps illustrates just how invested the Church has become in the whole celibacy/chastity message—and it's still centuries before the Middle Ages, when things really get serious. In this sentence, Tertullian touches on a tricky subject in the course of mounting a larger thesis. He makes an assumption about the alleged virginity of Mary, mother of Jesus, and this time he's not playing the game. His assumption, firmly grounded in New Testament text, would seem reasonable, uncontroversial, at the start of the second century. By the late fourth it would have been forgotten—it was forgotten—until an otherwise obscure Christian writer named Helvidius, possibly a Roman priest, cites Tertullian as a source in his own essay questioning Mary's perpetual virginity. Then all hell breaks loose. What was once reasonable and uncontroversial, even to theologians, is now dangerously provocative.

What exactly did Tertullian say? The offending sentence appears in his anti-remarriage essay "On Monogamy": "It was a virgin who gave birth to Christ and she was to marry only once, after she brought him forth." The key words are "marry," synonymous with having sex, in concert with "after." Tertullian is saying that Mary was a virgin when she conceived Jesus (no one ever argues that point), and once he is born, she and Joseph have normal sexual relations. The next sentence concludes this bit of evidence, one of many he's using to support his position, by stating that Mary was chosen so that "both types of chastity might be exalted in the birth of Christ, born as he was of a mother who was at once virginal and monogamous." After Christ is born, his mother continues to be monogamous. She's just no longer virginal. There's no sign, from the way Tertullian frames the sentence, that he thinks he's saying anything provocative or surprising or heretical or anything other than a simple matter of fact, based on the primacy of his source, the New Testament. Since the writing of the New Testament follows Jesus's lifetime by a few generations, not a few centuries— before there was a legal Church to convene official councils, allowing the leaders to cast votes on the relative divinity and virginity of New Testament characters—it's difficult not to think that the New Testament may have the inside track. Given the multitude of references that appear not only in all four Gospels but also in Acts and Epistles, Tertullian's assumption of Mary and Joseph's sexual union after Jesus was born seems logical as well as natural. As a result, the fourth-century fathers panic, discredit Tertullian, demolish Helvidius, and dismiss the evidence.

Matthew, for instance, goes into a long explanation of the prenatal situation between the immaculate couple. They're engaged when "she was found to be with child from the Holy Spirit." Although Joseph doesn't yet know about the Holy Spirit, he figures she's no virgin and, "unwilling to expose her to public disgrace, planned to dismiss her quietly." Then an angel shows up in a dream to explain what's going on and how he should proceed. Joseph follows the instructions: "he took her as his wife, but had no marital relations with her *until she had borne a son* . . . named Jesus."[25] If you're Tertullian reading that at the turn of the second century—not very far removed from the alleged events being described, and well before the perpetual-virginity doctrine has solidified—wouldn't you assume what he does, without fear that it would be considered heresy?

Moreover, not only the Gospels but also Acts and Epistles mention that Jesus has brothers.[26] Some of the fathers (including Jerome, who leads the charge against Helvidius) explain this away by claiming the term refers to spiritual brethren. But the settings in which these brothers are mentioned, the frequency of the references, and the distinction some of the writers make between "brothers" and "disciples"—who would qualify as spiritual brethren—overwhelmingly suggest that Jesus and his brothers share the same parents and very possibly were nurtured in the same womb, however they got there. (They can't all be virgin births.) Two of several references: "While he was still speaking to the crowds, his mother and his brothers were standing outside, wanting to speak to him" . . . "After this he went down to Capernaum with his mother, his brothers, and his disciples." When Jesus preaches for the first time at the synagogue in Nazareth—his hometown, where he is known in the context of his family—people are astonished by the wisdom that the boy they remember has acquired in adulthood. They wonder, "Is not this the carpenter's son? Is not his mother called Mary? And are not his brothers James and Joseph and Simon and Judas?"[27] James becomes the leader of the Church in Jerusalem before he is martyred; one of the Epistles is attributed to him, and another to Jude, a variant on the name Judas. (This is not the Judas who betrays Jesus.)

Few defend Mary's once-and-forever purity more assiduously

than Father (and later, Saint) Jerome. A translator of the Bible into Latin (his version, known as the Vulgate, remains the Christian standard in the West until the Reformation), he brings the creed of virginity, celibacy, and so forth, to Europe through an avalanche of letters and polemical essays that express his unbridled revulsion for the baggage of marriage and its connection to "the flesh," from sex to nursing. His scornful, often hysterical antipathy, combined with his almost unseemly passion for monkish living, anticipates the medieval Church's seriously twisted take on conjugal life. Jerome, no virgin himself, believes that "the only justification of matrimony was that by bringing virgins into being it repopulated heaven." He writes many letters lauding young women who have opted for perpetual virginity (just like Mary!), enumerating what they've blessedly escaped: "the disadvantages of wives: pregnancy, a wailing infant, the torment of a husband's unfaithfulness, household cares, and how death at last cuts off all fancied blessings." (And that's Jerome being mellow; not a mention here of the "poverty" and "deformity" of wives, simply because they are wives.) But Jerome doesn't only hector wives; husbands don't escape his wrath, either. "It is disgraceful to love another man's wife at all, or one's own too much . . . There is nothing blacker than to love a wife as if she were an adulteress."[28] Because that makes her husband an adulterer—any man "who too ardently loves his own wife" qualifies for that label. But though this is a Stoic idea and Jerome himself gives the Stoics full credit, Jerome will be associated with it thereafter.[29]

Back to the Mary business: after calling upon Jesus "to guard the sacred lodging of the womb in which he abode for ten months from all suspicion of sexual intercourse," Jerome accuses Helvidius of "raging madness," of being "an ignorant boor" and "like a snake," burying him in an avalanche of insults.[30] Helvidius, a more extra in the early Church home movie, warrants all this attention from Jerome because he has not only taken the New Testament at its word on Jesus's brothers, but he also dares to say that marriage is preferable to celibacy. The fathers of the Church are developing a new conjugal ideal, and to sell it to the burgeoning Christian population they need Mary and Joseph. That ideal is "spiritual marriage," or, more prosaically, marriage without sex. Two perpetual virgins living together as husband and wife make an unassailable poster couple for the cause—as long as no one assails their perpetual virginity.

SIX

Original Spin

I T's been three hundred years since Paul prescribed marriage as the antidote to lust, time enough for the fathers to have reached a consensus on the treatment's effectiveness: Stronger medicine is needed, ASAP. They regard marriage with distaste and deepening suspicion, but have no plans to do away with it. They can only continue to promote lifelong virginity, chastity, and celibacy; oppose remarriage; and encourage husbands and wives to convert their sexual unions to spiritual ones. As for the people who insist on their conjugal rights—most people, unfortunately—the challenge is twofold: to disconnect the urge from the act, and to make that act as pleasure-free as possible. A master strategist will be needed; someone with the vision, the intellectual power, and the psychological astuteness to package the plan for public consumption and to build a spiritual framework to give it weight—God's word will have to be invoked—but the argument needs to be both simple enough to attract popular attention and compelling enough to convince people that nothing less than their eternal salvation is at stake. The people must be convinced, in other words, that it's all about them. Who among the fathers can get this job done?

Enter Augustine, the once-tormented lover of women, out-of-wedlock dad, and the man behind "Lord, give me chastity, but not yet." Augustine, who at age thirty-three finally takes what the Lord has to give, swapping secular stardom in the fashionable field of rhetoric for religious stardom—eternal religious stardom—in the Church; Augustine, whose command of Scripture, not to mention the art of persuasion, is second to none; Augustine, the genius who is to religion what Shakespeare is to literature; Augustine, who besides all that has the further advantage, the immense and not-to-be-underestimated advantage, of knowing the enemy. Intimately. He himself has been lust's willing captive, trapped in the dungeon of sensual delight, where his soul suffered unspeakable torture and his flesh kept clamoring for more. From adolescence to his early thirties, Augustine has been consumed by this raging inner conflict between soul and flesh; now it is over. If anyone can lead the world to victory over lust, it'll be the man who has already done it for himself.[1]

Augustine describes his personal struggle a decade after it ends in *The Confessions,* sparing no detail—the more excruciating, the better—and his compulsive self-exposure in these pages is enough to make Britney Spears seem as elusive as Thomas Pynchon. Written in 397, when Augustine has reinvented himself as the lust-free bishop of Hippo in North Africa, the work is at once an extended hymn of thanks to God and a brutal interior narrative—a narrative, as Augustine puts it, of "the revolting things I did, and the way my soul was contaminated by my flesh."[2]

The retroactive litany of self-laceration starts in infancy ("was it sin to work my mouth toward the nipple as I cried?") and moves on to childhood. Augustine berates himself for such heinous sins as being pleased by the praise of teachers, sneaking food from home "to pamper myself or to give to others," wanting to win in games, lying to his parents about having done his homework when in fact he'd been goofing off, and stealing pears to impress his friends. Imagine a kid doing any of that.

But that's just a prelude. The real trouble begins when he turns sixteen, "the time of my young manhood, when I burned to be engorged with vile things." The horror, of course, is what Augustine calls "my erupting sexuality." He feels himself "decomposing," "drowned in lust," and driven by "dark impulse," and he's not exaggerating. Looking back, he wonders if his erotic turmoil might have been tempered by the constraints of marriage. "But could I have limited myself to sex used only for begetting children, Lord, as your law commands?" Even if he could have, Augustine reflects, marriage would have meant sacrificing the opportunity, which he has now taken, to rise above the muck of desire. Why merely temper what you can wholly transcend? Paul's words about married couples float into his mind: "They have all these cares of the flesh . . . Better for a man not to touch a woman." And these: "The man who has no wife expresses concern for God, and wants to please him, while the man with a wife expresses concern for worldly matters, because he wants to please his wife." Not for the last time, he thanks God profusely for steering his path away from the nuptial bed.

Back to the young Augustine's life in Thagaste, now in Algeria, where those eruptions—due to lack of distraction—are about to get worse. His parents, who are far from affluent, have just summoned him home from school in a nearby town. Their son will get a better education in Carthage, farther away, but it will also be more expensive. They need to save the money they would otherwise spend on tuition at his current school, or Carthage will be out of the question. The boy has already demonstrated his potential to be a master of rhetoric, and his parents foresee a brilliant career in his future. In retrospect, Augustine wishes they had been less attuned to his academic performance and more attuned to his spiritual—and sexual—purity. However, his father, Patricius, a pagan, is hardly one to worry about purity. And though his devout Christian mother, Monica, worries plenty (she'll soon be following the boy around the hot spots of the Roman Empire, trying to save his soul), she too is focused on his professional future. The young Augustine is aware of his parents' mutual desire that he become "verbally fertile . . . They cared only that I might acquire rhetoric and sway others with my words."

Out of school, stuck at home with nothing to do, "the thorns of my own drives, with no one to weed them out from around me, shot up above my head . . . I surrendered with ready hand all rule over my self, turning it over to mad cravings condoned by our debased humanity but condemned by [God's] law." On one of these idle, turbulent days, his father takes him to the baths, where he can't help noticing that the boy's sexual organs have matured. Patricius, "overjoyed with anticipation at having grandchildren by me," shares this wonderful news with his wife, who is anything but joyful. In private she speaks urgently to Augustine, begging him not to indulge in illicit sex, especially not with married women. But he dismisses her warnings as "old wives' tales, and too embarrassing to be taken seriously." Monica doesn't suggest marriage, even though as a Christian she knows that its purpose is to manage lust, because "she feared that her ambitions for me would be thwarted by a wife." Relax, Mom: there will be no wife, just illicit sex, illicit pleasure, and a heavy load of guilt.

Within months, young Augustine is in Carthage, and middle-aged Augustine takes up the whip of self-flagellation. He recounts how his soul, "sick and covered with sores, lunged outward . . . in a mad desire to scratch itself against some physical relief." Young Augustine seeks relief by going to the theater, a vile habit because "stageplays made me ecstatic . . . and fed my fires." He seeks relief through friends, with whom he discusses weighty collegiate matters like "truth," although the older Augustine puts it this way: "I descended into comradeship with the pride-maddened, the sensualists, the prattlers, whose words spread the devil's nets." And of course he seeks relief through sex, with the woman who will bear his son the following year—the same woman who will be his live-in "concubine" for more than a decade of mutual fidelity and, yes, mutual love. But "however loved I was, and secretly happy in that bondage, pleased with its entrammeling embraces—I was also tortured." Still, he does learn something. "My life with her taught me the difference between the restraint of the marriage pledge, formed for the sake of offspring, and a lustful sexual arrangement, where any children born were unintended." (Why doesn't he just marry her and end the torture? According to Augustine, "[she] could not be called my lawful wife, since my wild desire and lack of foresight had found her." Meaning she is no longer fit for matrimony, because she's already had sex with her would-be husband.)

Augustine finishes his schooling and begins to teach rhetoric, launching the luminous career of his parents' dreams. His shrewdness, braininess, and prodigious talent—not only as a teacher but also as a linguist, orator, writer, and logician—will carry him, apparently with concubine and son in tow, beyond Carthage, to coveted positions in larger cities, Rome and then Milan. But Augustine still finds no relief. In fact, the higher he climbs professionally, the lower he sinks internally. All the while, he's inching his way toward God. In Milan, Augustine meets Ambrose, the city's bishop and increasingly Augustine's spiritual mentor. Also in Milan is Augustine's mother, Monica, ever more devout and ever more concerned about the state of her son's soul. She and Ambrose become coconspirators in the fight for Augustine's spiritual health preaching and coaxing and showing the way, but they can do no more than that. The first time Augustine comes within reach of salvation, he panics and flees, muttering "give me chastity, but not yet." In context, there's nothing funny about that line.

So great is his panic, his despair, and his sexual need, that Augustine finally decides to take a wife. He knows he's "not so much eager for marriage as enslaved by lust," but if he is incapable of chastity—and after his close encounter with God, that's what he thinks—his only hope is marriage. Augustine is now around thirty and has been living with his concubine for a dozen years; at this point he believes he "would be wretched if deprived of a woman's embrace." Taking a wife won't free him from slavery, but he hopes it will lessen his self-loathing. Sadly, this means the end of the concubine, who cannot, for whatever reason, become his wife: "Since she was an obstacle to my marriage, the woman I had lived with for so long was torn out of my side. My heart, to which she had been grafted, was lacerated, wounded, shedding blood."

The concubine is no less traumatized by the breakup. Swearing her own vow of chastity, she returns to wherever she came from. Their son, Adeodatus, now in his early teens, remains—as is the patriarchal custom—with his father. And Augustine, bereft but determined, selects a young bride. So young is she that, ominously, she cannot become his bride any time soon: She's "two years below nubile age." Whatever that age is, their union will have to be delayed until she reaches it. Augustine, who says "she pleased me," agrees to wait. His libido has other plans.

Still grieving for his departed concubine, disgusted that he cannot control himself for two short years while she has sworn off sex for the rest of her life, and deeply ashamed, Augustine beds another woman. He's half hoping that "a woman's embrace"—any woman's embrace—will soothe his heartache, but the tryst proves to be "no cure for the wound of losing the one cut away from me." But this episode speeds Augustine's ascent out of the muck of lust and into the light of God more decisively than anything Monica or Ambrose, who have stuck by him all the way, could have done. Soon enough, the not-yet-nubile bride goes the way of the concubine. In 387, with Ambrose presiding, Augustine is baptized in Milan, with his mother by his side. (Monica, who dies within the year, will join Ambrose and Augustine in sainthood.) Having freed his own soul and lived to tell the tale, Augustine is determined to free everyone else's. Onward, Christian soldier: The battle is joined, and Augustine's doctrine of original sin leads the charge.

Not that the idea of original sin is originally his—or Christianity's, for that matter. The Genesis writers dream up the sin and the characters who commit it. And as an intellectual point of discussion about behavioral control, the pagans—Stoics, Platonists—make it first. Paul lays out the basics for the Christian audience, writing in Romans that "sin came into the world through one man, and death came through sin, and so death spread to all because all have sinned," and the fathers take it from there. (Augustine himself quotes liberally from Ambrose's work on the subject, and he also acknowledges the influence of "the Platonists," who identified lust as a "perverted element" before he did.) But while the idea may be derivative, the formulation of it—the formulation that will forever after identify original sin as a Christian exclusive—is Augustine's achievement. He connects the concept of original sin to the problem of lust to the purpose of marriage, infusing this theological exercise with the emotional truth of felt experience (his own experience, naturally) to sublime effect. His formula powers his work on marriage and the management of lust. Augustine's thinking is so good, apparently, that no further thinking on the matter is necessary for a very long time. If there's a more useful argument against nonreproductive sex—and simultaneously against contraception, making it doubly useful—the now-Catholic Church has yet to hear it.

Original sin brought death into the world—that's Paul. Original sin brought lust into the world—that's Augustine. For him, the repercussions of lust are far more serious for humanity than the fact of death. Lust is the consequence that matters to Augustine, the one upon which he builds his enduring thesis. But who says lust is a consequence of original sin? The original source, and that would be Genesis, chapter 3, doesn't include lust on the list of original punishment. Hard work for men, hard labor for women, obedience to husbands, expulsion from paradise, mortality of course—all of those are mentioned. Lust is not.

Augustine is the one who says lust is a consequence of original sin, *the* consequence as far as he's concerned, and he bases this assertion on his reading of none other than Genesis, chapter 3. In other words, he interprets the text. In the grand tradition of biblical readers, he fills in the blanks and the ellipses, seeing what he wants, or needs, to see. Since this is Augustine, what he sees—all he sees, even before the Fall—is sexuality, although only in the aftermath of the sin does he see it erupting.

He lays out his vision with such authority that what is only an interpretation, and a rather liberal one at that, sounds like holy truth. In a voice of clinical certitude, like a psychiatrist presenting a marital case history, Augustine describes the still-pure Adam and Eve's relationship and even what they're feeling (he subtitles this section of his masterwork, *City of God*, "The emotions of the first human beings before their sin"), and by the time he's done, you're seeing it the way he's seeing it.[3]

We are to assume, first, that by creating man and woman (instead of man and man) God institutes marriage; the latter is implicit in the former. God creates man and woman as husband and wife. Want proof? In short, God pronounces the nuptial blessing, "Be fertile and increase," immediately after he creates them. (Augustine, cutting to the chase, is going by the simpler Genesis 1 account.) That blessing—it's the *nuptial* blessing, after all—confirms their conjugal union. It cues sexual intercourse. "It would be a manifest absurdity to deny the fact that male and female were created for the purpose of begetting children," lectures Augustine, given the "obvious evidence" of their notably different anatomies. Put the anatomical evidence together with the nuptial-blessing evidence, and you've got a husband and wife having sex—all the proof you need. But the sex they're having now is wholly different in nature, says Augustine, from the sex they'll have later. Sex now is wholesome and pure instead of icky and vile because lust does not yet exist. They engage in it not because they feel like it but because God commands them to. As long as they remain "at one with God's command," their minds won't be agitated and their bodies won't be "pained by any disorders," nor subject to injury, illness, dissolution, or decay. They'll never feel too hot or too cold, they'll never get hungry or thirsty (and they won't eat for any reason but hunger or drink for any reason but thirst). They'll never know sadness or fear or exhaustion or stress, they'll never be afflicted by—yuck—"frivolous jollity" or other mood disorders. All is tranquil and nothing is desired. (All is tranquil because nothing is desired.) As for the state of the conjugal union, it is "based on love and mutual respect," and—if you're wondering about how the sex is going without the urge, listen up—"there was a harmony and a liveliness of mind and body, and an effortless observance of the commandment."

Before the Fall, you see, the (especially male) sex organs rise to the occasion through a "calm act of will." In the absence of "lustful craving" there can be only one such occasion, the reproductive occasion. At such times, the man and woman "unite in the task of propagation as a deliberate act undisturbed by passion." (Whoever does the ads for the future campaign to make conjugal sex as dreary as possible might try "the task of propagation" as a slogan.) In Augustine's graphic analogy, the "male seed" gets "dispatched into the womb with no loss of the wife's integrity, just as the menstrual flux can now be produced from the womb of a virgin without loss of maidenhead." This benefit accrues not only to the womb- equipped, by the way: "Without feeling the allurement of passion goading him on, the husband would have relaxed on his wife's bosom in tranquility of mind and with no impairment of his body's integrity."

Augustine gleans all of this information from his reading of Genesis 2:25—"The two of them were naked, the man and his wife, yet they felt no shame"—juxtaposed with Genesis 3:7, after the taste of forbidden fruit: "The eyes of both of them were opened and they perceived that they were naked; and they sewed together fig leaves and made themselves loincloths." From those two lines Augustine determines that until the original sin is committed, the couple's movable body parts—hands, feet, eyes, vocal cords, genitals, and so forth—operate as the "obedient servants" of their owners. After the sin, only the genitals no longer obey. That's why as soon as they grasp their nakedness (Augustine mocks people who read the "eyes open" bit literally), Adam and Eve reach for the fig leaves and make loincloths. Not blindfolds, not shoes, but loincloths—it's eye-for-an-eye justice, Old Testament style, and Augustine finds it fitting. "When the first man transgressed the law of God, he began to have another law in his members which was repugnant to the law of his mind, and he felt the evil of his own disobedience . . . in the disobedience of his flesh." The punishment for the crime of disobedience is disobedience—the genitals now and forever will serve a different master, that master being lust, and no one will be able to deny it or escape the shame of it, because the evidence is physical. All they can do is cover up, just as Adam and Eve, "embarrassed by the insubordination of their flesh . . . excited by lust," hide their "offending members." Only after the Fall have those members been called pudenda, says Augustine, and rightfully so, because the word means "parts of shame."

The damage has been done, and no amount of fig leaves or Balenciaga can undo it. Still, Augustine approves the impulse to conceal almost as much as he approves of the word "pudenda," because "at the very least . . . a veil might be thrown over that which was put into motion without the will of those who wished it." That which was put into motion can also be put out of motion precisely at the time when motion is desired, Augustine continues, and this is just as dire. He, of course, isn't worried about anyone's sexual performance, or lack thereof, in the course of a hot date, but about the nuptial command being nullified, which would nullify as well "man's great function . . . the procreation of children."

No human being can escape the scourge of lust because lust is the avatar of original sin, and no human being can escape that. To be conceived through sexual intercourse is to be infected, at the moment of conception, by original sin. (Mary is the mind-boggling exception; Jesus, product of a "virgin birth," is obviously untainted, but he's been disqualified as a human being by the Nicene Creed.)[4] Thus far, none of this seems to bode well for marriage or for the nuptial blessing, and here it does get tricky, doctrine-wise. Trust Augustine to reconcile the contradictions.

Okay: Lust proceeds from original sin, not from marriage, and marriage should not be condemned along with lust. Lust is evil and nothing can make it good, but marriage makes it less evil—it makes "good use" of the evil that is lust—by redirecting it to procreation. However, if employed for any other purpose, namely the "bestial" purpose of using it to gratify lust instead of the desire for children, conjugal sex is fornication, and fornication is evil. Augustine explains this further in his essay "On Marriage and

Concupiscence": "Conjugal intercourse is not in itself sin, when it is had with the intention of producing children, because the mind's good-will leads the ensuing bodily pleasure, instead of following its lead; and the human choice is not distracted by the yoke of sin pressing upon it . . . the blow of the sin is rightly brought back to the purposes of procreation." That lets out any form of contraception, of course, along with any oral, anal, manual, or other nonreproductive acts. Augustine, drawing again on Stoic principles, is merciless on this point: "But if a man wishes to use that part of his wife's body that has not been granted for this purpose, the wife is more shameful if she allows this to happen to herself than to another woman."[5] The idea of nonreproductive sex so horrifies Augustine that he advocates marital defiance in this one arena, compromising his own standard instruction to wives: "be the handmaids of your husband; be subject out of deference . . . Be completely docile, just like the servants."[6]

In Augustine's construction, marriage isn't wholly good, but it has "some good"—"some" meaning three. These three goods of marriage are the same three things that marriage is good *for*, and they remain definitive for Roman Catholicism: *proles, fides, sacramentum*. Procreation, fidelity, sacrament.[7] Translation: *If* the couple makes a deliberate, "calm" decision (nothing spontaneous, mind you) to engage in sexual intercourse with the intent to conceive, and only the intent to conceive, à la Adam and Eve before the sin; *if* mutual fidelity, or "conjugal chastity," is the rule (which doesn't just mean they don't cheat, it means they don't contemplate cheating, even in the abstract; the wife can't fantasize about George Clooney, the husband can't fantasize about Angelina Jolie, they can't even fantasize about each other); *if* they do not separate, divorce, or in any way break the sacred bond—that's God's job, when death do them part—then they've gotten the upper hand over lust. They've mastered their master and forced him to obey their procreative will rather than their diseased flesh. For them, sex isn't sinful and their marriage can be called good(-ish), which is as good as it can get. They're still contaminated by original sin, and regardless

113

of how thoughtfully and dispassionately they engage in reproductive sex, their offspring will be similarly contaminated. But hey, such is the human condition.

Augustine, having been there and done that, provides for lapses. He knows firsthand how the demon lust works, how "overbearing" its will to power over those who manage to handcuff him. He knows that even the most sexually self-controlled couple will occasionally relax their guard, and—boom!—they'll be doing it just because they're horny. Assuming that lust-driven sex is the exception and not the rule, Augustine decrees that while it is "not without sin," gradient of sin is lowered to venial by by virtue of the conjugal bond as opposed to the damnable sin of adultery. In light of the alternative, Augustine recommends, none too enthusiastically, that "a certain degree of intemperance is to be tolerated within marriage."

The theologians of the medieval Church will out-Augustine Augustine in their attempt to stifle lust, parsing the degrees of intemperance to the point of absurdity. They'll stipulate when, where, how, and in what position sex may occur, doling out penances customized to each infraction, taking into account such factors as the husband's level of drunkenness at the time. Meanwhile, Galen's theory of "female seed" will be taken as medical fact until the eighteenth century. The theologians believe, like everyone else, that for conception to occur the woman as well as the man must climax in order to release their respective stuff of life.[8]

To recap: The babymaking urge and none other justifies the "nupital embrace"; babymaking won't happen in the absence of his-and-her orgasms; to climax is (generally speaking) to experience pleasure; to experience pleasure is heinous. Micromanaging conjugal sex turns out to be a tough job, but apparently someone's got to do it.

SEVEN

Never On Sunday. (Or Wednesday. Or Friday. Or Saturday.)

T HE empire has collapsed, leaving the West politically rudderless. With no one in charge, barbarians burn their way through the former Roman provinces of Europe, ravaging villages whose inhabitants are already terrorized by local warlords vying for power among themselves. Illiteracy is the norm for all classes, scholarship is mostly confined to the monasteries, artistic pursuits are history, manners are absent even from royal circles, and common existence reverts to a largely agrarian form, as if civilization never happened. Such is life in the early medieval period aptly known as the Dark Ages. They begin in the sixth century and last, aside from a brief and shining moment around 800 when Charlemagne rides to the rescue, until the eleventh.

For the Church, these are boom times for advancing its sexual agenda. With secular culture dormant and proficiency in the three R's a relic of the classical age, ordinary Christians have little on their minds other than survival. Many of them have only recently swapped their pagan gods for Jesus; their way of thinking is as primitive as their way of life, credulous and superstitious, with an abiding faith in miracles—they don't doubt that a virgin could be impregnated by the Holy Spirit or that hell is a literal place, exactly as pictured in scary religious art. With no competition for all that empty mental space, Church leaders have a free field of influence.[1] They control the form, content, and flow of information—which, *mirabile dictu*, is all about lust.

To be fair, the public does seem to need help in this area. "It would be difficult to find anywhere more vice and less virtue," says Edward Gibbon, the eighteenth-century historian, looking back on the medieval world. The medieval Church lessons on lust control come straight from Augustine, writ large—and in profoundly graphic detail. The object is not just to teach, but also to punish.

Beginning in the sixth century, the sexual agenda is made manifest in the handbooks known as the penitentials, which communicate the formulas of discipline to parish priests. These handbooks contain lists of sins, dominated by the sexual sort, with each sin matched to a suitable punishment. When a penitent confesses, the priest simply locates the act or thought specified—the lists are staggeringly comprehensive—and prescribes the penance that corresponds to it. Some of the possibilities, especially concerning marital relations, seem bizarre beyond belief, but the lists used in the confessional are based on information gleaned from the confessional. They reflect the behavior of local inhabitants, behavior that is common enough to be of moral concern.

The handbooks, which originate in Ireland, soon proliferate throughout Europe. Written in Latin by priests and bishops as well as monks, and produced in England, France, Spain, and Germany as well as Ireland, they remain the disciplinary standard throughout the eleventh century, and from there are incorporated into the formal system of canon law.[2] Through the penitentials, the Church imprints its sexual code into the collective brain. That brain accepts the idea that penance scrubs out the sin and that the reward for scrubbing out sins as they accumulate is eternal salvation instead of eternal torment; in the meantime, the newly scrubbed can commit the sin all over again, and repeat the process. Whether the penitentials raise anyone's moral IQ is irrelevant to the fact that for five hundred years they dictate what is and is not sexually permissible—shaping marital consciousness for centuries thereafter.

Aside from matching punishments to crimes, the handbooks make it easy for a priest to interrogate his parishioner, in itself a form of punishment. The priest can select an item from the list and pose it as a question, enabling him to extract details that the penitent might be hiding or forgetting—hopefully without giving anyone enticing new ideas. One of the best-known penitential collections is the work of Burchard, a German theologian writing early in the eleventh century. He recommends a series of questions specifically for women, to be posed "mildly and gently" by priests who suspect them of such crimes as bestiality, incest, lesbianism, abortion, contraception, and stimulation of the vagina by foreign objects.[3]

The sexual sins listed vary from one handbook to another, depending on the writer and the demographics of his intended audience; a fisherman's wife in Cornwall, apparently, will commit different crimes than a merchant's wife in Florence, so the Cornish priest will need one list and the Florentine another. In nature the punishments are for the most part the same: a fast of bread and water. (As Pope Gregory I explains in the late sixth century, "when the belly is extended, lust is aroused." Lust and gluttony are two means to the same sinful end, the satisfaction of bodily desire; starve one and you starve the other.)[4] What varies is the duration. The length of the fast is determined by several factors, including the circumstances in which the sin is committed, how often the penitent has committed it before—and whether the guilty party is a layman or a clergyman.

Alas, the penitentials reveal that the men charged with curing lust in the field are not immune to the demon themselves. Clergymen are supposed to practice chastity (no sex) as well as celibacy (no marriage), but so far in Church history, many do not. From the internal legislation passed at conclaves during this time (not to mention the ubiquity of fornicating priests as characters in medieval popular literature, most famously in *The Canterbury Tales*), clerics are no less inclined to be promiscuous lechers, gamblers, and drunks than anyone else.

The penitentials calculate clerical punishment in direct proportion to rank; regardless of rank, clerics receive a stiffer sentence than laymen committing the same sin.[5] Slipping an aphrodisiac to a woman in the course of seducing her, for example, means six months of bread and water for a noncleric, two years for a deacon, three for a priest. Add 240 days to each sentence and change the sin to murder if the woman consumes the substance unknowingly, happens to be pregnant, and loses the fetus. If she consumes it knowingly, she becomes an accomplice, and will be punished accordingly, often to the same extent as her seducer.

Herbal potion-making looms large in the lists, as can be expected at a time of widespread belief in the supernatural and the magical. With a few exceptions (including the example above) the penitential writers share an assumption that women will be the perpetrators of this crime—perpetrating it most often upon themselves.[6] The severity of punishment is linked to the woman's motive. If the potion is used as a contraceptive measure or to induce abortion, the writers further assume that the woman is trying to destroy evidence of adultery. She'll get ten years on bread and water (they must be joking), unless she is poor, so poor that she will not be able to feed the baby. The motive ascribed then becomes poverty rather than adultery, and the punishment is halved. Contraception and abortion are explicitly condemned as forms of murder and implicitly denounced as a subversion of a woman's God-given (and natural) role. Neither of which, apparently, is as bad as satisfying lust, as the presumably adulterous potion-drinker is doing by committing adultery in the first place.[7]

A test: Who is the worse sinner? The wife who spreads honey on her body to enfeeble her husband sexually, or one who mixes her menstrual blood into his food to turn him on? A man who commits murder, or a husband who practices coitus interruptus during conjugal sex? A man who copulates with his mother, or a woman who performs fellatio on her husband? The answer, in all cases, is the latter. Think Augustine: Reducing lust by any means is always better than increasing it. Conjugal sex is supposed to be solely reproductive, for one thing, and coitus interruptus thwarts God's will, for another. Incest is bad, but *seminem in os*—semen in the mouth—is as bad as it gets.[8]

Gratian, who translates the penitential codes into canon law in the *Decretum*, produced in 1140, describes the hierarchy of sexual sins in ascending order of evil: fornication, adultery, incest, and finally, back to Augustine, "what is done contrary to nature, as when a man wishes to use a member [orifice] of his wife not conceded for this." (Incest, apparently, is not considered contrary to nature.) In the penitentials, punishment specified for either oral or anal (*in tergo*) sex is generally equal to that for murder, seven years, but can be double that or more, ranging from fifteen years to life. Even so, the idea of a husband depositing *seminem* in his wife's *tergo* barely fazes the penitentialists compared to his doing it in her *os*. Writing in the late seventh century, one major contributor to the genre expresses the universal sentiment when he calls *in os* "the worst of evils."

That contributor is Theodore, archbishop of Canterbury, whose list of marital sins is lengthy indeed. On the mild end it includes seeing one's wife in the nude (the punishment for this infraction isn't specified). A man can dismiss his wife for adultery and marry another woman without penalty, but if he stays with the adulteress, the sentence is two years of twice-a-week fasting—so much for Jesus's teaching on forgiveness. A woman can't dismiss her husband even for adultery, "unless perhaps to enter a monastery." Forty days on bread and water goes to the wife who tastes her husband's blood "as a remedy," apparently for medical purposes, and three years to the one who "mixes her husband's semen in food"—for aphrodisiac purposes.[9]

The last of the great penitentialists, and surely the most entertaining, is Burchard, Bishop of Worms. He has developed a complex formula to judge the degrees of aphrodisiac abuse, meting out four degrees of punishment to four married women trying to achieve the same end: to stoke the libidos of their husbands. That end is bad enough, but Burchard is focused on the means: Wife one mixes menstrual blood into her unsuspecting husband's food or drink; wife two suffocates a fish in her vagina, roasts it, and serves this delectable dish; wife three has a servant knead the daily bread on her naked buttocks before baking it; wife four mixes hubby's own semen into his meal. The sentences are as follows: five years for the menstrual-blood potion, two for the suffocated fish, two as well for the bare-ass bread, and—upping Theodore's ante—seven years for the semen mixture. Compare that to the unfaithful wife who, enraged at the idea that her lover is about to marry another woman, seeks revenge by mixing up a potion (no ingredients mentioned) designed to render him impotent. Despite her adultery, she gets a mere forty days. From Buchard's lust-fearing point of view, lenience is in order because there's a big upside to the case. All three players—the wife, her former lover, and his bride—will for the moment be sorely sex-deprived, always a favorable outcome.

Departing ever so subtly from the Augustinian playbook, the penitentials treat intercourse between infertile, menopausal, and already expectant wives and their husbands with relative leniency— provided that the sex is vaginal, of course. The awkward reasoning goes something like this: It can't be procreative, but it *could* be procreative; the potential is there. Naturally, abstinence would be the superior choice, but as long as penetration and ejaculation occur *inter vas*, "inside the vessel," the penalties range from light—forty days, increased for repeat offenders—to none.

So a lawfully wedded, fertile, not-expectant couple who lust only for babies and never for each other can have vaginal sex in any position they choose, right? Wrong. The only position not considered a "sin against nature" is man on top. Rear-entry vaginal sex, according to the penitentials, is "bestial." Dorsal sex—woman on top—is also out.[11] No reason is given, but here's a not-so-wild guess, it reverses and therefore subverts the order of superior male–inferior female that is mandated by God, and everyone else.

Early in the eleventh century the Church's stance on the dorsal position will be conveniently reinforced with medical logic from an unimpeachable authority. He is Avicenna, the pre-Renaissance Renaissance man from Persia—a theologian, mathematician, statesman, warrior, philosopher, scientist, physician, founder of pharmacology (and aromatherapy, no less)—whose *Canon of Medicine* becomes the standard reference work in Europe for no less than six hundred years. Avicenna maintains that ejaculation in the dorsal position can cause lesions in the male organ, endangering its reproductive function, and upends the cervix, so that "what was in it poured out."[12] Good news for the Church.

It seems that no aspect of sexual life, no matter how minor, escapes the penitentials. There are restrictions on time of day, days in the month, and seasons of the year, some of them inspired by the early Church fathers. Back in the third century, Clement of Alexandria decreed that married couples could not engage in sex during daylight, after returning from the marketplace, or at any other time when they should be devoting themselves to prayer, although Clement was kind enough to allow mutual payment of the marital debt after the evening meal. In the penitentials, restrictions multiply by a factor of nine million or so. Typically, conjugal sex is permitted only on Monday, Tuesday, and Thursday. Wednesday and Friday are set aside for fasting and prayer, as per early Church tradition. Never on Sunday—too sacred. Saturday is too close to Sunday. Also off-limits: sex during menstruation, pregnancy, 33 days postpartum (for a boy) or 56 (for a girl), and 40 days each before Christmas and Easter.[13] Taking into account only the prohibitions that persist across the penitential board, historians estimate that the number of days per year on which sex is allowed adds up to 175. Out of 365, that's less than half.[14]

As if acknowledging the impossibility of enforcing any of these demented rules, much less all of them, penalties for noncompliance are minimal. (They're also a challenge to calculate: one handbook recommends a 10-day fast for doing it during pregnancy, double that if the baby has quickened, quadruple that if the act occurs on a forbidden day—and reduce it by half should the husband be drunk when the act occurs.)[15] But there are other ways to leach physical pleasure and intimacy from married life. However they behave, medieval men and women believe. When people hear from no less an authority than the pope that the child conceived on an off-limits day will be born with hideous deformities, they're not likely to doubt it—especially not if they have faith in the magical properties of semen and menstrual blood. Some will take their chances, but others are bound to be affected.[16]

The pope responsible for circulating the deformed-baby story is Gregory I ("the Great"), a former monk who reveres Augustine almost as much as he despises the flesh. The last of the fathers and the first of the popes, Gregory is austere, mirthless, and as pious as they come. He adds yet another layer of complication to the already twisted carnal guidelines. This is a man who regards excessive laughter and harmless gossip as sins; his approach to restoring marital morality includes telling tall tales of young women who find themselves possessed by the devil because they enjoyed sex with their husbands the night before.[17]

But his special animus is sexual pleasure. In *The Book of Pastoral Rule,* intended for clergymen who deal with the public, Gregory launches his lecture: "Husbands and wives are to . . . remember that they are joined together for the sake of producing offspring"—how could they forget?—"and, when giving themselves to immoderate intercourse, they transfer the occasion of procreation to the service of pleasure, to consider that . . . in wedlock itself they exceed the just duties of wedlock." Such depraved couples should devote themselves to prayer and "supplications" so that they can make up for "having fouled with their admixture of pleasure the fair form of conjugal union." Reiterating the principle that "virginity surpasses wedlock" (you'd think he'd be preaching to the choir but clerical celibacy and chastity won't be mandated for another four hundred years, not that compliance will be universal even then), Gregory invokes Paul: "Wherefore the mind of married Christians is both weak and steadfast, in that it cannot fully despise all temporal things . . . it lies low in the delights of the flesh." The Christian husband should be taught to think of sex with his wife as something he "endures of necessity" while keeping his focus on God and death, "the fruit of the journey's end."

In the three centuries following Augustine, the Church's attitude toward marriage has turned increasingly negative and the teaching on sex ever more convoluted and shrill. Now Gregory explicitly goes after pleasure. He makes his position clear in a letter to the Anglican archbishop, noting that the Church does not "account wedlock as sin. But"—and as buts go, this is a big one—"since even the lawful intercourse of the wedded cannot take place without pleasure of the flesh, entrance into a sacred place should be abstained from, because the pleasure itself can by no means be without sin." Marital intercourse is not "iniquity in itself," the iniquity is "in truth only the pleasure of the intercourse." That said (again), Gregory takes up the archbishop's earlier question of whether a husband in a postcoital state can enter a church without bathing first. The pope responds that as long as that man "makes use of his wife not as seized by the desire of pleasure, but only for the sake of producing children" he may indeed enter a church— after he bathes. But "when not the love of producing offspring but pleasure dominates in the act of intercourse, married persons have something to mourn over." Couples such as this, Gregory writes to the archbishop, should take their mourning elsewhere.

Augustine did his damnedest to remove marital sex. The penitential writers have attempted to supervise the act itself in all its particulars. Gregory, with his scare tactics and life-rejecting sensibility, ratchets up the insanity. They've all been talking out of both sides of the *os*; they claim that marriage is good because fornication is worse, and by the way, the best of all possible worlds is lifelong celibate virginity. The best of all possible conjugal worlds (if such a world must be) is one in which both spouses swear off sex, and not just for brief intervals in order to devote themselves to prayer (as Paul recommends in the New Testament) but permanently, in "spiritual marriage." Alas, the best of all conjugal worlds is a place most people don't want to inhabit or are incapable of it.

The men of the Church must know this on some level, but so far they can't or won't back off. Maybe it's all about making sexual life so hellish, so dreary and unnatural, that people will give it up of their own accord. In some ways it's a wonder that the paradoxes of Christian wedlock don't lead to universal celibacy after all—but then again, with all that forbidden fruit the Church has defined and described, with so many rules and so many ways to transgress them, from the sublime to the ridiculous, it's possible that marital relations have never been hotter.

EIGHT

The Making of a Sexless Marriage

To understand just how deeply and for how long the Church's pro-celibacy propaganda affects common life, specifically the sales pitch on "spiritual marriage" fronted by Joseph and Mary, behold Margery Kempe. A thousand years after Augustine and Jerome, twelve hundred years after Tertullian, and nearly fourteen hundred years after Paul, this English wife who has always enjoyed having sex with her husband, decides to give it up for God.

In the year 1413, Midsummer's Eve falls on the twenty-third of June. By noon on that Friday, the village of York shimmers under a blistering sun, and most people try to move as little as possible. Margery and John Kempe, however, will not be deterred from their pilgrimage. Around midday they set off from York for the countryside, equipped with minimal provisions: a cake that John holds against his chest, and some beer, carried by Margery.

A man on pilgrimage should be thinking about the state of his soul. He should be thinking about the sins he has committed and the means of redemption—humbling the self, mortifying the flesh, telling the priest. Yet John Kempe isn't thinking about these things. John Kempe is thinking about sex. And not with shame or contrition, but with longing. He is thinking about how bad it feels not to be having any.

He's been conscious of little else ever since that Wednesday morning in April, during an Easter week he would not soon forget—for it was the first time in two decades of wedlock that John, inexplicably, had been unable to make love to his wife. Now it is nearing the end of June, yet still he remains powerless; still he cannot explain why. As a result, he is deeply distressed. Oddly, Margery is not, and that bothers John most of all.

Discrepancy in desire has been as foreign to their marriage as sexual dysfunction has been foreign to John. (Neither he nor Margery seems to have considered that the concurrence of these phenomena might be other than coincidental.) For eighteen of their twenty years together, the giving and taking of pleasure between them has flowed in equal measure and with equal delight. That their mutual ardor has endured for so long despite the tedium of domestic life, not to mention the rearing of fourteen children, would have been an enviable feat for any couple in any century. But then, in the course of a single night during their nineteenth year of marriage, the Kempes' sexual synchronicity—though not, as yet, their sexual contact—ended precipitously. John's obsessive thoughts on this sweltering midsummer's eve can be traced directly to what happened that night.

The Kempes were in bed together drifting into sleep, as ordinary couples do on ordinary nights, when Margery experienced something extraordinary. As she later described the transforming moment, referring to herself in the third person, "she heard a melodious sound so sweet and delectable that she thought she had been in paradise." God, she was convinced, had drawn her close and blessed her with an aural taste of heaven. The melody she heard was exquisite beyond words, and so incomparably joyful that it put all earthly melodies (all earthly everything, as it would turn out) to shame. With the glorious notes still humming in her brain, Margery leaped out of bed and cried: "Alas that ever I sinned!" It's easy to imagine how John, thus rudely awakened, must have stared at his wife in disbelief; perhaps he muttered the Middle English equivalent of "What the fuck are you talking about?" For these were strange words indeed, coming from Margery Kempe.

For all of these years, John knew her to be a merry, good-natured, forthright woman who shared his appetite for food, ale, and sex, a woman who had never been one to equate pleasurable sensations with sin. But that was a different Margery. Now, steeped in remorse, she seems a virtual stranger to her husband. Her joie de vivre has been eclipsed by a rigid asceticism that John neither shares nor comprehends.

Margery is illiterate; she recounts the process of her conversion, in the third person, to an accommodating priest. Their collaboration results in *The Book of Margery Kempe.* "And after this time," it reads, explaining the effect of that first divine encounter, "she never had any desire to have sexual intercourse with her husband, for paying the debt of matrimony was so abominable to her that she would rather, she thought, have eaten and drunk the ooze and muck in the gutter than consent to intercourse, except out of obedience." Though she could not deny him his conjugal rights, she could (and did) pressure John to renounce them voluntarily in order to create a "spiritual"—that is, sexless—marriage, à la Mary and Joseph—a still-admirable achievement in the eyes of the Church this late in the day.[1] Margery argued her case with passionate conviction, sure that it was based on divine authority, and ceaselessly lectured John about how they had so often "displeased God by their inordinate love, and the great delight that each of them had in using the other's body." In Margery's view, the path to atonement and eventual salvation was clearly marked. "It would be a good thing," she recalled telling John, "if by mutual consent they punished and chastised themselves by abstaining from the lust of their bodies."

John, however, lacked his wife's assurance. Though he listened patiently to her arguments and her pleas, though he even agreed, echoing Augustine, that chastity could be a good thing, but not quite yet, Margery's word wasn't enough to convince him that God wanted them to give up sex. He needed independent evidence, he said. In the meantime, he asserted his marital rights. As Margery puts it, "He would have his will with her, and she obeyed with much weeping and sorrowing." Poor Margery, forced to honor the vows of wedlock. Poor John, forced to force himself upon a once-eager bedmate who now endured his lovemaking grimly, and only because she knew it was her duty.

Outside of bed, Margery was no less estranged from her former self. She woke at 2 or 3 A.M. and went to church, where she prayed until well into the next afternoon. She kept vigils. She fasted. She slipped into the confessional booth as often as three times a day. From a local kiln she procured a haircloth, "the sort that malt is dried on," and wore it discreetly inside her gown, successfully concealing it from John's notice. About other matters she was more forthcoming. "I may not deny you my body," she told him repeatedly, "but all the love and affection of my heart is withdrawn from all earthly creatures and set on God alone." Nevertheless, John seemed to prefer a wooden bedmate to none at all: "he used her as he had done before, he would not desist." Maybe he hoped that she might yet come to her senses. This past April—at the beginning of Easter week, just two months ago—God came to her rescue instead.

As Margery knelt in prayer, asking for chastity for the umpteenth time, God entered her mind. He promised to orchestrate a marital intervention—"I shall suddenly slay [all sexual desire in] your husband"—and on Wednesday of that week, when John next sought sexual congress with his wife, God did just that. Margery doesn't say how, exactly; her description in the book is maddeningly opaque, perhaps because she didn't want to offend the priest to whom she dictated her account. Whatever the reason, this crucial turn in the narrative hangs on just a few suggestive words: John lost his "power to touch her . . . with carnal knowledge."

And that is how things stand between the Kempes on Midsummer's Eve, 1413.

At some point, as they sweat their way through the countryside, John tests his wife with a hypothetical question. "Margery," he says, "if there came a man with a sword who would strike off my head unless I made love with you as I used to do before, tell me on your conscience—for you say you will not lie—whether you would allow my head to be cut off, or else allow me to make love with you again, as I did at one time?"

"Alas, sir," Margery protests, "why are you raising this matter, when we have been chaste for these past eight weeks?"

But John will not be sidetracked. He demands to know "the truth of your heart."

"Truly," she says, meaning it, "I would rather see you being killed, than that we should turn back to our uncleanness."

This is the truth John seeks, but evidently not the one he desires. "You are no good wife," he cries.

Margery thinks his reaction unfair. Has she not lain beside him every night during the last two months, her body available for the taking? If John wants sex, what stops him from having it? John reminds her—as if she needed reminding—about the events of Easter week, when he was "made so afraid when he would have touched her that he dared do no more." Margery sees her opening and grabs it. His fear, she says, is the corroborative evidence he's been waiting for, a sign from above that he must "mend his ways and ask God's mercy . . . make a vow of chastity."

Not so fast, John says, and not now—"because now I can make love to you without mortal sin, and then [once the vow is made] I wouldn't be able to." Margery listens in dread, suspecting that her hard-won celibacy might not outlast the heat of the day, praying for God to prove her wrong. In silence, the Kempes resume walking. As they approach the village of Bridlington, John spots a cross planted by the roadside and sits down beside it, beckoning to his wife. "Margery," he says, "grant me my desire, and I shall grant you your desire." He offers her a choice of three: "that we shall still lie together in one bed as we have done before [that is, resume sexual relations] . . . that you shall pay my debts . . . that you shall eat and drink with me on Fridays as you used to do."

"No, sir," she says to the latter, mindful that her fasting, unlike her pursuit of chastity, began at God's specific request. "I will never agree to break my Friday fast as long as I live."

"Well then," John shoots back, "I'm going to have sex with you again." It is clear that he means right here, right now.

Margery, sobbing, asks him to wait a few minutes so that she can pray. She kneels at the foot of the roadside cross and asks for guidance: Should she give up the Friday fast in order to preserve her chastity, or vice versa? God wastes no time responding. "I no longer wish you to fast, and therefore I command you in the name of Jesus to eat and drink as your husband does."

Thus equipped with divine marching orders, Margery is able to complete the marital negotiation with dry-eyed confidence. "Grant me that you will not come into my bed," she says to John. "Make my body free to God, so that you never make any claim on me requesting any conjugal debt after this day as long as you live." In return, she promises to feast with John on Fridays instead of fasting without him. The Kempes have finally reached an agreement, on which John pronounces benediction: "May your body be as freely available to God as it has been to me."

They would have lived together in "spiritual marriage" until the end, but nasty rumors dog them. The neighbors whisper loudly that John and Margery "enjoyed their lust and their pleasure as they did before," spreading the word that the couple's vow of chastity is a sham. Apparently because of the gossip, the Kempes separate. But though John plays no part in Margery's book for a number of years, the narrator is not entirely without a husband. God takes over the role. "I must be intimate with you, and lie in your bed with you," Margery recalls God telling her, "and you may boldly, when you are in bed, take me to you as your wedded husband . . . take me in the arms of your soul and kiss my mouth, my head, and my feet as sweetly as you want."

Whether John finds comparable comfort is anyone's guess. By the time he resurfaces in the narrative, he is over sixty and in critical condition after a bad fall. He is found at home, "lying with his head twisted under himself, half alive, all streaked with blood." Margery, still his wife and next of kin, is notified. She rushes to John's side, where she encounters another bunch of hostile neighbors, who, in an irony not lost on Mrs. Kempe, hold her accountable for John's misfortune because she has been living apart from him. Margery summarizes the complaint against her: "She could have looked after him and did not." If John dies from his injuries, the locals threaten to hang her for murder.

In despair, Margery turns as usual to God. Will he save her from "slander" by keeping John alive for a year? Okay, God replies, provided that Margery takes John into her home and looks after him for the rest of his life: "He has made your body freely available to me so that you should serve me and live chaste and clean, and therefore I wish you to be available to help him in his need, in my name." God gives John not one but several more years under Margery's roof. Things go smoothly enough (Margery indicates nothing to the contrary) until John's final days, when he regresses dramatically. "He turned childish and lacked reason," Margery dictates, "so that he could not go to a stool to relieve himself, or else he would not, but like a child discharged his excrement into his linen clothes as he sat there by the fire or at the table—wherever it was, he would spare no place."

Consumed by the physically arduous roles of laundress, butler, chambermaid, cook, and round-the-clock geriatric nurse, Margery has no time for the sustained periods of contemplation that absorbed her during the separation from John. She might have resented this; instead, she is grateful. Ministering to her ailing husband offers her something more valuable than solitude, more essential than prayer. She feels that every bit of soiled linen she scrubs is a special gift from God, a penance customized to fit her signature sin: "She thought to herself how she in her young days had had very many delectable thoughts, physical lust, and inordinate love for his body. And therefore, she was glad to be punished by means of the same body."

In those two sentences, the illiterate Margery Kempe neatly distills a millennium's worth of warnings about the perils of sexual pleasure insinuated repetitively by religious leaders into the collective consciousness of Christian Europe. Her account is uniquely detailed for its era, and uniquely revealing of a married woman's inner struggle to suppress a basic human instinct (and a basic conjugal activity that has brought her much joy) in the name of faith—at a time when married women's inner, or outer, struggles are rarely, if ever, revealed by the women themselves. And Kempe is far from alone in this particular struggle. "I wear a hair shirt because of the silken undergarments and precious stuffs with which I used to clothe myself," writes another once-contented wife later on in the fifteenth century. This woman has also experienced a "conversion." that compelled her to follow an exacting course of self-mortification. Along with the switch from silk to horsehair there are also the "thirty-three stones . . . [I] put in the soles of my shoes because I have so often offended God with my leaping and dancing." Far worse than leaping and dancing, as this woman sees it, is her desire for her husband: "I flagellate my body for the impious and carnal pleasures with which I indulged it during my marriage."[2]

These days, carnal pleasure is celebrated as part of the popularly acclaimed calculus that adds up to a good marriage, and the pejorative use of the word "inordinate" to modify "love," especially love between husband and wife, is close to unthinkable. The modern, secular version of John and Margery Kempe—a couple who remain sexually passionate after twenty years together, even despite the famously dampening effect of parenthood—would have reason to be smug, not to flagellate themselves. That shift in perception will take awhile. For now, but not for long, people like the Kempes still take direction from the celibate men of the Church, who continue to show unseemly interest in what married couples are doing in bed.

NINE

Cuckold's Lament

CARICATURES of cuckolds, fables about wives who can't get enough, vicious attacks on marriage: If the major themes of medieval secular culture are any indication, more than a few men (still the ones who set the themes, establish the tone, deliver the content) have sex on the brain and brain and not in a good way. The ancient conviction that women's carnal hunger is incessant percolates throughout the medieval period, one of several factors that point to an exceedingly high level of male performance anxiety, especially in marriage.

The fear of impotence—and possibly worse, that if it occurs all the world will know—is widespread, under the transparent cover of fiction.[1] There's no Viagra, but there's magic. Wives use it as the penitential writers (and the ancient Romans before them) have already reported inside and outside the Church, men's preoccupation with the idea that women can manipulate their sexual functioning will only grow more pronounced, culminating with the Inquisition's witch hunts. Not that men themselves don't pursue magical cures for impotence wherever they may be found. One antidote—apparently lifted from Pliny, the first-century Roman naturalist—involves taking the testicle of a cock (the feathered variety), somehow enclosing it in a ram's skin with a soupçon of goose fat, and tying it on the arm. The caveat: if this amulet falls under the bed, forget the erection.[2]

The assumption that women are nymphomaniacs is nothing

new, but the popular literature of medieval Europe seems inordinately preoccupied by the subject.[3] One typical fable, "The Fisherman from Bridge-upon-Seine," concerns a man who is certain that his usefulness to his new bride begins and ends with his sexual prowess.[4] She brings to their marriage a respectable dowry—wine, wheat, five cows, ten sheep—as well as an avid libido. He feeds her well, buys her good shoes and nice dresses, and "screwed her the best he could." But he worries that his best won't be good enough for her. He knows that "a young, well-fed wife / Would like to be screwed frequently," and that if he cannot meet her standards she will leave him.

One night in bed, he asks what she loves about him. Faking modesty, she says not a word about what she loves most—the erect penis she holds in her hand. No, she loves him because he loves her, treats her well, and feeds and clothes her generously. Her groom knows better: "If I didn't screw you well, / You would hate me worse than a dog." She swears he is mistaken, calling his member an "outhouse organ" and claiming, "I wish a sow had eaten it / Except that you would have died." He says, "If I had lost my prick . . . / You'd never love me." Again she protests: "I wish it had pleased the true heart of God / That a dog had choked on it."

She's insistent enough to plant a seed of doubt, and the fisherman determines to find out the truth. A golden opportunity soon presents itself. While the fisherman is doing his business from his boat on the Seine, the body of a dead priest happens to float by. (The narrator fills in the backstory: A knight found the priest in flagrante delicto with the knight's own wife, "male above female, together, naked flesh to naked flesh," and as per medieval literary convention, the priest got what he deserved: He leaped into the river, "the prick extended," and drowned.)

When the fisherman spots the cleric's bloated corpse, he remembers what his wife said—"that she hated nothing / Living in this world / As much as she did his tool." He takes his knife and cuts off the priest's penis, washes and dries it well, puts the thing in his lap, and rows to shore. At home he pulls "a very long face / As if he were about to die then and there." He tells his wife about being overpowered by three evil knights who plan to amputate a part of his body but have the grace to let their victim choose which part will go. "I told them to cut off my prick," he explains, "Because you said / That you didn't want anything to do with it." Then he throws the priest's penis onto the floor for his wife's inspection. She fails the test, as her husband knew she would: "Fie!" she says. "What an outrage! / May God send you a short life! / Now there's nothing I hate worse / Than I do your body, / Now we will have to separate!" Instantly she instructs her servant to pack her belongings.

Just before she leaves, her husband calls to her. "Sweetheart," he says, and proceeds to make her an inexplicably generous offer. She must take half of his money, for to deprive her of a fair share would be to betray his duty as her husband, however short-lived that role has turned out to be. But with the castration and all, he'll need her help retrieving the cash from the pouch slung on his hips. Her fingers, searching for the pouch, encounter instead "a robust prick / Throbbing in his britches; She felt it in her palm and weighed it, / And could feel it hard and hot. / Her whole heart leapt with joy." What miracle is this? Her man promises that it's "my prick . . . / Just the way I used to have it," but she needs more convincing. "How did it come back to you?" Her husband says, "God has done this by His power, / Because, I think, he didn't want / You to leave me." That does it. The young woman shrieks ecstatically to her servant that they won't be leaving after all: "My lord has found his prick again! / Our Lord has taken care of it!" Then she grabs the cherished organ, dropping all pretense that anything else matters, and the narrator leaves this pair in the happily ever after to convey his message:

> *I say at the end of my story / That if a wife had a husband / The handsomest and the cleverest / And the best admired that could be, / And if he were a knight, by his deeds, / Better than Gawain ever was, / And if he were castrated / She would immediately want to*

have him exchanged / For the worst man in all his house, / As long as she found one / Who would screw her soon and often.

The author of this tale is speaking generically: The one thing that "a wife," any wife, presumably cannot do without is a serviceable penis, and "serviceable" means perpetually raring to go. On the other side of that presumption is, obviously, a concern with male sexual performance—or rather the lack thereof. That impotence in a husband will lead the sexually ravenous wife to other men is the literary if not actual expectation; the variable lies in the husband's response. Will he seek vengeance, or will he fail to notice—or feign obliviousness to—her infidelity? To medieval society, obliviousness is far worse, even if the vengeful husband acts on a mere suspicion that proves invalid. To be less than vigilant about a wife's sexual behavior is to be perceived as less than manly, and to be less than manly invites public ridicule, compounding the emasculation. Better to err on the side of paranoia.

In one well-circulated cautionary tale (cautionary to women, instructive to men), a betrayed husband preserves his manhood by acting swiftly and harshly: He kills his wife's lover, cuts his heart out, and tricks her into eating it. Only after the savory morsel has been consumed does he reveal its provenance, inducing his unfaithful spouse to kill herself by self-starvation. In a similar but more gruesome tale, twelve husbands learn that a single knight has slept with all of their wives. They find, murder, and mutilate the knight, removing his heart and genitals to serve as the basis of a tasty stew. This they feed to their unsuspecting wives, who also choose self-starvation when informed of the ingredients.[5] (Death by starvation seems to be the preferred fate for fictional adulteresses even in the kinder, gentler marital era following the Reformation. In Thomas Heywood's 1607 play, *A Woman Killed with Kindness,* a husband discovers his wife's infidelity, but instead of cutting up her lover and cooking his body parts, he simply throws her out of the house. In exile, she too starves herself to death.)[6]

The presumed sexual voracity of the female further presumes

that within every so-far-virtuous wife is an unfaithful one looking for an excuse to break out. Such is the scenario of another contemporary tale, "Dame Sirith." A fetching young woman is left alone at home by her husband (always a bad move). In his absence, a fetching young man with seduction on his mind just happens to drop by. She turns him down, exclaiming, "It shall never come to pass that a man, through propositioning or through pride, shall cause me shame!" The would-be lover departs, but only to strategize with a neighbor, Dame Sirith, who apparently has nothing better to do; she assures him that he'll soon have his prize. The Dame cooks up a tall tale about how her daughter has been turned into a dog, weeping day and night, by a rejected suitor, and feeds the story to the young wife. Lo and behold, she changes her mind—even asking the Dame if she could find the man and bring him back, no problem there—and the mission is accomplished, proving that the woman's virtue was mere pretense. As long as the husband knows nothing, the lover and his genitals need not be separated.[7]

But it's the oblivious cuckold, not the vengeful one, who plays the most poignant role in these narratives. His plight encompasses all the familiar aspects of the basic male nightmare: loss of virility, fear of aging, the inversion of the male-female hierarchy, and public humiliation. (The humiliation can take many forms in the fabliaux—in one, a husband is forced to kiss his wife's crotch in front of a jeering crowd, and in another, a queen tells the inexperienced knight who hopes to become her lover that "it is easy to judge from the state of the hay," referring to his measly chin hairs, "whether the pitchfork is any good.")[8] Most of all, and by definition, the theme is uncertainty about paternal identity.

The word "cuckold" derives from Old French. Its first appearance in English is thought to be in the anonymous poem "The Owl and the Nightingale"(1250), rendered as "cuckeweld."[9] A double meaning pertains: cleverness (for the cuckoo, who lays its eggs in another bird's nest) and stupidity (for the duped bird, who feeds what it believes is its own progeny). The latter definition applies to the husband who is, or pretends to be, unaware that he has been duped, even to the point of raising another man's child as his own. He has been emasculated, the fate worse than death for the stronger sex. And to close the loop, his wife's extramarital activity is justified by his impotence.

Whenever the marital order is threatened—in any era, regardless of what the terms may be—the social order is threatened. Medieval European society manages such threats by mocking them en masse through various rituals, most notably the masked parades known as charivari. These rituals are designed not only to shame the offender but to relieve the collective discomfort that he (or she) causes by distancing it, and also to reassert the proper order visually, for all to see. Nothing causes more discomfort than the subversion of marital roles, and at a time when male performance anxiety is acute, nothing exemplifies that subversion more than the cuckold. Only a deceived husband would be paraded through the streets wearing phallic horns on his head, the cuckold's symbol—and also the fool's, for a deceived husband is the fool of fools. He might also be subjected, as the husband dominated (or worse, beaten) by his wife would be subjected, to a backward-facing ride on a donkey, led through the streets by a raucous crowd; or to being pelted with tripe or frying pans, pulled by his beard, or even kicked in the genitals. (As Protestant marital ethics take hold of the culture, the target of humiliation will shift to the husband who mistreats and—especially—beats his wife.)[10]

The two master craftsmen of the cuckold as fictional character, Geoffrey Chaucer and Giovanni Boccaccio, portray him as too old, too weak, and too sexually anemic to fight his fate—perhaps because the writers (and no doubt their readers) approve of a wife's pursuit of her natural right to pleasure. After all that Church propaganda, the attitude these authors convey feels surprisingly modern and refreshingly sane. Boccaccio's narrative masterpiece of mid-fourteenth-century sexual politics, *The Decameron,* is an imaginary account of ten days in the lives of its characters—a mixed group of young Florentine aristocrats who have fled that plague-infested city for their country villas, where they proceed to regale one another with tales of erotic adventure. Through these stories, Boccacio reveals his contempt for chastity, trashes moral hypocrites, and of course assaults clueless cuckolds—infusing the standard view of the raging female libido with more admiration than fear.

The narrator of one tale begins by noting the "stupidity" of men "who are given to thinking . . . that while they are gadding about in various parts of the world with one woman after another, the wives they leave behind are simply twiddling their thumbs." One of these stupid men is a rich judge from Pisa named Ricciardo di Chinzica, "who had rather more brain than brawn, and who, thinking perhaps he could satisfy a wife with the same talent that he brought to his studies, went to a great deal of trouble to find himself a wife who was both young and beautiful." After the wedding, to a young beauty named Bartolomea, comes the wedding night—and a pathetic performance by the groom. "He only managed to come at her once in order to consummate the marriage, and even then he very nearly fell out of the game before it was over. And next morning, being a skinny and a withered and a spineless sort of fellow, he had to swallow health drinks, energy tablets and various other restoratives."

With "a better notion of his powers," Chinzica tries to conceal his sexual shortfall from Bartolomea by teaching her "a calendar which schoolchildren are apt to consult, of the sort that was once in use in Ravenna."[11] Ravenna, according to a footnote, is known to have as many churches as there are days in the year, which means, as Chinzica patiently but futilely explains to his wife, who (like everyone else) knows better,

> that there was not a single day that was not the feast of one or more Saints, out of respect for whom, as he would demonstrate by devious arguments, man and woman should abstain from sexual union. To the foregoing, he added holidays of obligation, the four Ember weeks [following the first Sunday in Lent, Whitsunday, September 14, and December 13], the eves of the Apostles and a numerous array of subsidiary Saints, Fridays and

Saturdays, the sabbath, the whole of Lent, certain phases of the moon, and various special occasions . . .

Chinzica's version of the proverbial female headache limits conjugal relations to, at most, once a month. It also gives him exclusive possession of the moral high road while keeping "a close watch" on Bartolomea, "lest anyone else should teach her as good a knowledge of the working-days as he had taught her of the holidays." Meanwhile, his "fair lady" experiences "chagrin" at the prospect of routine sexual deprivation, but she can't protest the logic of religious devotion.

Then a heat wave strikes Pisa. The judge yearns for the cooler air of Montenero, where he keeps a villa, so he and his wife make their escape from the sweltering city. He is thoughtful enough to arrange a fishing trip during their sojourn, thus providing Bartolomea "with a little recreation." Monsieur Ricciardo and the fishermen he hires go off in one boat; Bartolomea's fun consists of sitting in a second boat with other ladies, watching the fascinating activities of the men. Whereupon the "notorious pirate" Paganino da Mare intercepts the ladies' vessel, spots the beauteous Bartolomea, and carries her off.

Bartolomea weeps bitterly all day, and Paganino tries to console her with words; this doesn't work, so he "turned to comforting her with deeds"—of a sexual nature. Miraculously, she stops weeping, "so effective were the consolations he provided." Unlike her flaccid, faux-devout husband, Paganino "was not the sort of man to pay any heed to calendars, and he had long since forgotten about feasts and holy days." Bartolomea promptly falls passionately in love/lust with her captor. Before these two even reach Monaco, the pirate's hometown, "the judge and his laws had faded from the lady's memory, and life with Paganino was a positive joy." On land, Bartolomea's bliss continues, for "in addition to consoling her continuously night and day, Paganino treated her with all the respect due to a wife."

Time passes. Chinzica learns of his wife's whereabouts, and

with a purse of ransom money he sails alone to Monaco, finds Paganino, and tells the pirate to name his price and hand over the lady. Money, explains the canny loverboy, isn't the issue. The lady should decide the men's fate: Which one does she want? But Bartolomea pretends not to recognize her husband. The judge begs for some time alone with her, which Paganino grants. "Oh, my dearest," says Judge Chinzica, "my dear, sweet darling, my treasure, now do you remember your Ricciardo who loves you more than life itself?" The lady laughs, interrupting his babbling:

> "You are well aware that I possess a sufficiently good memory to know that you are my husband . . . But you showed very little sign of knowing me, when I was living with you, because if, either then or now, you were as wise as you wish to pretend, you should certainly have had the gumption to realize that a fresh and vigorous young woman like myself needs something more than food and clothes, even if modesty forbids her to say so. And you know how little of that you provided. If you were more interested in studying the law than in keeping a wife, you should never have married in the first place."

She refuses to go back with him. Crazy with grief, the judge returns to Pisa, where he dies; Paganino marries the widow, and they live happily ever after. End of story, which promptly causes the company to erupt in peals of laughter.

Chaucer, writing a few decades later, is slightly more sympathetic to the parade of pathetic husbands who limp through *The Canterbury Tales*—a good thing, since in the Chaucerian universe, being wronged is the universal state of married men: "It's he who has no wife who is no cuckold."[12] Chaucer's not condemning marriage, he's simply expressing a matter of fact that other men should keep in mind, the better to minimize the aggregate danger to manhood. The author seems to think that conjugal life could be enjoyable, provided that a man chooses his wife wisely and with full self-knowledge. But Chaucer has no patience for graybeards who are delusional enough to think that frisky young wives will rejuvenate them sexually, and these oldsters are all over the Canterbury landscape.

In "The Merchant's Tale" a bachelor geezer in the deep winter of his life, appropriately named January, suddenly wants to experience the "spiritual bliss" of marriage. He shares the ancient and ever-mistaken assumption that a very young wife will be docile and malleable—you can see Chaucer rolling his eyes—and so he believes that if anyone is likely to stray, it'll be him. With the ludicrous thought that a young, attractive wife will deter his infidelity, January marries May (as in the lusty month of), who promptly sets him straight.

Most memorably, the redoubtable Wife of Bath demonstrates that a middle-aged wife can shatter male illusions of potency as well as a teenaged one. This Canterbury character is still robustly sensual, with a zest for life that makes even the more youthful husbands of Chaucer's tales seem wan and ineffectual in comparison, as if they too have already given up. None of the Canterbury females are particularly virtuous or modest (who needs more of those?), but they have all the vitality their male counterparts lack—and that alone renders the men impotent, one way or another.[13]

Still, the Good Wife lives on in the dreams and works of men. Boccaccio is responsible for her medieval incarnation, under the name of Griselda. Her tale concludes the Decameron, although it's not confined to that text. Petrarch translates his protégé's work from Italian to Latin, then the linguistic common denominator; this enables Chaucer to spin his own version in *The Canterbury Tales*, namely that of the Clerk, perhaps to serve as a counterpoint to the Wife of Bath. From there the story of Griselda filters into popular culture in simplified form—the better to mold marriageable daughters and malleable brides into proper wives.

In one typically middlebrow retelling of her tale, Griselda is a peasant girl who attracts the eye of the lord of the land.[14] He wishes to marry her, but she must promise to submit to his will in all things. Promise she does, but though the lord marries Griselda, he still feels it necessary to subject her to a grueling series of Good Wife tests. Immediately after their first child, a daughter, is born, the royal husband says he must "take" the newborn, implying infanticide. Griselda asks no questions then or later; the baby disappears, with no discernible reaction from the mother. Four years later Griselda bears her lord a son. Again he asks her consent to "take" this child; again she says he need not ask. "Thou art lord of me and of my children," she assures him. "Do therefore as thou wilt with thine own and ask not my consent." That baby disappears, too, and the lord's next move is to inform his forcibly childless but ever-uncomplaining lady that he plans to divorce her and marry someone else. When Griselda makes no objection even to this, her husband finally reveals that the apparent double infanticide, followed by the pronouncement of divorce, were all ruses designed to measure just how submissive she is capable of being. The children have been safe and sound all along, placed in the care of a relative. The lord has no other woman in his life, and now that Griselda has more than lived up to his exacting marital standards, he intends to keep her. This is supposed to be a neat little morality play, an illustration of the principle that the writer himself summarizes as "by good obedience a wise woman gains her husband's love."

Somehow, though, the paradigm seems to be the worse for wear. While Griselda's ancient predecessors, Alcestis and Lucretia, embodied grace and nobility at least as much as virtue and service to their husbands, Griselda's main claim to fame is slavish obedience. If this has become the dominant characteristic of the Good Wife (and of a "wise woman") as defined by medieval culture, either men's imaginations have dimmed over time or their insecurity has intensified. Or both.

It would be nice to know what women are thinking about the men who are griping about women, but with a few notable exceptions the record remains blank until the Renaissance approaches.[15] One of those exceptions might be "The Wife's Lament," a tenth-century Anglo-Saxon dramatic monologue—if it is indeed written, as presumed, by an anonymous female author and not by a man posing as one.[16] Given men's complaints about wives during the Middle Ages, the lament in question might be expected to sound something like this: A good Christian woman spends her days slaving for an alehead of a husband who mounts her when drunk and leaves her for months on end. When he returns, his first comment is that his supper is cold, and his first act is to box her ears or worse. She tries to endure these assaults in Griselda-like silence, while secretly wishing that he would drop dead. Alternatively, she's a domineering shrew or has a lover to console her.

In fact, the wife doing the lamenting appears to be none of the above. She is faithful, and she doesn't want her husband dead; she wants him back. She mourns not his presence, but his absence. The couple has been forced apart by her vile in-laws, for unexplained reasons, and she has no hope that the two of them will ever be reunited. (She calls him "my lord," in the medieval marital vernacular.) Her husband's kin have spirited him away, across the "wild waves" of perhaps the English Channel. Now he lives on foreign land somewhere far away, and she must exist in "friendless exile" on hostile territory—her husband's family's lands. Her in-laws have thrown her out of the house, banishing her to an "earth-cave" in a wooded grove, where she pines for her lord day and night. "Now is destroyed, as though it never were, our friendship," she writes of the marriage. "Full oft we pledged, save death alone, naught should divide us else; that is altered now . . . Friends there are on earth, lovers living, who lie abed, when I, at daybreak, walk alone, under oak-trees, through these earth-caves." She and her "much-loved one," she thinks, both "dwell wretched." She feels his pain as sharply as her own, knowing that "too often he will think upon a happier home," which would be the marital home that no longer exists.

If the author of this piece is indeed a woman, and if her account is in essence accurate—in the sense of telling the emotional if not factual truth—then we should all admire what she rightfully laments: an unusually loving marriage at any time, and a bloody miracle at this time, given what little is known of it. That's why the authorship beggars belief. A woman who is not an aristocrat produces an artfully written and deeply felt eulogy of her marriage, amazingly enough; even more amazingly, her work is preserved. And she writes it in the tenth century—the brutish tail-end-of-the-Dark-Ages tenth century, when illiteracy is standard even for male aristocrats, the people most likely to be educated outside of the clergy; when the production of secular writing is minimal at best, the preservation of it undervalued at best, and the odds of a woman producing such work is virtually nil. For such a work to be preserved, figure less than zero. The author of "A Wife's Lament," then, may very well be a man.

If so, he's fantasizing about another Good Wife, but not as a model for the edification of women. This is more personal. It seems to be a man's fantasy of the perfectly loving wife he wishes he had, a wife to whom he means everything—or maybe he had a perfectly loving wife and she's the one who disappeared, which makes this a husband's lament. Either way, the piece expresses what no man in the tenth, or for that matter the twenty-first, century would want to reveal—unseemly, unmanly emotional need and dependence—so the author takes female cover. Just a guess.

TEN

The Golden Age of Adultery

For all the bitching, brooding, legislating, theologizing, and delusional thinking about marriage since God told Eve to shut up and submit to her husband, there's been just one major shift: the Christian alignment of sex with sin, turning marriage into the dumping ground for lust. But not to worry. The next shift is already in the works.

The dark days of the Dark Ages vanish in the dazzling light of the twelfth century, when cultural life revives, learning becomes fashionable once again, and knights put on their shining armor. As new ideas begin to circulate, one in particular takes hold. It takes hold of the only segment of society that rivals the Church in arrogance, power, wealth, personal mobility, and access to secular knowledge from outside Christian Europe—and is also accustomed to circumventing religious authority. That segment would be the aristocracy. The idea its members fall in love with is just that: love. Not spiritual love for God (the only kind that counts for the Church), not cerebral love between men (the only kind that counted in the classical world), but love of the erotic kind, men's for women. This is about heterosexual desire, romance, and frankly sexual passion—hardly unknown in life, but never before promoted in the West as an aspirational ideal, the supreme form of human love, equal to if not greater than love of God. Nothing could be more subversive to the Church, especially considering that the locus of this love is extramarital, as in adulterous. And nothing could have more potential to transform sexual awareness, and inevitably—although it is not yet in the cards—marriage.[1]

The religious imperatives that rule the times clash head-on with the traditions and vital concerns of noble families, whose members resent and resist clerical meddling in secular life, especially in marriage. At this level of society the principle of indissoluble, sexually exclusive wedlock is untenable, the very antithesis of what aristocratic marriage is designed to accomplish—the accumulation and preservation of wealth, land, and political power across generations. Highborn unions are brokered through an intensive and protracted series of negotiations, with all the hairsplitting compromises that might go into a Middle Eastern peace agreement or a multinational corporate merger today. Each side works to maximize its political and economic advantages with an eye to the long-term future as well as the present. As in ancient Athens, "feelings" are deemed irrelevant. Bride and groom are commodities to be exchanged or dangled; their value is measured in terms of holdings and titles, and later in their ability to breed sons.

"Do you love Maria?" asks one male aristocrat of another in John Marston's play *The Malcontent*. The other man replies that he has "no great affection" for the highborn woman he seeks to wed, but esteems her "as wise men do love great women, to ennoble their blood and augment their revenue." That's a fair description of the aristocratic status quo circa 1600, when Marston wrote the play, but it would also be accurate in 1100, or for that matter, when Charles marries Diana in 1981. Great affection within a royal marriage would be a lucky accident; it's what a king gives to his mistress, while his wife gets the crown. Once she fulfills her end of the deal, she too could seek "affection" elsewhere—discreetly. As a certified virgin of noble birth, equipped with ancestral titles and lands of her own and with plenty of childbearing years ahead of her, Diana could have produced unquestionably legitimate and thoroughly royal heirs, keeping the throne within the family: That was her value to the House of Windsor. There may have been no divorce and no lethal accident if she had understood and accepted at the outset that marriage to a king, future or current, is a business transaction and not a romance.

Young women surely know this in the Middle Ages, even if they don't belong to the castled class. The daughter of a minor landowner or a well-to-do tradesman comes into sexual maturity well aware of the nature of wedlock. Her lineage and the quality of the dowry her father settles upon her dictates the social level at which she will marry. This means that not everyone marries. Second and third sons, by the rule of primogeniture, are often forced to remain bachelors, and by the time a girl reaches marriageable age (puberty), the family coffers might have been drained by her older siblings. The best match her father can make for her might not be good enough: a suitor of dubious birth who will accept a paltry dowry in exchange for superior maternal bloodlines. And if Daddy's ancestral pride makes that bargain too painful or reprehensible, or if his daughter has obvious physical flaws that mark her as an unsuitable breeder, her only other option is the convent. Only the peasant class has some freedom of choice. With no goods or titles to exchange and no power to be gained through marriage, parents can be lax in their control. A son or daughter might even mate for love. That would be inconceivable for blue bloods—one reason that the courtly ethic so enchants them, especially the women, who keep the game going for three centuries.[2]

However it is made, Christian marriage in medieval Europe is theoretically unbreakable. According to canon law, not even a king can procure a divorce. But the aristocracy, though Christian, has long been accustomed to living by its own laws, which reflect a value system that directly opposes the Church's. Generational stability, political alliance, and economic interest greatly outrank religious considerations. Heirless nobles rebel against doctrinal meddling where it doesn't belong. They will not watch their patrimony disintegrate; if a wife fails to produce male heirs, she has to be replaced. And if a more lucrative or politically advantageous marital opportunity becomes available, aristocrats feel that the mere fact of already being married shouldn't stand in the way of cashing in. Indissoluble wedlock is unthinkable for them.

And they soon learn that money talks, even to the men in mitres. Throw enough of it at the right bishop and—voilà!—the sacred bond is magically dissolved. The strategy usually entails the sudden discovery, even after a decade of wedlock, that a man has married his fourth cousin twice removed. He confesses the unwitting sin in all Christian piety to a churchman whose greed is as formidable as his ecclesiastical connections. The cleric solemnly agrees that the nobleman's soul is in peril but can be saved by an immediate annulment. Cash changes hands, the pope is consulted, a decree is issued, and the matter is closed.[3]

It is just such a nobleman who imports the idea that will (eventually) rewrite the rules of marriage as thoroughly as the equation of sex with sin—only this time the changes will make sense. He's a formidable warrior and philanderer as well as the feudal boss of nearly a third of France, and he intends to teach his courtiers how to behave around women. This medieval Mr. Manners, as he styles himself, is William IX, Duke of Aquitaine, Count of Poitou.

Europe at this time is just dragging itself from the muck of the Dark Ages. Feudalism, the first secular power structure to blunt religious control in several centuries, has only lately stabilized. The trappings of wealth and luxury reappear at court, much to the delight of lords and ladies, but courtesy seems to be lost forever. Even at court, people eat with their hands and wipe snot on their sleeves. Forks and handkerchiefs won't be invented for six hundred years, and it'll be five hundred before Erasmus, the Christian humanist, advises young men to refrain from farting in public— or at least to cover the noise with a cough. No amount of fine silk or lace filigree can conceal the fact that those to the manor born are no longer to the manner born. There are exceptions, naturally, and William is reportedly one of them, which makes him intolerant of the boorish behavior demonstrated by his peers. Never mind that his own behavior may not be stellar. One contemporary writer calls him "a foolish and shifty man" who returns from the First Crusade "to loll in the slough of every vice," bragging about his sexual conquests. Rumor has it that the man credited with disseminating a code that idealizes women, ironically enough, is in fact a bit of a misogynist.[4] Nonetheless, he designs an elaborate series of etiquette lessons disguised as a game—the game of "courtly love."

If there is such a thing as an entirely new idea, this isn't one of them. William is a restless adventurer; he leads crusades; he gets around. Sojourns in the Middle East would expose him to Arabic love poetry, proliferating locally through the tenth century and currently filtering into the courts of Europe. But the literature of courtly love, including the King Arthur/Guinevere/Lancelot epics, is rooted in Latin poetry, above all in Ovid's magnum opus, *The Art of Love*. This work—which so offended the emperor Augustus, the man obsessed with promoting reproduction, restoring moral order to Rome, and deflowering virgins procured by his wife that it led to Ovid's exile—is probably William's major inspiration. *The Art of Love*, written at the start of the first century, sets the whole courtly tradition on track. It's an epic guide to pursuing, consummating, maintaining, and exiting an adulterous affair, addressing men in one section and women in another, and it's spreading like wildfire throughout the twelfth century.

A man should be eloquent, says Ovid, for "a woman, no less than populace, grave judge or chosen senate, will surrender, defeated," to a would-be lover who knows how to string a sentence together. He should also be intuitive: "What she asks, she fears; what she does not ask, she desires." And once he's succeeded in his quest, the last thing he should do is treat her as an inferior. In fact, he should "let her play the powerful lady," while at the same time making sure that "she thinks you spellbound by her beauty."

Ovid's mastery of the psychology of seduction, whether of men or women, makes *The Art of Love* a gold mine for a man bent on refining the way other men conduct themselves around women— not least because it helps them understand how women's minds work. (Incredibly, Ovid seems to think that women actually have minds.) William himself could pick up a few tips. Hell, we could all pick up a few tips. And since Ovid refrains from portraying women as babbling idiots, breeding machines, treacherous manipulators, and nymphomaniacs, this can only help elevate relations between the sexes—in Aquitaine, if nowhere else.

Whatever his sources, William is as devoted to playing the game as he is to teaching it. Allegedly, his shield bears the image of his own mistress, with a line that reads, "It was his will to bear her in battle, as she had borne him in bed."[5] As the troubadour duke of Provence, he writes and performs some of the first chansons de geste—the rhythmic narratives on which the tradition is based— heard in Europe, and though the system of courtly love never filters down to the rest of the population, the idea behind it does, straight to the heart of marriage.

While the Church continues to fixate on sex, the court is fixated on love, specifically a man's love for a woman. Many scholars claim that Mary, as in the allegedly perpetual virgin, is the model, but there's nothing virginal about courtly love. Even though it often celebrates unconsummated passion—at least the delayed gratification of it, on the principle that denial ennobles the lover and elevates the beloved to celestial heights—seduction is always in the air. How could the spotless Mary, born free of original sin, be cast as the object of erotic desire? (And how could someone born free of original sin also be conceived through sexual intercourse? If one is true, the other isn't, but this is never explained.) There are actually two traditions—one in which consummation is beside the point and the other in which consummation is the entire point—and two forms, the game and the literature.

The game of courtly love (in practice something like a two-character play) is an elaborate blueprint for the building of desire, as opposed to the quenching of it. The higher it builds without fulfillment, the more perfect a lover the knight proves himself to be. It's not meant to be real; it's all an act, with demanding parts to be played by the bachelor knight and the always highborn, purposely elusive lady who is the wife of another man, often the knight's overlord. The conventions are expressed through tightly structured rituals and scripted rhetoric. Many of the rituals proceed on the jousting field, where knights show off their prowess with lance and spear, barreling down the field on horseback trying to pluck each other off the saddle. Before the battle, a knight rides up to his chosen lady, there to watch the jousts, and asks for an emblem—a scarf, a flower, a kiss—to inspire him in the jousts. Everything is scripted, from the way he phrases his request to the manner in which she fulfills his request. The literature, which develops from the troubadours' lyrics, is just as stylized, if not more so, with layers upon layers of allegory—not the kind of thing to read on a bus or in an airport terminal today.

Take *The Roman de la Rose,* a thirteenth-century French production that percolated through Europe for three centuries, in which every one of the characters and their actions, even the objects—the garden, the arrows, the fountains, and of course, the rose—represents something else. There's Beauty, "a lady of great worth . . . neither dark nor brunette, she shone as clear as the moon, to which the other stars are like tiny candles . . . as simple as a bride and as white as a fleur de lis." Then there is Wealth, "a lady of great dignity, worth, and moment," who is not simple and wields power over men, as the text states: "all the greatest and humblest have done honor to Wealth . . . each one called her his lady, for everyone feared her: the whole world was in her power." Wealth wears a robe of purple, the royal color, and while Beauty's beauty is described in detail, Wealth gets the detail—a page of it—for her robe, on which every stone (one cures toothache and also provides protection to whoever glimpsed it), belt buckle, clasp, thread, you name it) is more than it seems. Wealth has a lover, "a young man, full of great beauty," who appears to use her for her money but does it beautifully, so she doesn't mind. And Generosity . . . but that's enough.

Consummated or not, courtly love is by definition adulterous. The knight who jousts on horseback, sword in hand, competes against other knights for a highly desirable lady. But they're not fighting for her hand in marriage, or even for the privilege of courting her. She already has a husband. Initially, at least, they're not even fighting for the privilege of sleeping with her. They're fighting for the privilege of *loving* her—synonymous with serving her. Courtly convention stipulates that the knight must not expect anything in return from the lady. He can only ask for permission to worship her. If she makes outrageous or life-threatening or humiliating demands on him, all the better. The higher she places the bar, the greater his opportunity to ennoble himself.

What begins as manners lessons masquerading as lyric poetry ends up as a full-fledged, trans-European literary genre that rises and falls with feudalism and chivalry. But it falls only in the sense of its literary progress, not its social impact. People stop churning out new works by the sixteenth century, when the middle class takes over the power structure, but the literature lives on—Wagner makes an opera out of Tristan and Isolde, Lerner and Loewe make a musical out of King Arthur and his crew—and its true legacy, the legacy of love, is all over the place.

The troubadours' tales of genteel knights and their delicate ways of wooing fair ladies can be neither genteel nor delicate. The celebrated "poem of the red cat," for instance, concerns two noble wives looking for action with a man who won't talk about them later. They find one who's only pretending to be mute, but after they drag a cat's claws across his back and he doesn't cry out, they figure he's safe. Once they have their way with him, trading him back and forth, they return to their husbands. He proceeds to write up the carnal encounter for public recitation:

> *How often I screwed them you will now hear: One hundred and*
>   *eighty-eight times!*
> *So that my tackle almost broke*
> *And my harness,*
> *And I cannot tell you what great sickness*
> *Overtook me from all that.*[6]

But a little crudeness can't stop courtly love from sparking a fad, then a fashion, then a sensibility, and finally a broad-based social revolution. Many nobles contribute to the archive, following William in profusion for the next few centuries; they write and perform their compositions, or they hire professionals to do so—the most sophisticated courts have their own troubadours-in-residence. Among the two thousand-odd courtly love songs that still exist, several hundred of the authors' names are known to historians, most famously that of Richard the Lionheart, William's great-grandson.

Courtly love is in fact a family affair. Its development from a formal series of elite extramarital rituals to the defining principle of contemporary Western marriage spans four generations of one noble bloodline. William starts it, but it is his granddaughter, Eleanor of Aquitaine, and her daughter, Marie of Champagne, who transform a medieval edutainment into modern romance.[7]

Eleanor is born in 1122, fifty years after William IX's death. The court of Aquitaine still reflects the influence of the first troubadour, whose son, William X—Eleanor's father—has inherited not just the family titles and fiefdoms but also his sire's liberal views, his boldness in war, and his resistance to religious interference within his rightful domain. The court in which Eleanor grows up reflects the vibrant worldliness of the paternal character. Few young girls of the Middle Ages, aristocratic or otherwise, experience as Eleanor does the free flow of ideas, the stimulating conversations, the unconflicted celebration of the senses. By her era, the sophisticated game of romance introduced by her grandfather has spread throughout the courts of Europe. Noblemen are putting quill to paper and scribbling lyrics; the gentling of manners and the love of love in upper-class circles have become conventions of their own.

Like her father and grandfather, Eleanor is a strong-willed secularist of great charm, a seeker of sensation engaged in life, not in the afterlife. Asceticism apparently fails to penetrate her bloodline or the soil of her ancestral lands, heated by the Provençal sun and perfumed by thyme and lavender. Of all the noble French families that clash with the Church, hers is among the most troublesome and the least compliant. Eleanor shows every sign of continuing that tradition.

William X dies violently and prematurely at the age of thirty-eight. Eleanor, his eldest daughter and heir, is just fifteen when she is designated Duchess of Aquitaine, Countess of Poitou. Now she controls more territory than Louis VI, the French monarch. Eleanor has beauty and youth in spades, but what instantly makes her the most desirable bachelorette in Europe is the geography she brings to the high-stakes merger known as marriage. The lucky nobleman who captures her and her lands will automatically overpower his feudal rivals. Eleanor, naturally, has no say in the match, this being the medieval aristocracy. Her feudal overlord, who happens to be King Louis himself, will select her husband-to-be. Louis VI (aka "Louis the Fat," for obvious reasons) is a pious fellow who runs a pious court in Paris; he is the antithesis of William IX. He is also politically shrewd. Making a *shiddoch* for Eleanor is easy: his self-interest and the national interest are perfectly aligned. The king chooses his own seventeen-year-old son and future successor, also named Louis.

The future arrives sooner than expected. Two weeks after the grandiose wedding, Louis the Fat dies, a victim of his own obesity and general ill health. The teenaged newlyweds are now the king and queen of France. Eleanor leaves the scented beauty of Provence for the chill grayness of Paris and a court more familiar with priests than troubadours. Louis, now Louis VII, has ascended to a throne that would have been his older brother Philip's had he not been killed in a freak accident six years before. Louis has been groomed for a different life, as was then typical for the second son of royalty; his ascension was to occur in the Church. At twelve, when his brother dies, Louis is pulled from the cloister at Notre Dame and told that his destiny has unalterably changed. Schooled in religious law and ritual, he is hastily educated in the temporal subjects necessary for good kingship; although prepared for celibacy, he is forced to marry. If he and his young wife ever get along, it lasts about three seconds.

Louis and Eleanor arrive in Paris in 1137, when the city is known more for its intellectual ferment than its glorious aesthetic. Theological debate rages in the universities. Peter Abelard, shorn of his manhood and his Heloise, is a teaching master at Notre Dame with an avid student following. Students flock to Abelard, now a monk, whose bracing oratory about the Trinity makes him a pied piper to them and an evil influence to the Church. Exposed to nondoctrinal thinking, people begin to question the absolute nature of religious authority, and to reject it.

Eleanor, for her part, tries to impart to the somber court at Paris a taste of her grandfather's elegant style and fetching rituals, but she is blocked by the boring King Louis. Hardly the type to tolerate love songs, he certainly doesn't want his wife promoting such frivolity in or around his castle. Poor Eleanor. Day after day she is guilty of one of the seven deadly sins: sloth. When Louis feels the need for spiritual redemption, which he hopes to achieve in crusade, Eleanor insists on joining him—not as a loving wife, of course, but as an adventuress seeking new vistas. They travel, arduously, to Jerusalem, but not together; Eleanor and her retinue are "kidnapped" along the way by her dashing uncle, just eight years her senior. According to chroniclers' gossip, Uncle Raymond of Antioch is the first of her many lovers.

After fifteen years of a marriage that has produced two daughters (one whose paternity is not exactly clear) but no sons, Louis—well aware of her dalliance with Raymond—finally gives Eleanor her freedom. She comes up with the excuse for an annulment: She and Louis are cousins in the fourth degree, their souls are in jeopardy, and so forth. The pope himself has to approve an annulment at this level of royalty, which he promptly does before a formal audience of solemn bishops. It is now 1151.

The newly single Eleanor, once again the most valuable trophy in Europe's marriage market, doesn't stay single for long. She's snapped up eight weeks later by Henry Plantagenet, Duke of Normandy. He is eighteen; Eleanor is close to thirty. Henry is also Louis's archrival in the ongoing battle royal over the lands of France, which will soon be resolved—in Henry's favor. With Louis's ex-wife as his bride, Henry triples his feudal territory. Soon Eleanor presents him with the prize she has denied Louis: a son and heir. The first three years of this marriage have been a vast improvement over her fifteen dreary ones with Louis. Having added the titles of Countess of Anjou and Duchess of Normandy to her royal resumé, with their respective courts hers to mold, a permissive husband whose secular inclinations are as strong as hers, and the worldly sophistication she's acquired during her travels, Eleanor now has the ability and the autonomy to continue—on a much grander scale—what her grandfather started. Wherever she is in residence, French royalty follows her. She orchestrates glittering entertainments, vibrant conversations, and enchanting games of seduction in her "Courts of Love." She encourages and patronizes a new generation of troubadour poets, who refine the rhetoric of *courteisie* while immortalizing her in song.

At least one of them, Bernard de Ventadour, is clearly obsessed with Eleanor well beyond the call of literary convention. Inflamed with unbridled ardor, Bernard's lyrics survive as a model of the genre, and it seems likely that his object of desire allows him the ultimate favor of becoming her lover. Even the laissez-faire Henry, off in England, understands that Bernard's erotic fervor—requited or not—isn't mere art. Delicately, without making an unseemly fuss, Henry summons Bernard and his lyre north to England. This court, Henry communicates, is much in need of musical enlightenment. Bernard has to comply with his king's wish, but writes a torrent of anguished verses about Eleanor during his forced absence, begging to return to her side. When he finally gets there, she has lost interest.

Henry, already the Duke of Normandy and Count of Anjou, is destined for bigger things, as is his wife. In 1154 he captures the English throne as Henry I, making Eleanor a queen for the second time—and bestowing upon the English court a resident expert on the rules of the game. From there the aristocratic ideal of love, minus the formalities and with a few tweaks, will be converted into the middle-class ideal of marriage: the melding of two minds, bodies, and hearts into one. Ideals are ideals, not to be confused with the real thing. But any which way, Eleanor and her kin would find it next to unimaginable that the heady quality of adultery would one day converge with the dutiful, dispassionate quality of marriage as they experience it.

Maybe that's what finally enables the convergence: Love enters marriage through the extramarital back door. As C. S. Lewis noted in his study of courtly doctrine, *Allegory of Love*, "Any idealization of sexual love, in a society where marriage is purely utilitarian, must begin by being an idealization of adultery." In the *Roman de la Rose*, there's a brief scene that seems to posit conjugal union as the endpoint of romantic love, involving a young man who falls deeply in love with a rosebud (translation: innocent young woman). Tenderly, he plucks her—not to adore her from afar, not for purposes of seduction, and not for an adulterous affair, but to make her his wife.[8] In hindsight, that's a big conceptual leap, but hard to notice in the din of antimatrimonial, antifemale sentiments being uttered at the time. Take the anonymously penned and sarcastically titled *The Fifteen Joys of Marriage*—not a big help in the performance-anxiety department—from which one relatively mild quote should suffice: "every wife . . . whether she's honorable or otherwise, believes and esteems her husband to be the world's most paltry and least potent practitioner of the secrets of love."[9] Between the antimarital and the extramarital themes, there's not much room for promarital anything.

The element of sexual self-renunciation that runs through courtly-love doctrine isn't enough to mollify the religious establishment, which finds it threatening and heretical. The lover sublimates his lust, yes, but for another human being, not for God. That's the heresy: The idea that human love is its own salvation, an absolute good, right now, right here, on earth; at the same time both spiritual and erotic, loving and lustful, high and low, all in the same relationship—with a woman, no less—is threatening. The doctrine of courtly love breaks with the past by elevating heterosexuality to celestial turf; it breaks with medieval Christian doctrine by placing human love on the same level as (if not above) love of God; it destabilizes the masculine tradition by suggesting that a man who devotes himself to a woman enhances rather than compromises his identity as a man.

C. S. Lewis hyperbolically claims that the troubadours "invented" love. Not so: way back in the Bible, passionate love, or passion anyway, was the instrument through which Delilah brought about Samson's downfall, and also the device used by Homer to set off the Trojan War. Between the first millenium BCE and the chivalric romances of the Middle Ages, plenty of lives, in fact and in fiction, have been wrecked by love.

What the troubadours bring about is the reinvention of love. They make its pursuit desirable, even admirable. Previously, epic tales of sexual desire ended in mutually assured destruction for all concerned. The lesson was negative: Only nutcases or fools would be so reckless in their disregard for social order and family preservation to risk everything for a few fleeting moments that could never be worth the price. But as the courtly ethic advances from an amusing game for French aristocrats to a new model of human intimacy, the cost-benefit analysis drastically changes. To gamble all you have, even your life, on romantic rapture becomes the route to transcendence. The most memorable romantic lovers of courtly literature—Tristan and Isolde, Lancelot and Guinevere, Troilus and Cressida—meet tragic ends, but noble ones. They martyr themselves for the glory of the faith. The new religion of love is a wedge to the future.

Planted within the courtly ethic are the first tiny shoots of modern secular culture—the beginning of the struggle to humanize love, to extricate sex from sin, to merge sex and love instead, ultimately in marriage. The courtly code gives life to the now-familiar thesis that human happiness naturally resides in the couple, bonded by love, united in law, and embraced by society.

A pretty picture, but to get anywhere inside the frame, the traditional assumptions about female nature will need some adjustment—starting with their sexuality. Clearly, this won't be happening for a while.

There are still two female paradigms, the same two as always, but the medieval Church, ever in line with Augustine, has deepened the chasm between them. How could any real-life woman measure up to the Virgin Mary? Possibly the idealized object of knightly passion, the Lady, comes close. She almost seems—depending on the courtly lyric in question—intended to inspire devotion, lust, respect, and love, all in a single male heart. That's something new.

Scholars have spent the last century arguing over the meaning of the Lady. She is glorified for her inaccessibility; is that just a newer, subtler way of marginalizing the female, of placing her on a pedestal rather than in the kitchen while still removing her from the world of men? Is the esteem in which she's held real or fake? If she represents perfection, how is that less dehumanizing than viewing her as inferior? Isn't it obvious that she is modeled on the only other female openly worshipped in the Middle Ages, Mary? Etc.

Whatever it means, at least the weaker sex is getting some decent press for a change. And if the Lady seems inhumanly cold and distant at first, she acquires flesh and blood as the literature of courtly love evolves—the mooning knight and the untouchable Lady become romantic equals as well as passionate lovers. Somewhere in the medieval fog is a bridge to the future, but a fantasy female stands guard at either end. One is too good to be real, and is worshipped; one is too evil to be real, and is feared. So far, there seems to be no middle ground.

ELEVEN

The End of the World?

HALFWAY through the year 1347, several crews working for an Italian commercial fleet board ships at Venice, Genoa, and Messina, off the Sicilian coast, and set sail for trading ports in the Eastern Mediterranean and the Black Sea. All told the voyage will take several months—nothing unusual by the standards of business travel in the fourteenth century—and the men will return to their families with time to spare before winter sets in. The first of the vessels to reenter Italian waters docks at Messina in October, right on schedule. But this is no ordinary homecoming.

The sailors rowing into the harbor are sweating profusely, less from physical exertion than from fever. Frightening growths, some the size of apples, nestle in the moist warmth of their armpits and groins. Blackened patches of skin cling to bare forearms. What causes the symptoms is a mystery to these men, but not the effect: They'll die in agony, and soon—just like their comrades. Somehow, somewhere, this malady came aboard at sea and spread from one person to the next with the relentless speed of fire through dry kindling. (This is the first outbreak in the West of the bubonic plague pandemic, which will ultimately kill about 75 million people. It seems to have began in China a decade before, spreading to Central Asia and thence to Europe.) Of its provenance and means of transmission, the sailors have no clue. They don't suspect that the small brown rats endemic to medieval ships harbor the germs, or that fleas pick up those germs while snacking on rat flesh and pass them on to humans, who become carriers in turn. So the men who come ashore at Messina, and shortly afterward at Venice and Genoa, bring deadly cargo with them unwittingly. Those already infected are dead within hours, a few days at most, but a few minutes or less is time enough to contaminate their families. All they have to do is sneeze.

Then winter sets in, and the rate of transmission slows almost to a stop. People don't know that these germs get lazy in cold weather; they think the madness is over. But come spring, the plague surges back with murderous efficiency. Borne by ship along the heavily trafficked coastlines and interior waterways of Europe, it sluices through Italy and over the border into Marseilles. The contagion travels through southwestern France, spreading south to Spain, north to Paris, east to Bordeaux and Burgundy, and crosses the channel from Normandy into Britain. By late autumn it has vaulted the Alps to penetrate Switzerland and Hungary. Another winter arrives, bringing another illusory end to the wave of death. In 1349 it washes over the Netherlands, Belgium, Germany, Austria, Scandinavia, Greenland, and Russia, while doubling back over old territory. The force of contagion doesn't slacken until after 1350, ultimately killing off about a third of the total population of Europe.[1]

This is the first and worst visitation of plague, but not the last. Over the next two centuries there will be recurrent outbreaks of what is initially called "the Pestilence," or more starkly, "the Great Mortality." Around 1400 someone puts together the only two elements of the scourge that are self-evident—symptom and prognosis—and christens it "Black Death." The source of contagion and the means by which it spreads won't be explained for another five hundred years, at which point scientists will affix the adjective "bubonic" (the symptomatic swellings are known as buboes) to distinguish this plague from others.

The fleas that carry the plague are ubiquitous in medieval homes from hovels to castles, judging by the contemporary housekeeping how-to books that rarely fail to include techniques for dealing with them. Just one person needs to be bitten by an infected rat or flea to put others at risk, especially in close quarters like a ship or a busy market square. Casual contact with someone else's diseased snot, spit, sweat, or other bodily fluids will do, and in the Middle Ages such contact is impossible to avoid in ordinary life. Personal cleanliness isn't even a concept, let alone a concern. Handkerchiefs, nightclothes, forks don't exist. Picking a shred of meat from where it sticks between your teeth is the extent of dental care; rotting teeth are a universal annoyance for young as well as old. There are wooden serving spoons and multipurpose knives, which might go straight from eviscerating a hen to the dinner table, but no individual utensils. Runny nose? Wipe it with your sleeve, or better yet, your servant's. No sleeve? Use your hand, the same hand that fishes your dinner out of the communal pot and brings the food to your mouth. All of this is customary. But washing that hand, or the other, is not customary—even after fertilizing a field with cow dung, splashing pig slop into a trough, skinning an animal, milking a goat, delivering a baby, or defecating.

Bathing the body is no more common than washing the hands. Changing clothes is not, in the Middle Ages, a daily or even weekly routine, and many people have only one set. Keeping apparel dry is far more critical than keeping it clean. Sleeping naked en masse—servants, kids, elderly relatives, married couples, houseguests, and the occasional farm animal, all tumbling onto the same enormous mattress—is another custom. For opportunistic germs, it's heaven. All that sneezing, coughing, drooling, snoring, ejaculating. And bedwetting—the average consumption of beer per person, children included, is a gallon a day, and getting up to go to the bathroom before there are bathrooms requires a semiconscious and possibly still-inebriated person to climb over his bedmates in darkness, then try to locate a chamber pot in which to relieve himself. But with no concept of either manners or privacy, in the modern sense, why would anyone go to such trouble when there's a perfectly good wall, or an unpopulated patch of floor, close at hand? There's always the great outdoors, too, although only the most preternaturally considerate person goes naked into that good night unless it is the height of summer warmth. For daytime use, city streets, the walls of public buildings, and local farmland function as community toilets. Systems of public sanitation are a few centuries away. Unpopulated rural areas aren't safe, either; you can be the only person around for miles, but if you aren't lord of the manor, you're probably in contact with animals. Fleas love horses and cows and pigs and dogs, all of which can catch the plague and pass it along to you before it kills them. Even if you somehow manage to avoid human and animal contact, you still have to breathe—and the most virulent form of bubonic plague enters the lungs from the air.[2]

This explains why the Black Death does its best work in cities, where lack of space means faster and more thorough transmission, and in cloistered communities like convents, monasteries, and prisons, mortality can approach 100 percent. As always, the rich and privileged fare better than the poor; nobles who own country estates, especially with private wells, have at least a chance of survival. Aside from the loss of human life, the Black Death also means the loss of humanity. A fatal, fast-moving contagion with no known cause or cure is not the kind of disaster that brings out we're-all-in-this-together unity. During the plague years, there are doctors who refuse to attend patients (even if the problem is a broken leg, you never know who in that household has a patch of black skin), magistrates who fail to procure deathbed signatures on the wills of the dying, brothers who refuse to bury brothers.

The central New Testament idea to "love thy neighbor as thyself" has always been easier to preach than to practice, but even the pretense is abandoned by the Christian majority of southwestern France. Seeking a tangible source for the pestilence that besieges their towns in the summer of 1348, they look first to the Jews, their neighbors and coworkers, accusing, convicting, and executing them for poisoning the town wells. (Not surprisingly, the mass lynchings fail to stop or slow the contagion, but no one expresses remorse.)

The spirit of Christian charity evaporates even within families, as Boccaccio bears witness in his introduction to the *Decameron*: "This scourge had implanted so great a terror in the hearts of men and women that brothers abandoned brothers, uncles their nephews, sisters their brothers, and in many cases wives deserted their husbands. But even worse, and almost incredible, was the fact that fathers and mothers refused to nurse and assist their own children, as though they did not belong to them."

At the time, people think the Black Death means the end of the world. In a way, they're right. It does signal the end of their world, a world of no questions, in which skepticism is anathema and obedience to one's master is all. Everyone has at least one master—and while the ultimate master is supposedly God, in reality it's the relevant Church authority. For most people, the relevant Church authority is the parish priest. For kings and emperors, its the pope. As for the pope, he answers to no one. Perhaps the most significant casualty of the plague is faith—faith in the Church.

The centrality of religion in medieval European life is impossible to overstate. No need to wonder what time it is when the ringing of parish bells segments each day into times for worship, work, and rest. Feasting, fasting, fornicating—everything is prearranged and relayed to the masses by the Church, personified by the pope, who may as well be God; he's the only human on Earth who has access to God's ear, or so the people have been told. If you want to pray, you go to your parish and submit to the direction of the priest. If you want to confess, you sit in the confessional and blurt your sins to the man on the other side of the partition, who pronounces judgment and penance. Clerics vet all messages sent heavenward, the way that prison officials vet convicts' mail.

Then along comes the Black Death, mowing down the sinful and sinless indiscriminately. People who believed the party line that there will be hell to pay in the afterlife if they don't follow the rules of the Church can see that there might be hell to pay no matter what. The groins of virgins breed black boils just as easily as the groins of whores, and they all look the same in death: limbs twisted, faces contorted, flesh putrid. You can be healthy on Monday, infected on Tuesday, and a corpse on Saturday, leaving precious little time to wipe the sin slate clean by confessing and repenting in preparation for your personal judgment day. The biggest hurdle of all may be luring the priest, any priest, to your deathbed of contagion in order to perform last rites, the final cleansing. If a cleric does show up, he might charge an outrageous price for mumbling a few prayers. Stories of deathbed fee-gougers also abound, adding to the popular perception that extravagance and greed motivate the clergy more often than not.

While the epidemic is in full force, such thoughts are held in abeyance; what counts is survival. So people pour money into local religious organizations and institutional charities because they're told by their priests that God will smile on them if they do so, even if they have reason to suspect that their donations go straight into the pockets of those same priests. But once the epidemic is over, the survivors increasingly turn away from organized religion. Instead, they put their faith in the saints, especially those associated with pain and suffering.

One modern historian conducted a comparative study of the most popular names for boys in Florence following the Black Death, in part to determine its effect on religious practice.[3] That effect appears to be, in a word, enormous. Virtually no Florentine born before 1350 was named "Antonio," after Anthony of Padua, the patron saint of the oppressed, the elderly, the poor, and the starving. After 1427 the name ranked second. At number six, also unknown preceding the plague, is Bartolomeo—after one of the original twelve apostles; he was purportedly flayed alive and crucified by the Romans, surely qualifying him for the pain- and-suffering category. (Michelangelo's *The Last Judgment* shows Bartholomew clutching his skin, the organ of the body that most visibly bears the signs of Black Death.) Also rising out of nowhere to the heights of post-plague fashion is Lorenzo. Here the inspiration is Lawrence of Rome, a third-century deacon who achieved martyrdom by being roasted on a gridiron. The sudden vogue for "Christopher," patron saint of pestilence, needs no further explanation.

The institutional authority of the Church reaches its peak under Innocent III, a rabid papal supremacist whose reign ends with his death in 1216. He spends eighteen years manipulating, harassing, forcing on crusades, and excommunicating kings and emperors as necessary to compel their submission to his rule, while violently suppressing anything that hints at heresy. This most powerful of medieval popes raises the fine art of loathing the flesh to a whole new level of derangement with his screed on the wretchedness of the human state, *De Miseria Conditionis Humanae*. From the end of the twelfth until the seventeenth century, it remains the most popular work on a most popular subject—with widespread public exposure guaranteed by the numerous secular as well as religious writers, Chaucer notably among them, who quote or refer to it in their own works.

Innocent doesn't draw the Augustinian line of corruption at the moment of original sin—too late. As far as the pope is concerned, corruption and creation happened simultaneously, when "God formed man of the slime of the earth, which is inferior to other elements" such as fire, which yielded the stars, or water, which yielded fish. Only men and beasts were made of "slime," which makes them the "most vile" of all God's creations. Adding insult to injury, the vileness is reproduced "from the filthiest sperm . . . in the stench of lust," a process repeated over and over again, each time resulting in another "mass of horrible putridness that always stinks and is filthy."

The pontiff hates the flesh. In fact he hates the human body in its entirety—in every respect—most of all in the female respect. Parroting Aristotle's mistaken theory of conception (soon to be parroted everywhere as the Renaissance approaches), Innocent explains gestation: "Notice what food the fetus is fed in the womb: with menstrual blood, of course, which ceases in the woman after conception so that with it the fetus is fed inside the woman . . . This blood is said"—by an unidentified source—"to be so detestable and unclean that 'on contact with it crops do not germinate, orchards wither, plants die, trees drop their fruit; if dogs eat of it, they are transported into madness.'"[4] (To be fair, dark and detailed fantasies about menstrual blood go back further in Western tradition than Christianity does. Innocent may be citing Pliny, who claimed back in the first century that fruit and wine will sour in the presence of a menstruating woman, and "hailstorms, whirlwinds and lightnings even will be scared away by a woman uncovering her body" at that time of the month. To this lore Thomas Aquinas, the Augustine of the thirteenth century, will add, "The gaze of a menstruating woman can dim and crack a mirror." Who knew that the weaker strength could be so strong?)[5]

The fathers and the popes have come and gone over the centuries, only some of them lunatics. But regardless of the men in charge, the Church's view of human sexuality has done anything but brighten. For a thousand years the overwhelmingly Christian population of Europe has been a captive audience for this kind of instruction, and even if people aren't actively listening, they can't help but absorb some of it. For a thousand years they've been told to deny, suppress, transcend—mortify—"the flesh." How fitting that bubonic plague, a disease that mortifies the flesh like none other, should hasten the end of mass obedience, first the pope's authority, later the king's, and still later, the husband's.[6]

TWELVE

What a Man Wants

T HE Black Death won't be receding from experience, let alone memory, any time soon. Seemingly random outbreaks are destined to recur every generation or so until—not coincidentally—the 1700s, which mark the turning point between the age of faith and the age of reason.

Whether with conviction or by rote, observance of the daily rituals prescribed by the Church has long grounded the nerves as well as the lives of even the most indifferent participants, lulling kings and peasants alike into thinking that such observance builds a firewall against the worst. Now that the worst has happened to 25 million men, women, and children in the West alone, another sort of contagion spreads, only this one has no visible symptoms and will take several centuries to run its course. This disease infects the psyche. It's the the onset of mass disillusionment with the powers that be, political and social as well as religious.

Gradually and at first unconsciously, people begin to search for security, guidance, and comfort in unfamiliar places. Instead of looking outward to the Church, they are compelled to look inward. They look to themselves, to their families, to hearth and home, and at the heart of it all, to married life—destined to develop into the promised land of unreasonable expectations. This will take many moons, but signs that the process is underway appear before the traumatic fourteenth century breathes its last.

In 1393 a prosperous Parisian gives his new bride a special wedding gift, although he seems to be the real beneficiary. It's a homespun manual of instruction in the fine art of husband tending, subtitled *A Treatise on Moral and Domestic Economy,* written by none other than the husband to be tended.[1] The Frenchman is a merchant by trade, with so few literary pretensions that he identifies himself only generically, as "*Le Ménagier,*" translated as "Goodman" or "Citizen." Nevertheless, his guidebook is a priceless bit of social history. It exemplifies the principle that the more things change, the more they stay the same.

On the one hand, the Ménagier is definitely looking inward for comfort, specifically to his wife. On the other hand, the wife he intends to cast from the bridal clay is a dead ringer for Griselda. Indeed, this medieval Pygmalion lovingly retells the tale of the peasant girl who marries a prince and utters nary a sigh when he "murders" their children, holding her up as the aspirational model for his audience of one. Seeking to immunize himself against strife and dishonor, the twin dangers traditionally perceived to be inherent in wedlock, the sixty-year-old businessman makes a traditional choice based on traditional logic. He marries a fifteen-year-old, thinking she will be malleable and he will be safe.

Chaucer and Boccaccio, the Ménagier's contemporaries, would say that she will be frustrated and he will be a cuckold; such a May-December union is just the sort of mismatch they deride in literature. (How the marriage turns out is not for us to know; the Ménagier doesn't report back.) In life, these unions remain as conventional in medieval Europe as they were in ancient Athens. That convention will remain in place as long as the need for it exists—as long as society, still controlled by men, thinks it solves more problems than it creates. Chaucer and Boccaccio are the exceptions; they're visionaries, pointing the way down a long and winding road that ordinary men like the Ménagier—and they are the rule—can't yet see. Give them another two hundred years just to get ready for the trip that is still far from over as I write. No point in deluding ourselves on that score. To dislodge two thousand years of cumulative thinking may not take another two thousand, but anything is possible.

To begin with, the link between a man's honor and his wife's behavior has to weaken, and it's as strong as ever. The Ménagier figures that his wife's behavior is the key not only to his present reputation, but also to his posthumous one. He assumes, logically enough, that he won't be around all that long. When he dies she will surely remarry—her breeding years have only just begun—and if her second husband finds her marital conduct to be other than above reproach, her first husband's honor will be besmirched. Why this matters when he's six feet under would be obvious to anyone living in 1393. Besides, the Ménagier will try to get her pregnant before he kicks, and as the Bible and countless other sources indicate, both honor and dishonor transfer down through the male bloodline. The Ménagier is too bourgeois not to obsess about which it will be.[2]

Still, it must be said that what this aging fellow wants most of all from his pubescent bride is the timeless psychic dowry that all men—yes, all—pine for (and who wouldn't?). Three words: peace of mind.

Using the current term that signals spousal affection, the merchant addresses his mate as "Dear Sister" throughout, and if it's good enough for the redoubtable Wife of Bath, it's good enough for this babe. The Ménagier is no Chaucer, but he does an admirable job of distilling a billion years of male wishfulness into one little sentence: "His pleasure should come before yours." Once is never enough when it comes to indoctrinating an impressionable mind—maybe he learns this from the Church—and in any case, six words do not a treatise make. Thus, more of the same: "Let a woman watch well how and to whom she shall be wedded," the groom instructs, although it seems a little late for such advice, "for however poor or lowly he may have been before . . . for all time to come after the marriage, he ought to be and is sovereign." Dear Sister must never contradict him, especially not, as per usual, in public.

But it seems that Dear Sister wants this to work both ways, and is clever enough, and spunky enough, to have gotten her very old man to agree. She's aware of her husband's duty to correct her behavior, but at some point off the page she has already extracted his promise to do so "in our chamber," away from servants or strangers. Deal, the Ménagier agrees, provided that she will "strive to amend yourself according to my teaching and correction, and to serve my will in all things." (Even this early in marriage, he is pleased "that you tend rose-trees, and care for violets, and make chaplets, and dance, and sing.")

No middle-class woman's life is a total lark, however, especially in these labor-intensive times. Sis has her own gender-specific household tasks in addition to playing surrogate husband in the real one's absence. The Ménagier's detailed to-do lists cover the basics in both categories, from the management of servants to estate planning and feudal law. Culinary advice includes recipes for everyday suppers (snails, frogs, pastries) and elaborate menus (twenty-four in all) for "great occasions." When presentation really counts, the housewife might consider serving swans or pheasants "with gilded beaks and claws and their feathered skins sewn round them again." There are strategies for keeping the bed free of fleas (in summer) and the fire smokeless (in winter), and explications of more profound assignments—for in all seasons a wife is charged with hiding her man's "secrets" and preventing him from "acting foolishly." Next to the salvation of her soul, his comfort should be her number-one priority. If she applies herself to this task, she'll win nothing less than the married woman's holy grail: her husband's love. It's the New Testament marital exchange—love for service—and once the exchange becomes the currency of their daily life, Dear Sister will have secured for them both "that peace which should be in marriage" but so rarely is.

Service with a smile falls on the wife's side of the conjugal ledger, the Ménagier explains patiently, because men are in charge of "outside affairs." Men bear the heaviest burdens and endure the greatest hardships; on the road, on the battlefield, on the high seas, it is always men who must "journey hither and thither, in rain and wind, in snow and hail." A man can spend weeks, months, sometimes years in extreme deprivation—not for himself, naturally, but for God, king, or feudal lord—with only one thing to keep him going. That one thing is the sweet dream of homecoming, provided his wife isn't a harridan, and the Ménagier is going to make damn sure that his is anything but. When a man's on the road, he is "upheld by the hope that he hath of the care his wife will take of him on his return . . . the pleasures which she will do him, or cause to be done to him in her presence; to be unshod before a good fire, to have his feet washed and fresh shoes and hose, to be given good food and drink . . . to be well-bedded in white sheets . . . Such services make a man love and desire to return to his home and to see his goodwife, and to be distant with others."

But the right service performed with the wrong attitude will not a happy husband or a peaceful marriage make. The merchant illustrates this axiom by quoting a "rustic proverb" about the "three things which drive the goodman from home, to wit a leaking roof, a smoking chimney and a scolding woman." The man stuck with one of the latter can kiss peace of mind good-bye. All the men who have written about this matter so far have concurred that the opposite of a scolding wife—and the route to peace of mind—would be a submissive one. (Hopefully, men of the current century will have a different idea about how to get to the same desirable place. But what, as Freud famously asked, do women want? When they finally join the public conversation in a sustained way, sometime in the seventeenth century, women will prove that they can pontificate on marriage as volubly and voluminously as men—with none of the consistency. For women seeking to understand the ongoing reality of male psychology, even if they find the premodern adjectives objectionable, men's consistency is extremely helpful. For men seeking clues to female psychology, good luck. Confusion reigns, not clarity.) Instilling obedience is the real purpose of the treatise, and the Ménagier works this angle every which way, shifting from straight lecture to uplifting fables to chilling cautionary tales.

The story of saintly Griselda is included in the uplifting fable category, and when her tale has been told, the Ménagier explains its meaning—as if Dear Sister could possibly miss it: "by good obedience a wise woman gains her husband's love." And a wise man offers his wife more than one role model in this critical area, and they don't all have to be human. A dog, for example, "always has his heart and his eye upon his master; even if his master whip him and throw stones at him, the dog followeth." With that, the merchant completes his lecture on obedience and moves on to other aspects of behavior.

He expects Dear Sister to intervene when he's about to make a rash or boneheaded move, but she should proceed "subtly, cautiously and gently." No one—especially not her husband—should see a wife pulling the strings or hear her utter a negative comment or complaint, because—this will come as a shock—"the heart of man findeth it hard to be corrected by the domination and lordship of a woman." In the obligatory parable that follows, there are three characters: a canny wife, her slow-witted husband, and his easily manipulated mistress. One day the wife pays an ostensibly friendly call on the other woman (married men don't have to sneak around on Planet Medieval), who is too poor to provide the creature comforts to which her lover is accustomed. The wife is sympathetic. She suggests that the two of them collude, secretly, in their shared man's care and feeding, to which the naive mistress readily agrees. Soon the wife sends over a pail for washing his feet; clean socks; firewood for the stove; a bed dressed with fresh sheets, pillows, and blankets; and a supply of "linens," use not specified.

When the man shows up next, his girlfriend has everything ready for his pleasure. But he is not pleased when she, sworn to secrecy by his wife, won't reveal the provenance of the new goodies—he accuses her of stealing. In self-defense, she tells the truth. Her now ex-lover trots straight home to his victorious wife, confessing his dalliance and swearing off all other women forever. The moral is . . . well, let the Ménagier explain: "And thus did his wife reclaim him by subtlety."

"Subtle" doesn't quite describe the attitude with which a married woman ought to conduct herself in public—"scared" comes closer. Dear Sister should keep her eyes lowered, looking neither to the right nor the left of other passersby (even if they're female), and at the same time she should be on the lookout for "suspicious company," especially female. Her husband fails to elaborate on the telltale signs of delegates in either category, but tells her what to do if she comes into contact with unsavory characters: "Flee." To delay even for a second might have traumatic consequences. However undeserved, he drones, "ill fame" permanently taints a woman's character, so deeply that she might as well be dead—the Lucretia Solution. Which, of course, is included.

Suppose a wife receives a sealed letter, delivered in her name, when her husband is away. How can she best avoid the slightest imputation of "ill fame"? First, in front of witnesses, she must verify the handwriting of her name. If it's really her husband's, she must display the evidence "with great joy and reverence," and then retire to read it "secretly and all alone." But if the sender is anyone other than her rightful spouse, she must open it in front of the same witnesses and read it aloud on the spot to avoid the slightest suggestion of impropriety.

The Ménagier's treatise belongs to a new literary genre that springs from a new idea, or rather an old idea that hasn't occurred to anyone for more than a thousand years, so it may as well be new. The idea is self-help, which is not likely to be on the minds of people conditioned by religious authorities to think that the course of life on earth, and their place in life on earth, is fixed. The Church's ability to indoctrinate is slipping fast, but that is not the only factor driving the attitude shift. The Black Death has had a transformative effect on mass psychology, fostering a thirst for life in the moment—and the hope of making it better while the moment lasts. Hope: What a concept. As a palpable component of the zeitgeist, hope was last in evidence during the classical period, the human-centered, intellectually vibrant classical period. By no coincidence, the classical period is back.

175

At this very early stage, the producers of self-help literature are skittish, feeling their way around the market (to explode in less than a century, with the invention of movable type). The game is too new and the players too green to do much experimenting yet—to target the behavior of husbands toward wives, for instance, a topic awaiting the advent of Protestant ethics. For now, the behavior of wives is the default topic, and the key themes are, as always, submit and control.

If it's not a husband trying to shape up his wife, it's a father working over his daughter. Sir Geoffroy de la Tour Landry, author of the standout text in this category, has three. Soon after its publication in 1371, *The Book of the Knight of la Tour Landry* becomes the conduct manual of choice for well-born girls in England, France, and "such parts of Germany as were relatively civilized."[3] The nineteenth-century English translation makes it a best seller all over again. More pious and more affectionate than the Ménagier's and minus the Martha Stewart–ish detail, the knight's book stays tightly on message. It's the usual message, to be sure, as in "a good woman ought not to displease nor disobey her husband that God hath given her by his holy sacrament"; the wise wife should soothe her husband's wrath "by fair words," most crucially when it seems that he's about to commit some "villainy" from which, heaven forfend, "dishonor" might ensue. Once she has transformed him into a purring pussycat, he will be receptive to her guidance. Very gently and very privately, she should tell him where he went wrong and what he should do to rectify his mistakes. "And so," the knight—or is it the Ménagier?—concludes, "shall she keep the peace and love of her husband."

Shrewdly, Sir Geoffroy tells stories to help the medicine go down. One concerns an obscure young woman named Deborah, who is goodness personified, "full of patience . . . of holy life [and] great wisdom." Good enough to transform the "dispiteous and cruel" man she marries: "By her great wit and good governance, she could behave herself so well unto him that ever more she pleased him, and brought him out of his frenzy, and made him peaceable unto her and unto all other people." In this author's none-too-original opinion, wickedness in a man can be alleviated only by the goodness of his wife; the more wicked he is, the better she needs to be. "For the goodness of the woman maketh small and lesseneth the wickedness of the man, and assuageth the wrath of God." As his wife, she is bound "by the faith of marriage" to pray for him and to deter him "from every evil deed."

Abigail, another admirable representative of her breed, devotes herself to saving her reckless husband from the self-destruction that—without her in the picture—would have resulted from "his follies and his wicked speech." According to Sir Geoffroy, "at all times this good lady amended his defaults by her prudence and goodness . . . [and] suffered patiently the pain and sorrow that he made her for to endure." Abigail's faultless conduct demonstrates "unto every good woman how she is beholden to suffer her husband; and that she oweth to support him over all and to save and keep him, how be it that he be fool or diverse, since God hath knit them together by bond of marriage." Many, many paragons of womanhood later, the knight finally gets around to clarifying why such saintliness is, or ought to be, a feminine rather than a masculine attribute. He quotes an unidentified source: "And as the wise man saith, 'The woman . . . should be piteous much more than the man, for the man is of more hard courage than the woman.'" At least he should think of himself that way. "A woman that is not humble and piteous is mannish," the knight goes on, adding that it's a vice in womanhood to be rude or of haughty courage.

By way of negative example on that last point, Sir Geoffroy launches into a story that would give any girl a lifetime's worth of nightmares, about a young woman who gets mad at her husband. Off she goes to her father's house. But her father condemns her for deserting her spouse, regardless of the reason, and is relieved when his son-in-law shows up to take her home. On the way, the reunited couple stop for the night in a town that happens to be populated by "a great number of young people, wild and infect[ed] with lechery." These hooligans set upon the runaway wife. Ignoring the innkeeper's generous offer to barter one of his own daughters in exchange for a paying guest (Sir Geoffroy lifts this detail from the tale of Sodom and Gomorrah), they snatch her by force and proceed to rape her repeatedly. Next morning, the woman "saw herself so shamed and defouled, [that] she died for sorrow." (Can anyone say "Lucretia"?)

Now for the rough stuff. The husband carries his wife's corpse home, where he hacks it into twelve pieces, one for each of her friends. Along with a body part, each package contains a letter of explanation from the widower outlining the circumstances surrounding her death, "that they might be ashamed of her," and inviting them to seek revenge on her assailants. They accept en masse. All twelve of them travel to the town of iniquity and slaughter no less than thirty-three thousand inhabitants, both men and women. The author reveals nothing about how this astonishing David-and-Goliath rout is accomplished. Predictably, he fixates on the story's moral content: "Therefore, daughters, take heed such a vengeance was done for that lewd deed of her going away . . . she was dead, and so many men slain . . . And therefore every woman ought to restrain wrath, and to please and suffer her husband . . . and not to go away from him."

In theory, as we already know, the female is weak, childlike, emotionally unstable, airheaded, and incapable of love, friendship, or fidelity. In narrative, as we've already seen, she is a master of deception, outwitting men left and right (Delilah); has the power to make or break her husband's reputation, legacy, sexual performance, reproductive capability, his very identity as a man (too many to list); can bring about war (Helen of Troy); can bring down empires (Lucretia); can bring death to mankind (Eve); can bring trouble into the world (Pandora); and, according to Sir Geoffroy, has brought on the massacre of thirty-three thousand people. The shared purpose of the Ménagier and the knight is not to theorize but to instruct actual females in the art of the possible (they hope), but in the process they provide further evidence of the typically conflicted thinking of men on women. Maybe this is why the whole control thing never works very well: Ambivalence isn't the most helpful attitude for a general leading the troops.

The campaign to instill obedience in women represents a couple of thousand years' worth of concerted effort, yet there seems to be little payoff or even signs of progress. The psychic toll must be, by now, considerable. If the centuries of campaigning have had any of the desired effects—of raising the female docility and fidelity indices, or blunting female rage, or reducing the toxic level of "scolding" wives, or simply shutting them all up—would husbands and fathers be compelled to write prophylactic conduct manuals? Would the literature of cuckoldry be expanding rather than shrinking?

In the early 1430s, a literal Renaissance man—an architect, humanist, philosopher, mathematician, social commentator, courtier, and writer named Leon Battista Alberti—tries something different. Rather than inculcate obedience in women by hectoring them, Alberti crafts a series of self-important dialogues that attempt to teach men how to rule their respective roosts, a harbinger of the next wave in self-help books directed at men.[4] The title of his work, *Della Famiglia*, reflects its central theme: The family, specifically Alberti's own clan of wealthy and prominent Florentine merchants (in fact, the dialogues are conducted by semifictionalized male relatives). More broadly, Alberti concerns himself with the future of "the family" as a social institution, discussing everything from farm economics to the benefits of male friendship.

Alberti's alter ego is the avuncular Giannozzo, whose role is to impart the wisdom of experience to his much younger and greener cousin, Lionardo. Speaking as Giannozzo, Alberti frets that the family, as an institution, is in serious decline—hardly the first man to worry aloud about this. Some of his contemporaries blame the usual suspects: rampant adultery, fornication, women out of control, and so on. For his part, Alberti mentions the current pattern of late marriage for men (which usually implies high rates of illegitimate birth) as another threat.

Alberti is a bachelor, but that doesn't stop him from expounding on marriage at length, again using the long-wedded Giannozzo as his stand-in. (He can't very well speak for himself.)

Lionardo listens raptly as Giannozzo, by way of instructing him on the patriarchal method, offers the analogy of a spider spinning a web.

> All the threads spread out in rays, each of which, however long, has its source . . . at the center. From there each filament starts and moves outward. The most industrious creature himself then sits at that spot and has his residence there. He remains in that place once his work is spun and arranged, but keeps so alert and watchful that if there is a touch on the finest and most distant thread he feels it instantly, instantly appears, and instantly takes care of the situation. Let the father of a family do likewise. Let him arrange his affairs and place them so that all look up to him alone as head, so that all are directed by him and by him attached to secure foundations.

Lionardo swears that he has never seen "so apt or so useful" an analogy, but he has his doubts about how any one "master," no matter how diligent and organized he may be, can manage to be "all things at once." Not to worry, Giannozzo reassures him, for there is "a quick and excellent remedy" within reach. Lionardo is all ears.

> Since I find it no easy matter to deal with the needs of the household when I must often be engaged outside with other men in arranging matters of wider consequence, I have found it wise to set aside . . . the smaller household affairs . . . to my wife's care . . . to tell the truth, it would hardly win us respect if our wife busied herself among the men in the marketplace, out in the public eye. It also seems somewhat demeaning to me to remain shut up in the house among women when I have manly things to do among men . . . I cannot convince myself that men who are engaged in other concerns really ought to be or to seem so very interested in every little household trifle.

Giannozzo pauses for a moment of charming, if possibly dis-ingenuous, self-doubt: "I don't know," he says, "perhaps I am wrong about this."

Perhaps not. Giannozzo is "precisely of the opinion of the ancients," which means to a Renaissance-influenced thinker like Lionardo that his opinion is correct. The younger man goes on to summarize what "the ancients" well knew:

> [M]en are by nature of a more elevated mind than women . . .
> The character of men is stronger than that of women and can
> bear the attacks of enemies better, can stand strain longer, is
> more constant under stress . . . Women, on the other hand, are
> almost all timid by nature, soft, slow, and therefore more useful
> when they sit still and watch over our things. It is as though
> nature thus provided for our well-being, arranging for men to
> bring things home and for women to guard them.

But no masculine spirit, however gloriously accessorized and honorably directed, can fulfill its destiny without the right sort of wife (diligent, watchful, and so on). Fortunately, Giannozzo hap-pens to be blessed with one: "My wife certainly did turn into a perfect mother for my household," he tells Lionardo. Giannozzo credits in part "her particular nature and temperament" for this blissful state of domestic affairs. Mostly he credits himself: "it was due to my instruction." Lionardo, fully expecting to be a husband someday soon, pops the question: "How did you do it?" After a preliminary word about timing (a wise husband allows his bride time to adjust to her new surroundings and for "her first pangs of longing for her mother and family" to subside), Giannozzo explains the process—at length and in detail, over many pages, with perti-nent anecdotes, self-congratulatory asides, tips, and techniques.

For instance, a man should never tell a secret, large or small, to any woman. Giannozzo's voice joins the venerable chorus: "[Husbands] are madmen if they think true prudence or good counsel lies in the female brain [and] stupid" if they "blab to their wives and forget that women themselves can do anything sooner than keep quiet!" Not that Giannozzo ever doubts his wife's love, discretion, or modesty—she's virtue incarnate, according to him. But he seems determined to convince Lionardo that it is always "safer" for a married man to keep his wife in the dark, "to have her unable, and not merely unwilling, to harm [him]." From the beginning of married life, he determines "never to speak with her of anything but household matters or questions of conduct, or of the children." On those subjects alone he has more than enough to say, and happily, Mrs. G. is more than willing to listen. She assures her husband that "her father and mother had taught her to obey them and had ordered her always to obey me, and so she was prepared to do anything I told her to." To please her husband, Giannozzo tells her to follow three simple rules: "First, my wife, see that you never want another man to share this bed but me." (Hearing this, the lady "blushed and cast down her eyes," as a real lady should.) Next, "I said . . . that she should take care of the household, preside over it with modesty, serenity, tranquility, and peace." Finally—if somewhat redundantly—"she should see that nothing went wrong in the house." The woman's character is "the jewel of her family," sermonizes Giannozzo. Unless, of course, it's the shame of her family, in which case the husband is to blame.

A young man of Lionardo's background would know this drill already, given that "the ancient authors you like to read" (as Giannozzo teases him) loved to blather on about it. Actually, the dialogue between the two cousins sounds much like the one in Xenophon's *Oeconomicus* some two thousand years back, in which Socrates played the Giannozzo role. "When a sheep is ailing," said that earlier sage to his acolyte,

> We generally blame the shepherd, and when a horse is vicious, we generally find fault with the rider. In the case of a wife, if she receives instruction in the right way from her husband and yet does badly, perhaps she should bear the blame; but if the husband does not instruct the wife in the right way of doing

things, and so finds her ignorant, should he not bear the blame himself?

Even Giannozzo, who claims to have turned out a flawless spouse, broods about the harm women can do, lecturing Lionardo on the vigilance required—more than once. The younger man, when he can get a word in, doggedly seeks practical advice. What techniques are most effective? How will a wife handle the lessons? Precisely what allows a man to master his wife in all things, starting with cosmetics? Lionardo introduces this topic by referring again to those "ancient authors" who instructed their wives "never . . . to let themselves appear less virtuous than they really were . . . [and] for this very reason, never to paint their faces with white powder, brazilnut dye, or other makeup." As ever, Giannozzo has the answer, having developed a "fine method for making her detest the stuff." First he joins his wife in a locked room and tells her to kneel with him in prayer. They ask God to grant them, among other things, "many male children"; for him they request "riches, friendship, and honor"; for her, "integrity, purity, and the character of a perfect mistress of the household." The prayer session turns out to be a prelude to an extensive lecture, conducted by Giannozzo for the little woman's edification, on what does and does not incline God to grant one's wishes. "Unchastity" falls into the latter category: "God punishes nothing so severely in women as he does this . . . All their lives he makes them notorious and miserable." It is on chastity that "you . . . must set your whole will, all your mind, and all your modesty," for nothing else is "so acceptable to God, so pleasing to me, and precious in the sight of your children."

What does the above have to do with forbidding your wife from rouging her cheeks? Absolutely everything. She can be as pure as Mary, but if she paints her face, no one will applaud her for her virtue. Instead she will "offend" God, husband, and children; provoke disapproval from others; and cause herself irrevocable harm. Among the other horrific consequences of powdering her nose, Mrs. G. gets an earful about how women of such "immodest appearance" instantly trigger the worst instincts of "numerous lust-ful men." From there, ruin will surely follow: "Such men all besiege and attack such a girl, some with suddenness, some with persis-tence, some with trickery, until at last the unfortunate wretch falls into real disgrace. From such a fall she cannot rise again without the stain of great and lasting infamy upon her."

"Wise words," Lionardo finally supplies, "[b]ut did she obey you?" Not completely, Giannozzo admits. One time, at an Easter dinner that the couple hosted, "my wife . . . had covered her face with pumice, in God's name, and she talked all too animatedly with each guest on his arrival or departure. She was showing off and being merry with everyone, as I observed." Did he scold her? Lionardo asks. "Ha, ha," Giannozzo answers. "Yes, in the right way . . . This you can learn from me—it is much better to repri-mand a woman temperately and gently . . . A slave can bear threats and blows . . . A wife, however, will obey you better from love than from fear . . . It is best, therefore, to do as I did and correct your wife's failing kindly but in time."

What Giannozzo does is to wait until he corners the pumice-faced lady out of the guests' earshot. "Then I smiled at her and said, 'Oh dear, how did your face get dirty? Did you by any chance bump into a pan? Go wash yourself, quick, before these people begin to make fun of you. The lady and mother of a household must always be neat and clean if she wants the rest of the family to learn good conduct and modest demeanor." To this, Mrs. G.—trained from babyhood to please her superiors—reacts most satisfyingly. At once, her husband recalls, she began to cry. "After that I never had to tell her again." Cut to Lionardo exclaim-ing on cue, "What a perfect wife." His cousin assures him that such perfection can be within reach of any man. "All wives are thus obedient," he says, self-servingly, "if their husbands know how to be husbands."

A husband at the top of his game shows kindness, yes; but kindness should not supersede firmness. Giannozzo cautions that the slightest sign in word or deed of "self-surrender" during the course of wife training will elicit disdain rather than respect, and rebellion rather than submission. To reveal any "weakness" in the presence of a woman is to reveal a "spirit all too deeply . . . feminine," horror of horrors. To avoid this tragedy, Lionardo must follow Giannozzo's example: "Always, therefore, I showed myself virile and a real man."

Always? Not bloody likely, but a bachelor using a fake husband as his mouthpiece might not know that. "Always" encapsulates the burden of expectations men have placed upon themselves from the start. It's the impossible dream, the unattainable goal, the Sisyphean boulder they keep kicking up the hill of marriage—which is the site of maximum exposure for a man—exposure to the very person who is not supposed to see him in his naked human state, lest she use the evidence against him. Maybe the men of the Western world ought to cut themselves some slack already.

THIRTEEN

Season of the Witch

THE brain waves that began to pulse in the twelfth century, sparking thoughts of love in upper-class minds, are now electrifying everyone with thoughts of love—for the classics. The cultural and intellectual firestorm they call the Renaissance is in process, and values are shifting. Out: pessimism, fatalism, dread, ignorance, social stasis, carpe mortem, mortifying the senses, and God-centeredness. In: optimism, self-determination, hope, knowledge, social progress, carpe diem, reveling in the senses, and human-centeredness. As Europe learns how to read and rediscovers the thinkers of antiquity, the Renaissance brings on the modern world, albeit in ancient form.

The classical contagion, like the Black Death, spreads from fourteenth-century Italy to the rest of Europe. But fleas travel faster than ideas, especially when the ideas are embedded in thousand-year-old texts languishing in sometimes obscure and far-flung locations. The process can't really flourish until the Italians at ground zero become proficient in Greek. There can be no capital-R Renaissance of classical knowledge in its written form (the visual side is a whole other story) if it's based on Latin sources alone, because classical Roman culture itself derives from the Greeks. But fluency in Greek has been lost, along with both the Latin and Greek texts, for many centuries.

Ground zero is Florence, more specifically the heart and mind of Petrarch, an obsessive classics collector and scholar with a habit of writing letters to his idols—Homer, Virgil, and Seneca among others—and climbing the hills of Rome to breathe the ancient air while poking through the ruins, like some latter-day tourist. Both Petrarch and his protégée, none other than Boccaccio, are desperate to learn Greek. Sadly, even the local tutors are barely fluent. (Boccaccio presses his for a translation of Homer, and though the tutor does an execrable job, the student painstakingly copies the Latin renderings of the *Odyssey* and the *Iliad* over and over, circulating the copies among his peers.) By the time university officials in Florence finally locate a real Greek scholar and persuade him to join the faculty, Petrarch and Boccaccio are moldering in their graves. But they've planted the seeds of passion for a new generation to nurture across a fertile field, now expanding both geographically and socially. Between the twelfth and fifteenth centuries, the number of universities in Europe triple in size to accommodate the demands of a rising middle class, denizens of a society newly in love with learning. The sons of merchants are now educated along with the sons of royalty, and they're all gobbling up the classics (and, finally, learning Greek). With scholarship no longer limited to monks and princes, the academic craze for all things classical is destined to become a popular one as well—and the invention of the printing press in the mid-fifteenth century makes that a certainty.

All very exciting, especially compared to the intellectually dead Dark Ages. But the standard depiction of the Renaissance, this glorious resurgence of classical ideas bathing the West in sunshine and light, glosses over the unattractive shadows. Aristotle's theory of women as defective by birth and nature, Juvenal's toxic portraits of same in "Satire VI," Cato's warning that husbands who let their wives out of sackcloth will soon be covered in the ashes of servitude, mastered by those same wives—all of it newly exhumed, and newly available to an enthusiastic public.

By the late fifteenth century Christian humanism has emerged as the philosophical signature of the Renaissance. Some of its proponents have sparked, refreshingly, a pro-marriage mini-movement, expressed through what is called the "defense of marriage" treatise. "What could be happier and sweeter," trills one of these writers, "[than] where husband and wife are so drawn to one another by love and choice, and experience such friendship between themselves that what one wants, the other also chooses, and what one says, the other maintains in silence as if he had said it himself."[1] The passage is typical of the tone these writers take, newsworthy in itself. But their work tends to circulate within a small circle of like-minded intellectuals, and their voices are too few and too soft to compete for popular attention, already riveted on the ancient texts.

Theological attention has been riveted on those texts, especially Aristotle's, since the thirteenth century—which just happens to be as long as the Church has been waging war on heretics through the device of the Inquisition. Good old Pope Innocent III, he of the menstrual-blood phobia, helped spark the classical revival in the first place by spreading Aristotelian wisdom. Albert "the Great" of Germany, a vastly influential bishop, philosopher, and mentor of Thomas Aquinas during the thirteenth century, also dipped into that well for inspiration—and some useful bits of rhetoric. Here's one: "Woman is a misbegotten man and has a faulty and defective nature in comparison with his. What she herself cannot get she seeks to obtain through lying and diabolical deceptions. And so, to put it briefly, one must be on guard with every woman, as if she were a poisonous snake and the horned devil."[2]

The current leaders of the Inquisition, entering its third century at the time of the Renaissance, turn to the same pagan archive for assistance in—oh, the irony of it all—battling the resurgence of pagan behavior, which they call witchcraft. The classical writers furnish the key material for the *Malleus Maleficarum*, "The Witches' Hammer." This virtual CliffsNotes of ancient sources, arranged with psychotic precision, doesn't pretend to enrich Western culture nor to advance scientific inquiry. Its purpose is to guide the hunters and prosecutors of alleged witches, two of whom are named as the coauthors, during the Inquisition. Four out of five of the suspects rounded up are women,[3] true to the *Malleus*'s unoriginal thesis: "All witchcraft comes from carnal lust, which is in women insatiable."

It has the good fortune to be published in 1487, a decade or so after the advent of mass printing. Between 1487 and 1520 alone the *Malleus* goes through fourteen printings, with at least another sixteen between 1574 and 1669. (Even today, when the need to train professionals in the art of witch-hunting is presumably minimal, Amazon.com has it available to ship within twenty-four hours.) The preface to the first edition is supplied by the sitting pope, Innocent VIII; it is, in fact, the text of his notorious proclamation declaring war on witches, issued in 1484. Supposedly he handpicks the coauthors of the *Malleus*, James Sprenger and Heinrich Kramer, who also collaborate as the two chief inquisitors for northern Germany. Sprenger and Kramer already enjoy favored-son status at the Vatican, but political connections alone won't secure this very special, very elite assignment. The pope chooses the two because they happen to be classical scholars, as well as highly placed, hyperfanatic inquisitors—ideal for the project.[4]

Their *Malleus* is structured as a trick Q & A, though the questions—Why are married men most at risk from witches? Why must justice be swift and harsh?—are perfunctory, mere props for the answers, which are culled from a wide range of ancient sources. To take one example: Why is it that "a greater number of witches is found in the fragile feminine sex than among men"? Good students Sprenger and Kramer know the answer: The female is naturally susceptible to corruption, being "more credulous . . . more impressionable, and more ready to receive the influence of [the devil.]" Once that happens, all other females are exposed. "[Women] have slippery tongues, and are unable to conceal from their fellow-women those things which by evil arts they know; and, since they are weak, they find an easy and secret manner of vindicating themselves by witchcraft."

Sprenger and Kramer move from predictable standbys like the Old Testament, Greek mythology, and Roman legend to the big guns of ancient and early Christian society: Aristotle and Seneca, Cicero and St. Paul, Jerome and Juvenal. As an anthology of male writers warning other men about women with startling consistency through two millennia, the authors' work reveals (however inadvertently) why the marital dynamic stalled for as long as it did. The authors skip around the continuum from the relatively mild to the outrageously hostile, at one point channeling the bachelor wit St. Jerome—who in turn was channeling that beleaguered husband Socrates—on a connubial conundrum that no bachelor was likely to comprehend in full: "If you do not [marry], you are lonely, your family dies out, and a stranger inherits; if you do, you suffer perpetual anxiety, querulous complaints, the garrulousness of a mother-in-law, cuckoldom, and no certain arrival of an heir."

Sprenger and Kramer, apparently worried that the point of this is too subtle to grasp, supply an anecdote that could have been the basis for a hilarious episode of *The Honeymooners*. It involves a none-too-bereaved man forced to recover the body of his wife, who drowned in a river. The widower conducts the search by walking upstream, which would seem to be counterintuitive, until he explains: "When that woman was alive she always, both in word and deed, went contrary to my commands; therefore I am searching in the contrary direction in case even now she is dead she may preserve her contrary disposition."

No Renaissance take on the woman problem would fail to include the Athenian expert Aristotle. His theory of female inferiority has not been challenged in two thousand years, and the authors have no intention of breaking with tradition. Woman is inferior to man because she is in fact an inferior man, remember? "There was a defect in the formation of the first woman, since she was formed from a bent rib, that is, a rib of the breast, which is bent as it were in a contrary direction to a man. And since through this defect she is an imperfect animal, she always deceives." Citing Theophrastus, the authors warn: "If you hand over the whole management of the house to her, but reserve some minute detail to your own judgement, she will think that you are displaying a great want of faith in her, and will stir up strife; and unless you quickly take counsel, she will prepare poison for you, and consult seers and sooth-sayers; and will become a witch." Marriage, since it involves woman, is a no-win scenario for the man, even if his wife never morphs into a witch. As usual, a long-dead sage pronounces sentence, this time it's Cicero: "Can he be called a free man whose wife governs him, imposes laws on him, orders him, and forbids him to do what he wishes, so that he cannot and dare not deny her anything that she asks? I should call him not only a slave, but the vilest of slaves, even if he comes of the noblest family." The wife of a rich man, says (the presumably unmarried) St. John Chrysostom, the Tertullian of the eastern Church, "does not cease night and day to excite her husband with hot words, to use evil blandishments and violent im-portunations. And if she have a poor husband she does not cease to stir him also to anger and strife. And if she be a widow, she takes it upon herself everywhere to look down on everybody, and is in-flamed to all boldness by the spirit of pride."

Sprenger and Kramer don't neglect the literate but largely unschooled reader, thoughtfully providing the occasional history lesson. "If we inquire," they write, "we find that nearly all the king-doms of the world have been overthrown by women." Examples are duly cited. "The rape of one woman" led to the destruction of Troy; the "accursed Jezebel and her daughter Athaliah" brought an end to "the kingdom of the Jews"; the Romans "endured much evil through Cleopatra . . . that worst of women"; and unspecified "oth-ers." The authors conclude, "it is no wonder if the world now suf-fers through the malice of women."

All of the above is just Muzak. The "inquiry" doesn't get up to full volume until it addresses the authors' (and their corporate sponsor's) obsession, the source of women's greatest weakness and most insidious power, the heart of darkness in marriage: sex. Woman, they explain, preys on "the carnal desires of the body it-self, whence has arisen unconscionable harm to human life."

What to do, then, with the entire human race confronting "unconscionable harm"? Here the authors can suggest no better solution than what Cato the Censor fantasized about back in pre-Christian Rome: "If the world could be rid of women, we should not be without God." The authors validate the idea by appropriating the words of another ancient Roman, Valerius, as he tried to alert his apparently naïve friend Rufinus to a painful truth: "You do not know that woman is the Chimaera, but it is good that you should know it: for that monster was of three forms; its face was that of a radiant and noble lion, it had the filthy belly of a goat, and it was armed with the virulent tail of a viper." If any present-day Rufinuses need further clarification, Sprenger and Kramer interpret Valerius's metaphor in these terms: "a woman is beautiful to look upon, contaminating to the touch, and deadly to keep."

Once the inquisitors have identified their witches, according to the guidelines approved by the pope and outlined in the *Malleus,* the process is fairly rote. Confessions are extracted through various, often ingenious forms of torture (exhaustively described in these pages); rubber-stamp convictions follow. Then it is simply a matter of firing up the barbie. What is at stake, metaphorically speaking, is supposed to be heresy, but that is only the cover story. For Church executives the real issue is control, and theirs is slipping fast. One way to delay if not reverse the crash is to obliterate any sign of resistance to Church policy, which means that anyone Christian who questions some aspect of it might be executed as a heretic. The division between faith and Church has been sharpening through the Middle Ages, but what matters to the leadership—which administers the faith and monitors the faithful—is less commitment to the faith than obedience to the institution. If its rules are challenged, the faithful are deemed heretics, stretching the definition of heresy to the point of meaninglessness.

Why is it, the authors ask, that "Women are chiefly addicted to Evil Superstitions"? The concern isn't *whether* women are addicted. That's a given of Inquisition logic: Women are the chief perpetrators of witchcraft; witchcraft is evil; ergo, women are the enemy. However derivative the arguments, the procedure is something new: a multinational "womanhunt" instigated, organized, and operated by society's highest governing body, which also happens to be its only source of law-enforcement. Taming the shrew, killing the witch, solving the "woman problem"—and protecting the loins and fruit of men (a point made explicitly in the Bible, if you remember the penalties for women who do damage to a man's testicles in the course of trying to stop a brawl) the *Malleus* solves it.

It's a mystery why the presumably unmarried, chaste leaders of the Church would be so concerned about an anatomical part of no use to them. But the authors of the *Malleus Maleficarum* certainly are. "Carnal lust . . . is in women insatiable," Sprenger and Kramer assert; there is no way to satisfy "the mouth of the womb." Ergo, "it is no matter for wonder that there are more women than men found infected with the heresy of witchcraft." Because of this gender-specific "infection," the authors go on, the heresy at issue is that of witchcraft rather than "wizardcraft . . . since the name is taken from the more powerful party." The idea of women as the "more powerful party" would seem to contradict their traditional identification as substandard men, but the *Malleus* acknowledges no contradiction. In fact, the preponderance of witchcraft over wizardcraft does credit to men. To Jesus, too. "And blessed be the Highest Who has so far preserved the male sex from so great a crime: for since He was willing to be born and to suffer for us, therefore He has granted to men this privilege."

So Jesus died for "the male sex" alone. As a result, men are likely to be innocent of the crime of heresy, but only as long as they shun "infected" women. Generously, Sprenger and Kramer don't insist that all women are necessarily infected. Lust is insatiable in all women, the authors claim, but to be a witch, two other qualities are essential: infidelity and ambition. "Since of these three vices the last [lust] chiefly predominates, women being insatiable, etc., it follows that those among ambitious women are more deeply infected who are more hot to satisfy their filthy lusts; and such are adulteresses, fornicatresses, and the concubines of the Great." (The latter is not specified.)

Of the seven methods used by wicked women—Sprenger and Kramer's list is lifted from the papal bull that appears as the book's preface—"injuries towards men" is discussed first. At this point in our history, it should surprise no one that marriage makes any man injury-prone, because marriage involves sex, and women being insatiable, and so forth, well, you can imagine. And if not, Sprenger and Kramer will do it for you. Matrimony is instituted by God, the *Malleus* says, "yet it is sometimes wrecked by the work of the devil." To explain why God would permit marriage, his own work, to be sabotaged, the authors channel Augustine: "Since the first corruption of sin by which man became the slave of the devil came to us through the act of generation, therefore greater power is allowed by God to the devil in this act than in all others." Huh?

Next they theorize—and apparently their theory is embraced widely enough, at least by those who make it their business to hunt witches, to make the *Malleus* a best seller for two centuries— that the devil, working through his female instrument, manipulates copulation and reproduction. He can prevent an erection, block the flow of semen, make conception impossible, or force a miscarriage. The devil can also cause marital discord. "Witches can . . . stir up such hatred between married couples that they are unable in any way to perform the procreant functions of marriage; so that, indeed, in the untimely silence of night, they cover great distances in search of mistresses and irregular lovers."

A witch can also be a wife, naturally, and her unlucky husband won't know until it's too late. Sprenger and Kramer tell a story about a "certain well-born citizen" whose wife is "of such an obstinate disposition that, though he tried to please her in every way, yet she refused in nearly every way to comply with his wishes, and was always plaguing him with abusive taunts." One day the poor fellow returns home from some activity or other, is immediately greeted by "his wife railing against him," decides he's had enough, and reaches for the door. But his wife has already padlocked it. Now she demands that her beleaguered spouse beat her; refusing to do so, she says, will prove that there's "no honesty or faithfulness" in him. Since brutality is not in his nature, as the wife well knows, the man can only manage to stretch out his hand and lightly tap her on her butt with his open palm, "whereupon he suddenly fell to the ground and lost all his senses, and lay in bed for many weeks afflicted with a most grievous illness."

Obviously, the authors conclude, his wife bewitched him—"and very many similar cases have happened." Among them, the *Malleus* reveals, is that of a German aristocrat who marries a young woman of equal rank. That should be enough, in the fifteenth century, for happiness ever after, but the count is unable "to know her carnally, on account . . . of a certain charm which prevented him." Understandably panicked, the man prays to every saint he can think of, to no effect. Three years into this trauma, while traveling on business, he is strolling through a strange city when he runs into his ex-mistress. He greets her warmly "for the sake of their old friendship," and she asks about his health. Fine, he replies. She is stunned into silence, but finally blurts: "Curse that old woman who said she would bewitch your body so that you could not have connexion [sic] with your wife! And in proof of this, there is a pot in the well in the middle of your yard containing certain objects evilly bewitched, and this was placed there in order that, as long as its contents were preserved intact . . . you would be unable to cohabit." With this valuable information, the count returns home, drains the well, retrieves the pot, burns its contents, "whereupon he immediately recovered the virility which he had lost." The countess celebrates by inviting all the nobles in the area to a second wedding bash, at which she announces that she is now, finally, "the Lady of that castle and estate, after having for so long remained a virgin."

Just as married couples shouldn't delude themselves into believing that the bond of wedlock, though sanctified by God, will immunize them against witchcraft, men with reliably functioning sexual organs shouldn't feel safe. Consider the husband and wife who enjoy normal and frequent conjugal relations, yet for six years of marriage the wife has been unfaithful—with an "Incubus devil," every Sunday, Tuesday, and Thursday, "and on some of the other more holy nights." She entertains her demon lover in the conjugal bed, "when she was lying . . . by the side of her husband." Somehow the inquisitors bust her; "she was . . . condemned to the fire, and having truly and completely confessed, is believed to have obtained pardon from God" but still dies at the stake. Sprenger and Kramer don't mention whether this particular husband is aware of being cuckolded so flagrantly, but in general the scenario goes like this: "Husbands have actually seen Incubus devils swiving their wives, although they have thought they were not devils but men. And when they have taken up a weapon and tried to run them through, the devil has suddenly disappeared, making himself invisible. And then their wives have thrown their arms about them . . . and railed at their husbands, mocking them, and asking them if they had eyes, or whether they were possessed of devils."

The devil's primary function is to "destroy the unity of the Church, and in every way to subvert the human race." What better way than by procreating baby devils? But the evil one can't produce his own semen, apparently, so he has to steal it. According to Sprenger and Kramer, the highest-quality semen is produced during sexual intercourse, as opposed to masturbation or "nocturnal pollution." The devil collects the stuff this feat by using either a fertile witch, an unsuspecting wife, or a fertile wife who is also a witch. "Even in the case of a married witch who has been impregnated by her husband the devil can, by the commixture of another semen, infect that which has been conceived."

This brings us to question 9: whether witches may work some prestidigitatory illusion so that the male organ appears to be entirely removed and separate from the body—a rhetorical exercise, because of course the answer is yes, witches can "truly and actually remove men's members." Indeed, say the authors, separating a man from his penis is nowhere near as difficult as (to make a rather odd comparison) turning Lot's wife into a pillar of salt. The devil doesn't have to resort to such archaic methods. He tricks the mind, or the senses, or both, leaving the victim unable to feel or see his organ; it seems to have vanished. "There is no doubt," the authors note, "that certain witches can do marvellous things with regard to male organs." So while the devils rush about scooping up fresh semen, witches collect

> male organs in great numbers, as many as twenty or thirty members together, and put them in a bird's nest, or shut them up in a box, where they move themselves like living members, and eat oats and corn, as has been seen by many and is a matter of common report . . . a certain man tells that, when he had lost his member, he approached a known witch to ask her to restore it to him. She told the afflicted man to climb a certain tree, and that he might take which he liked out of a nest in which there were several members.

The dismembered man (could anyone be taking this seriously?) climbs the designated tree and finds the nest. "But when he tried to take a big one, the witch said: You must not take that one; adding, because it belonged to a parish priest."

The equation of woman with unbridled lust, outré pagan rituals, and all the rest, passes from the ancient world to the medieval one virtually intact, taking on the colors and patterns of Christianity. It isn't much of a leap from there to the Inquisition, which substitutes satanic evil for heathen magic and converts the salacious-female image into a devil-mounting witch. If the literature is any reflection, men at this time already fear that their wives control their sexual functioning—both ways—either through magical means of their own or with the help of another woman skilled in the black arts. (Midwives always make good suspects.) Husbands skulk in the woods, tailing their wives to the laboratories of local witches, or doing some surreptitious shopping on their own, buying herbs and potions to stymie their wives' attempts via similar methods to render them impotent, infertile—or, for the insatiable ones, ragingly, continuously potent.

An earlier medieval theologian, Peter of Palude, is credited as the source for the five methods of generative "obstruction" described in the *Malleus*. The simplest calls for the devil to "so darken [a woman's] understanding that she considers her husband so loathsome that not for all the world would she allow him to lie with her." This ploy works in reverse just as well; the devil "disturbs" the husband's imagination so that he won't go near his wife. Though every so often the wife may be "obstructed" (caused to miscarry or fail to conceive), Sprenger, Kramer and their source, Palude, agree that the male organs are easier to "bewitch," by preventing an erection or blocking the flow of semen. The power of such suggestion must have been bewitching indeed, considering the ultrasensitive emotional antenna that the penis so often is. And it must have been tempting for a man experiencing temporary sexual dysfunction (all that swilling of ale, and no Viagra for centuries) or unknowingly firing blanks (no infertility specialists around besides the devil) to blame it on witchcraft or his wife. The authors pose this question, too: how to know if a man's impotence is caused by witchcraft or by something less sinister—"coldness of nature, or some natural defect." Typically, they appropriate someone else's answer, one Hostiensis: "When the member is in no way stirred, and can never perform the act of coition, this is a sign of frigidity of nature, but when it is stirred and becomes erect, but yet cannot perform, it is a sign of witchcraft."

As a Renaissance text, sharing the field with work not only by Petrarch and Boccaccio but also by Cervantes, Machiavelli, Montaigne, Donne, Shakespeare, and other luminaries, the *Malleus* is quite obviously trash. But it's unmistakably Renaissance trash, as emblematic of its time as the Mona Lisa's smile—even aside from its association with the Church's own signature Renaissance product, the Inquisition. The *Malleus Maleficarum* is a compendium of classical knowledge boiled down to its most malevolent essence; at the same time it's a one-stop historical survey of the more extreme trains of thought that have been running through the minds of the men who built and led the Church for nearly fifteen hundred years.

It also exemplifies another negative effect of widespread exposure to ancient pagan views: The Renaissance extends and exacerbates the medieval belief in magic, which is to say the pagan belief in magic—the vast Christian population of the West, after all, was originally a vast pagan population, converted en masse within a few centuries. The Inquisition is supposedly about heresy, and in some cases (such as Galileo's insisting that the earth revolves around the sun), from the Church's point of view, it probably is. But the *Malleus* is explicitly about hunting and interrogating witches who perform magic at the devil's behest—and the magic that overwhelmingly concerns the authors of the most widely used professional handbook during the Inquisition involves sexual magic performed by women on men.

Not that the average husband actually expects his penis to disappear at any moment, or suspects his wife of having the intent or the ability to shoo it away. But from those sculpted erections in Athenian public life to the medieval fables of penis-stewing cuckolds seeking revenge on their unfaithful wives, to the tips for trapping semen-stealing witches that the *Malleus* elaborates on ad nauseam, it would be fair to say that penis anxiety centered on women has been kept alive in the collective male mind, however subliminally, for way too long—and that the marital relationship has suffered as a result. Throw in a thousand years of pro-celibacy preaching, the consistent view of women as men's natural inferiors, and so forth, and it's not all that surprising that these attitudes seem frozen in place. What's surprising, in hindsight, is that they change so quickly, given their longevity.

Those "defense of marriage" essays at the end of the fifteenth century signal that change, but the signal is missed by the general public. Breaking through the psychic ice floes accumulating across society after all this time will take something, or someone, impossible to ignore. It won't be long before that someone materializes.

FOURTEEN

Be Fertile and Increase—The Sequel

THE thousand-year reign of celibacy over marriage is about to end, and the man about to end it is, miraculously, a 40-year-old virgin wearing a monk's cowl. Martin Luther has seen for himself what happens to clerics who experience the carnal urge—the overwhelming majority, he thinks—yet are forbidden to marry. Unable to slake the urge through the conjugal act, all they're left with is fornication. So they fornicate: with prostitutes, with live-in mistresses, and for some priests who serve the public, with female parishioners. Those who avoid such depravity will suffer involuntary "nocturnal pollutions"—Luther's term for wet dreams— rendering them unworthy to receive Communion the next day. Far from quelling lust so that clerics can attend to matters of the spirit instead of the flesh, the celibacy mandate in place for centuries has accomplished precisely the opposite. All of this clerical sin, Luther suspects, is ultimately to the pope's benefit, thanks to the system of indulgences.

The word (from the Latin *indulgeo,* to be kind or tender) originally referred to an act of kindness, later on to the remission of a tax or debt. In the ecclesiastical sense, "indulgence" means the remission of temporal sin in exchange for cash, with the price tied to the gravity of the sin. (The unmarried clergy has its own price structure. Patronizing a prostitute, for example, incurs a one-time, pay-as-you-go fee. Keeping a mistress is assessed annually—the lay population is so inured to this sort of union that the woman involved is commonly addressed as "Mrs. Priest," "Mrs. Bishop," or whatever title applies—and siring a child can be excused by paying a cradle tax.) People who can't pay the freight are stuck with the old bread-and-water penitential routine, but otherwise it's a simple process of confessing the sin and forking over the requisite fee to the priest. This system has allowed unscrupulous Church leaders (all the way up to "those miserable bags of maggot fodder," as Luther calls the popes[1]) to bilk salvation-minded clergy and laity alike for centuries. An especially egregious use of indulgences is what drives Luther into open rebellion against his ultimate boss, Pope Leo X, and he won't be rebelling in a vacuum. By 1517 the assumption that venality and immorality guide decision making in Rome—regardless of the man on the papal throne—is widespread. Popular rage has been building up like dominoes ever since the plague years of the fourteenth century. The stack is ready to topple.

At this time the pope is directing a massive campaign to raise funds for the renovation of St. Peter's Basilica in Rome, so he's delighted to hear that a Saxon prince named Albert of Brandenburg wants to buy himself a high office in the Church. After heated negotiations, the men strike a deal: Albert becomes the archbishop of Mainz, and Leo gets ten thousand ducats for his pet project.[2] It's a big chunk of change, but not enough for Leo's needs. He commissions Johann Tetzel, a Dominican priest who is, more to the point, a world-class hawker of indulgences, to hawk as many as possible in Saxony. (Rumor has it that Tetzel is brazen enough to include as part of his sales pitch the widely known couplet, "When coin in coffer rings, a soul from purgatory springs.") Tetzel can't ply his trade in Luther's province, where the ruling prince has banned the sale of indulgences. But Archbishop Albert, deeply in debt after parting with those ten thousand ducats and, conveniently, the prince of a neighboring state, is willing to let Tetzel dupe his own subjects—as long as he shares the profits.

Enter Luther, now the parish priest in Wittenberg, who

doesn't know what's going on—at first. It's possible that he never would have found out, and history might have taken a different turn, if not for his job. He's the go-to guy for confession. His parishioners do know what's going on: salvation is for sale in Albert's province. In fact, some have taken advantage of the opportunity for themselves. When they show up for confession insisting that they've already repented and holding the receipts to prove it, their priest is outraged—though not at them.

That's it for Luther. He scribbles a list of ninety-five accusatory statements and has them duplicated on placards, thanks to the infant technology of the printing press. On October 31, 1517, he posts the list on the door of Wittenberg Castle Church, commonly used as a bulletin board by local clerics and religious scholars. He also sends copies to the out-of-towners concerned, Albert of Mainz among them. But Luther doesn't intend to go public with his protest. His goal is to expose the papal shell game to insiders; the *Ninety-five Theses* are to be used as points of argument in anticipation of an open debate at the University of Wittenberg. However, the printer circulates them throughout Germany, the sleazy archbishop sends one on to Rome, and Pope Leo goes ballistic. Even so, the real action doesn't start for four years.

In the interim, Luther takes every opportunity to mock the "crawling mass of reptiles" that constitutes the current papal regime in the course of attacking them all. In a series of highly visible essays and speeches, Luther hurls insults at "His Avarice" (that would be the pope) and his "lackeys and bullies," the "soul-murderers" who have turned the church into a "filthy privy" and "flooded the whole world with unchastity"[3]—much to the delight and approval of his ever-widening fan base. All the while, Luther's waiting for the pope's SWAT team to arrive and bump him off.

But Leo dithers, possibly because he's too busy pursuing such sacred pleasures as hunting, gambling, throwing dissolute fetes, and generally squandering Church resources, none of it lost on the public.[4] When the pope finally takes action against Luther in 1521, it's too late to bump him off. By then Luther has become a folk hero well beyond his native Germany, with broad popular support; a catastrophic PR scandal is the last thing Leo needs. Instead of burning Luther at the stake, the pope formally excommunicates him, burns his books, and accuses him of heresy, demanding that Luther recant forty-one of his ninety-five theses. The trial takes place in Germany, without the papal presence, and with Luther refusing to recant any of the supposedly heretical items. His defiance at the Diet of Worms, as the trial is called, marks the symbolic start of the Reformation.

After that the pope stops harassing Luther, but Luther will never stop harassing the pope, whoever he may be. (Leo will be dead in two years.) Having dispensed with indulgences, Luther—still wearing his monk's cowl—starts hammering the hell out of celibacy while praising the goodness, indeed the "godliness," of marriage with relentless force. He wants to liberate the "wretched multitude"—his celibate peers, nuns included—"who now sit in shame and heaviness of conscience" over their sexual sins. As their would-be savior, Luther must convince this multitude to trade the "villainy and wickedness" of celibacy for the God-given glory of marriage. Luther has no plans to do so himself, mind you. He doesn't see himself among the wretched multitude. Although he freely admits to experiencing occasional "nocturnal pollutions in response to bodily necessity," this monk doesn't "feel much desire."[5] Thus he has no need for a wife. What he needs is to spread the gospel of marriage for the benefit of everyone else.

"For the estate of marriage does not set well with the devil, because it is God's good will and work," Luther preaches to the multitude. "This is why the devil has contrived to have so much shouted and written in the world against the institution of marriage, to frighten men away from this godly life and entangle them in a web of fornication and secret sins." Forming the center of his argument are those four critical words from Genesis 2:28: "Be fertile and increase." Luther can't stop referring to them in one fashion or another: "[M]an and woman should and must come together in order to multiply . . . it is not a matter of free choice or decision but a natural and necessary thing, that whatever is a man must have a woman and whatever is a woman must have a man."⁶ The physical act of intercourse between husband and wife, says the expert, is "more necessary" than "emptying the bowels and bladder." (*As* necessary, maybe, but *more*?) God created bowels and bladders to serve their respective functions just as he created man and woman to serve theirs: "It is a nature and disposition just as innate as the organs involved in it, and wherever men try to resist this it remains irresistible nonetheless and goes its way through fornication, adultery, and secret sins, for this is a matter of nature and not of choice."⁷

Within a year of his trial, Luther is urging drastic action: "Priests, monks and nuns are duty-bound to forsake their vows whenever they find that God's ordinance to produce seed and to multiply is powerful and strong within them." In case any of the priests, monks, or nuns think they are exceptions to the rule, he invokes the New Testament guidelines on the matter: "There are eunuchs who have been so from birth, and there are eunuchs who have been made eunuchs by men, and there are eunuchs who have made themselves eunuchs for the sake of the kingdom of heaven."⁸ For the vast majority of people who exist outside of those three categories, Luther concludes, the only alternative to a life of "heinous sin"—or at the very least, excruciating inner torment—is marriage. (Since Luther doesn't qualify for the first two groups and has no intention of marrying, he seems to consider himself eligible for the third.) He points to Augustine, still complaining about "nocturnal pollutions" in old age; Jerome, who "beat his breast with stones" when in the grip of desire and still couldn't quell it; St. Benedictine, founder of the Benedictine order, who "lay down on thorns"; and another saint, who "macerated his harassed body until it stank horribly."⁹

In marriage, however, all will be well—as long as God's command to "Be fertile and increase" is fulfilled. But if one spouse proves unfit for duty in the reproductive department, Luther has some startling advice for the other. Should the laggard turn out to be the husband, in which case Luther assumes a physical cause—one way or another his equipment's not functioning, apparently on a permanent basis—he must accede to the wife's natural rights of sex and maternity and allow her a surrogate partner. Luther's savvy enough to know that the average man might balk at this idea, but that doesn't mean he's sympathetic—although he's no fan of the Jews, he supports a woman's right to maternity as rabidly as they do. If accession is not forthcoming, then the wife should force the issue. She should say, "Look, my dear husband, you are unable to fulfill your conjugal duty toward me . . . in the sight of God there is no real marriage between us. Grant me the privilege of contracting a secret marriage with your brother or closest relative, and you retain the title of husband so that your property will not fall to strangers. Consent to being betrayed voluntarily by me, as you have betrayed me without my consent."[10] And if that little speech doesn't produce compliance, Luther blithely advises deception, abandonment, and bigamy. The hypothetical wife should "secretly flee from him to some other country and there contract a marriage."

In sketching the reverse scenario—unfit wife, deprived husband—Luther assumes that her affliction isn't physical, but mental: She has an attitude problem. "One finds many a stubborn wife who will not give in, and who cares not a whit whether her husband falls into the sin of unchastity ten times over. Here it is time for the husband to say, 'If you will not, another will; the maid will come if the wife will not.'" He shouldn't bed the maid just yet, though. First he must warn his wife of his intentions, more than once, and also alert the neighbors. If she continues to refuse him despite his warnings and, Luther assumes, community censure, he should "get rid of her." He's not talking about divorce, either. If she cannot be compelled to do the right thing, "the civil government must . . . put her to death." He backs up this astonishing statement with a quote from St. Paul—"the wife does not rule over her own body, but the husband does," comparing her crime to theft, of "robbing the other of the body she has bestowed upon him."

Should the wife be physically "incapable of fulfilling the conjugal duty," this rule doesn't apply. Instead, her husband must practice forbearance. (Women, of course, are incapable of self-control.) "Let him serve the Lord in the person of the invalid and await His good pleasure. Consider that in this invalid God has provided your household with a healing balm by which you are to gain heaven." For once, Luther seems unconcerned about the threat of fornication posed by involuntary conjugal celibacy:

> But you may say: I am unable to remain continent. That is a lie. If you will earnestly serve your invalid wife, recognize that God has placed this burden upon you, and give thanks to him, then you may leave matters in his care. He will surely grant you grace, that you will not have to bear more than you are able. He is far too faithful to deprive you of your wife through illness without at the same time subduing your carnal desire.

There's something refreshing, even comforting, about Luther's pro-marriage activism. Instead of the usual never-married celibate theologian ranting about the evil twinship of sex 'n' marriage that he himself has vowed never to experience, here's a never-married celibate theologian ranting about the evil twinship of celibacy 'n' chastity that he himself has intimately experienced. Yet there's also something odd about the man himself—a personal disconnect. Luther still lives in a monastery. He goes about in his monk's cowl exhorting his celibate peers to flee their houses of shame (as far as Luther's concerned, the difference between a monastery and a brothel is that money changes hands in only one of them) and get married already, without feeling obliged to lead the way. So far, he appears to be unaware of the strangeness—some might call it the hypocrisy—of it all.

FIFTEEN

Love Meets Marriage: A New Idea

MARTIN Luther's message does not fall on deaf ears. An escalating number of monks and nuns respond by ditching their communally celibate lives for marriage, sometimes to each other, and with little hesitation—as if they'd been waiting for their prince to come all along. Meanwhile, the prince spends close to four years pushing the matrimonial cause before he grasps his credibility problem. In 1522 he wryly acknowledges the awkwardness of his position: "I will not mention the other advantages and delights implicit in a marriage that goes well, lest somebody shut me up by saying that I am speaking about something I have not experienced." Then, apparently forgetting what he's just said, Luther proceeds with his lecture on the thing he has not experienced, and no one shuts him up. He still has no plans to experience marriage—even after his excommunication, Luther remains a monk—or to stop proselytizing it. Having acknowledged the problem, he assumes that the problem has been solved.

It hits a little closer to home the following year, when Luther becomes personally involved in the consequences of his own preaching. A local herring merchant seeks his collusion in the rescue of a dozen nuns, one of whom is the merchant's daughter, from a nearby cloister. Luther can hardly say no. He feels responsible for the welfare of these women, and besides, he still believes that sooner or later the pope will have him burned at the stake for heresy. If freeing these women accelerates his destiny, so be it.

So the plan proceeds: The fishmonger arrives at the cloister in his wagon and makes (or appears to make) a routine delivery. His daughter and her fellow runaways sneak into the back of the truck, concealing themselves inside empty herring barrels, and the merchant drives off.[1] He takes his daughter home with him; two of the others return to their own families. That leaves nine to be housed in Wittenberg. Luther has agreed to serve as their guardian—don't forget that females, married or single, can't be responsible for themselves—until they find husbands to take his place. At some point while these young virgins are in Luther's charge, a colleague of his suggests the obvious: Why doesn't Luther himself marry one of the refugees? Luther mutters something about how the pope will be executing him any day now, and there's no point in taking a wife only to make her a widow.

But the pope does not oblige. Luther is still very much alive two years after the convent caper, with only one runaway nun under his supervision. She is twenty-six-year-old Katherine von Bora, whose betrothed has recently dumped her for another woman. Luther hastens to assure Katherine that he will find her a suitable husband, and soon does, but his idea of "suitable" doesn't suit her. Even though at twenty-six she is regarded as spinsterish, Katherine won't settle for someone she can't stand, and tells Luther just that. She also tells him that she's already decided on the man she will marry: Martin Luther. He doesn't miss a beat. Out comes the pope defense, plus the new argument that he, now forty-two, is too old for marriage.

But destiny catches up with Luther not long after, when he visits his aging parents. During this visit, his father reveals a secret wish. Hans Luther doesn't want his name to die out with him. He wants grandchildren. A severe and critical parent at the best of times, Hans was infuriated by Martin's decision to enter the monastery, and at the time, his son felt the full force of his wrath. Enticed by the prospect of pleasing this notoriously hard-to-please man, not to mention annoying the hell out of the new pope, Luther finally gives Katherine's proposal some thought. Beyond the personal satisfaction of making one father happy and another miserable, the idea makes obvious political sense. Luther has finally decided that the time has come to practice what he preaches. He still hears the executioner's song, but the tune has changed: if his time is short, he may as well experience what he has urged everyone else to try. And he could give Katherine the social identity she lacks—no longer a nun, still not a wife—and a respectable position in life. Such are his calculations. If Luther feels anything for Katherine besides responsibility, he doesn't admit it. When he returns to Wittenberg, his mind is made up. Barely a month later, on June 27, 1525, the ex-monk and the ex-nun become husband and wife.[2]

Luther adjusts to marriage with what appears to be astonishing ease for a forty-two-year-old virgin bachelor. The quotidian shocks to the system during the first year together are felt, but he's not fazed; later he describes them, offhandedly, as little more than "strange thoughts." Sitting down for dinner with Katy, as he calls her, he looks across the table at her, faintly astonished that "Before I was alone, now there are two." Waking in the morning, he'll notice "a pair of pigtails lying beside him which he hadn't seen there before." And like countless other married men before him, Luther discovers early on that "wives bring to their husbands, no matter how busy they may be, a multitude of trivial matters." Years later, he recalls from his newlywed days the arbitrary interruptions: "My Katy used to sit next to me . . . while I was studying hard and would spin and ask, 'Doctor, is the grandmaster the margrave's brother?'"[3]

As time passes, the once-exotic practice of sharing bed and board with a woman becomes a habit that no longer stirs "strange thoughts"—or much thought at all. As a man of the sixteenth century, Luther could wish for nothing more from marriage than not to have to think about it, to have settled into a cozily predictable routine that contents both husband and wife. Thus Luther, who states shortly before his wedding that he's not the least bit "infatuated" with his bride-to-be, has come to love her deeply after six years of marriage. "I wouldn't give up my Katy for France or for Venice," he crows in 1531, "first, because God gave her to me and gave me to her; second, because I have often observed"—sweetly, if patronizingly—"that other women have more shortcomings than my Katy (although she, too, has some shortcomings, they are outweighed by many great virtues); and third, because she keeps faith in marriage, that is, fidelity and respect."[4]

She gives him children, too—six of them. His delight in parenthood is sweetened by a smidgen of schadenfreude. Following the birth of one of his sons in 1532, Luther gloats, "That God has hated the pope appears from this, that God has deprived him of the fruit of his body." While observing another son toddling around and making "a joyous nuisance of himself," Luther announces, "These are the joys of marriage of which the pope is not worthy." (By "the pope," Luther seems to be speaking generically—the pope in 1532 is Clement VII, as opposed to His Avarice, Leo X, who put Luther on trial in 1522.)[5]

So happy a husband is he that he sometimes worries he's overdoing it. "I give more credit to Katherine than to Christ, who has done so much more for me," he frets, perhaps needlessly. One could reasonably question how anyone, even Christ—or for that matter the industrious wife of the thirty-first Proverb—could have possibly outdone the staggeringly competent and energetic Katherine. She bears Luther's six children and raises them, along with four foster children, and has no problem shepherding this brood on a barefoot odyssey through the Holy Land. Aside from the minor task of caring for ten children, Mrs. Luther tends orchards, along with the herb and vegetable gardens that yield not only food for the table but ingredients for the homeopathic medicines she makes as the family's resident pharmacologist; plays exterminator-in-chief to the beaver-sized mice threatening the vegetables; nurtures the barnyard animals she later slaughters, and the fish pond's trout and perch she later guts, all to be cooked and served by her; cultivates the vineyards from which she produces the evening wine; and makes high-quality beer for sale and private consumption in the brewery on the family's property. And that's not to mention converting the Black Cloister monastery—where Luther himself lived as a monk—into the family's home which doubles as a hostel (run by Katy, naturally) that accommodates up to thirty guests. These include an unmarried aunt of hers, various nieces and nephews of Luther's, and a motley crew of young scholars who get room and board in exchanging for providing clerical and secretarial services to the much-in-demand Doctor Luther.[6]

Government officials, academics, disciples, and colleagues from near and far seek his counsel, along with a constant stream of clerical black sheep, male and female, who have fled or been exiled from their orders with his encouragement. They stay at the Luthers' home-cum-B&B, crowding around the table for Katy's five o'clock suppers, engaging in conversation that seems to continue long after dinner is done. Much of it is in monologue form, although Luther's language is too pungent and his statements too outrageous to be boring; his audience seems fascinated no matter what. (Even when the doctor waxes melancholy or morbid, not infrequently in either case, he still manages to get off some zingers.) He holds forth on everything from the nature of God to the nature of his recent enema, from Hungarian politics to the superior quality of hospital care in Italy, from the theory of predestination to the fact that his wife is pregnant with one child while nursing another. Domestic matters often interrupt: An infant son sitting on Daddy's lap might soil himself just as Daddy launches into an attack on, say, Erasmus, the Dutch humanist. Katy might appear out of nowhere to announce an invasion of field mice proceeding somewhere on the property, or to complain about disobedient servants—to which Luther responds either by humoring her or by teasing her, sometimes both. (The guests take copious notes, which are collected in multiple volumes of *Table Talk*.) In addition to feeding her husband's entourage, Mrs. Luther provides them all with comprehensive medical and pharmaceutical care, while serving as her husband's round-the-clock masseuse and personal physician—a full-time job in itself, for Luther suffers from multiple ailments. Katy sharply limits his consumption of wine, because it exacerbates his insomnia and kidney stones. Instead, she plies him with her home-brewed beer, which alleviates both conditions.

At one of these suppers during the winter of 1542–1543, Luther frets about how much his head hurts. Turning to Katy, he says that if it doesn't feel better the next day, they should send for their seventeen-year-old son, away at school, "for I'd like to have him here at my end." Mrs. Luther has been hearing this stuff from her husband since the day she proposed to him. Her tart comment: "See to it, Sir, that you don't imagine things." The doctor tops that with a killer metaphor that would occur only to a man with a life-long history of intractable constipation: "I'm like a ripe stool and the world's like a gigantic anus, and so we're about to let go of each other."[7] (They let go of each other three years later.)

Luther's theological view of marital sex, consistent since his celibate days, is textbook Augustine. (A steadfast admirer of the original spinner, Luther chose to enter the strict Augustinian order at the start of his monastic career.) The text spills out of his mouth: Sexual intercourse "is never without sin, but God excuses it by his grace . . . he preserves in and through the sin all that good which he has implanted and blessed in marriage." Lust is a disease and marriage is the cure—check; couples should not "permit them-selves to be governed by their bodies in the passion of lust"—check; at the same time, they must not practice restraint to excess, lest one or the other be exposed "to the danger of fornication and other sins"—check.[8] But from there, Luther breaks free.

Fundamentally (and obviously), he elevates marriage over celibacy, but Luther goes further than that. He concurs that sex is sin unless redeemed by marriage, without stipulating that the pro-creative impulse alone justifies the act or panicking about the poten-tial for pleasure. Luther has his own way of dealing with the details of conjugal sex: He doesn't. Beyond insisting on mutual fidelity, Luther seems to think that what couples do in bed is their business. Not a word from him about unacceptable positions or unnatural orifices—in fact, he tells couples to ignore restrictions placed on "holy days or work days" by the "filth-preachers."[9] The abiding fascination with carnal matters that so many of his predecessors share is not shared by Luther. Six children demonstrate that his equipment functions, but he's no more interested in his own sex life than he is in anyone else's.

While celibate, Luther imagined marriage as nothing more than "a hospital for the cure of lust." Personal experience, he's delighted to say, has proven him wrong: Marriage is a "school for character." This is the role that the Church claims exclusively for the monastery, but as a veteran of both institutions, Luther can state with confidence that the monastic routine of prayer and solitude is child's play compared to the rigors of wedlock. "What a lot of trouble there is in marriage!" he marvels. If character building really mattered to the Church, he says, all monks would have wives; the challenge of living day in and day out with a woman breeds fortitude, patience, humility, tolerance, and tenderness.[10]

As it happens, the subject of women and the Church often provokes a rant against institutional misogyny from Luther, complete with illustrative quotes. Many are historical—"If you hear a woman speak, flee from her as if she were a hissing snake," one of his favorites, comes from a third-century theologian[11]—but Luther also draws on more contemporary sources. His old nemesis, Albert, the archbishop of Mainz, is one of them. Luther has new reason to fume about the man, having heard about Albert's pet peeve: "the stinking, putrid, private parts of women."[12] Such sentiments, and worse, have issued from the mouths of Church officials before, as Luther well knows, but Albert is a special case. "That godless knave, forgetful of his mother and sister, dares to blaspheme God's creature through whom he was himself born," bellows Luther. It's one thing to attack the behavior of women, something that Luther himself often indulges in, but "to defile their creation and nature is most godless." It is, he says, "as if I were to ridicule man's face on account of his nose! For the nose is the latrine of man's head and stands above his mouth. As a matter of fact, God himself must allow all prayer and worship to take place under this privy."[13]

Luther can refer to his wife as "my lord Katy," or himself as "an inferior lord" to her "superior" one, because everyone, including Mrs. Luther, has no doubt that he's joking. He knows that she knows how to behave. Even at home, she addresses him as "Sir" or "Doctor"; to do otherwise would be to challenge his authority.[14] The inferior-superior construct of women to men remains the general assumption for all classes of society, held by both sexes. Luther subscribes to the principle as heartily as anyone else. "Girls," he claims one night at table, "begin to talk and to stand on their feet sooner than boys because weeds always grow up more quickly than good crops."[15] When a non-German-speaking envoy sent by Henry VIII of England finds himself at Luther's table unable to understand a word of the conversation, Luther suggests his "very fluent" wife as a tutor. "She's such a ready speaker that she's much better at it than I am," Luther explains, with a show of uncharacteristic modesty that he immediately seems to regret. "However," he hastens to add, "eloquence in women shouldn't be praised; it's more fitting for them to lisp and stammer." Luther's radical thinking does not extend to the relationship between husband and wife, that's for sure.[16]

Luther prizes his wife (who wouldn't want someone like Katy around the house?) and sings the praises of women: "Imagine what it would be like without this sex. The home, cities, economic life, and government would virtually disappear. Men can't do without women. Even if it were possible for men to beget and bear children, they still couldn't do without women."[17] Channeling Aristotle, he confides a favorite theory to his acolytes in 1531, seven years into marriage: "Men have broad shoulders and narrow hips, and accordingly they possess intelligence. Women have narrow shoulders and broad hips. Women ought to stay at home; the way they were created indicates this, for they have broad hips and a wide fundament to sit upon."[18] He can't imagine a role for women outside of maternity. No one can, man or woman. It's too soon for that.

When Luther refers to the "truly golden and noble works" performed by a wife day after day, he means that "she suckles the child, rocks and bathes it . . . busies herself with other duties and renders help and obedience to her husband." Most golden and noble of all is the work of childbirth, Luther imagined back in his monastic days. In an essay from that period, he urged expectant dads to cheer on their laboring wives with a little pep talk, for which he provides a truly hilarious script. "Dear Grete," writes Luther—feel free to substitute the name of your choice—"remember that you are a woman and that this work of God in you is pleasing to him . . . Should it mean your death, then depart happily, for you will die in a noble deed and in subservience to God. If you were not a woman you should now wish to be one for the sake of this very work alone, that you might thus gloriously suffer and even die in the performance of God's work and will."

If Luther felt entitled in his celibate state to offer obstetrical advice, all the more reason to regard himself as a lactation expert once he becomes a husband and father. Many years after "Dear Grete," Luther leads a discussion at the table about the goodness of mothers' milk, which turns into a discussion about women's breasts. When are they "an ornament to women" and when are they not? Proportion is the deciding factor. And pity the women who have "large and flabby breasts." No ornaments they, and besides, "they cause unhappiness . . . because they promise much but produce little"—little in the way of lactation. Or maybe he's talking about (could it be?) sex. Whichever, "firm breasts" win the contest.[19]

Luther manages to be an authority on marital conflict, along with everything else. He is so often asked for his opinion by clerics from near and far who mediate such disputes for the public that mock trials are staged in the family residence. Once the case is presented, Luther performs the dual role of judge and jury. One scenario concerns a Frankfurt schoolmaster moonlighting as a preacher—quite successfully, as it happens. The man so captivates the congregation that its leaders ask him to become a deacon, an honor that the man happily accepts. The problem, according to the person presenting the case, is the man's wife, who has a "haughty spirit . . . [and] simply did not want to have a parson for a husband."

There's no doubt in anyone's mind about who should prevail in this case, but for the record, Luther paraphrases the Old Testament principle "A wife is bound to follow her husband, not a husband his wife." This wife, thunders Luther, has defied biblical law, "a wicked woman, indeed a devil, to be ashamed of the ministry in which the Lord Christ himself and the dear angels were."[20] The issue to be decided is whether her husband should bow to pressure and decline the ministry, thus undermining his own position as domestic commander in chief, for the sake of preserving peace at home. Or should he dump his wife—violating the New Testament sanction against putting asunder what God has joined together—take the job, and find a more supportive spouse? Luther responds that neither course would be necessary in an ideal world; the government would step in and "compel the old hag" to stand by her man. In reality the government will do no such thing. Nonetheless, this husband must not surrender his God-given authority by acceding to his wife's demand, which would upend the domestic order on which society depends for its very stability. If the hag cannot be controlled, she must go. Thus Luther concludes that preserving the rule of the husband is more important than abiding by the rule of Christ, and his conclusion is accepted by all who are present. The alternative remains unthinkable.

Luther's vision of marriage includes sex, but there's nothing heady about it. He's original enough in his thinking—original in comparison to all that's gone before—to allow that marriage might begin in passion, but passion doesn't interest him. "It's the greatest blessing of God when love continues to flower in marriage," he says, but it can't begin to flower until "the intoxication has been slept off." (He has a point.) Luther doesn't go near the very modern, or maybe that should be postmodern, idea that conjugal sex could or should be adventurous, that its quality (or quantity) matters to the relationship, but then sex doesn't interest him either. Married love, as Luther conceives it, seems to be an exalted form of love-thy-neighbor. It's the domestic component that counts: A man has no neighbor more dear to him than the woman who shares his bed, his name, his future, and the fruit of his loins. The New Testament obliges the husband to love his wife; Luther couldn't agree more, but telling a man to love his wife doesn't mean he will. The key, he says, is "to love her with constancy."[21]

Constancy in love, neighborly or otherwise, has already been established as a literary theme by those subversive troubadours who dared to elevate heterosexual passion above the godly sort (a Christian heresy) and the homoerotic one (a classical heresy). But the lyricists of chivalry left love where it has always been—outside the conjugal gates. The Renaissance humanists who tried to fuse love and marriage had the right idea at the wrong time; they were fifty years too early. Luther shares many of their ideas. When he unveils his own match-up between love and marriage, his timing—as usual—is spot-on. In place of the adultery, celibacy, and forbidden eroticism that have roiled wedlock thus far in history, his vision of "holy matrimony" offers deadly earnest elements: piety, propriety, sobriety, fidelity, sincerity, and duty. Add them together and you've got "the dearest life."

In Luther's framework, constancy can emerge from passion, but only when the flames have subsided. Constancy—the steady, sustaining warmth of affection—is to his mind the very essence of conjugal love. The primary challenge (and peril) of conjugal life, the critical transition point for every couple, is the ability to move out of the fire and into the embers without feeling bereft.

At dinner one night, Luther launches into this topic by way of a story about a young man named Lucas Cranach the Younger. It seems that Lucas is a recently married local artist who spends the first postnuptial months enslaved by love and unable to bear even a moment's separation from his bride. A wise friend encounters Lucas at the height of his frenzy and advises him to calm down. "Before a half-year is gone, you will have had enough of that. There won't be a maid in your house whom you won't prefer to your wife." Luther then extracts the moral. "And so it is," he duly explains.

"We hate the things that are present and we love those that are absent. This is the weakness of our nature."

The love-crazed groom might find it incomprehensible that such an internal shift could occur in a mere six months, but the long-haul spouse knows that when love stops being effortless, the struggle for constancy begins. And then, Luther says, "the devil comes and introduces hatred, suspicion, and concupiscence on both sides, and these cause desertion." Luther naturally has some tips on averting this fate, starting with mate selection. Children should be guided by their elders, as always, but Luther strongly disapproves of parents who try to bully or otherwise force their child into a match that he or she actively resists. He doesn't go so far as to suggest that young men and women should be allowed free choice in the matter, but he does help to bring about the day when that will be the standard. And though Luther shares the prevailing view that physical attraction as a motive for marriage is a recipe for disaster, he also contributes to the demise of that view. Mate choice is destined to become the primary province of the two people involved. When that happens, physical attraction will be the first criteria—and the idea that love follows marriage instead of the reverse will seem quaint indeed.

Luther emphasizes that "there must be harmony with respect to patterns of life and ways of thinking."[22] He also advises that the couple should be close in age, breaking with the still-routine pattern of middle-aged men selecting young brides just beginning their reproductive lives. In addition to following those steps, the couple should enter their union reverently, as befits the "holy estate of matrimony"; they must, of course, be virgins, and have the assent if not the blessing of both families; and finally they must commit to mutual cooperation, goodwill, and fidelity. According to Luther, these are the raw ingredients most necessary to the development of marital love—and, along with constancy, to ward off the devil's assault.

By emphasizing compatibility and closeness in age over practical concerns such as money, status, and breeding potential, Luther points to the future. Companionship, compatibility, some degree of personal choice—these are relatively subjective, secular, emotional values that will become part of the current ideal of married love. It won't be neighborly love, and it won't develop after marriage. Without the benefit of hindsight, Luther can't know that he's opened the conjugal door to the wolf that has always been barred from entry: Sexual passion. Erotic love. Romance.

Luther dies in 1546, but his idea of marriage does not vanish into the grave along with him. As the Protestant influence spreads across Europe in the wake of the Reformation, so does its marital synthesis—essentially Luther's, give or take a few details. It proceeds from three central values, updating Augustine's three "goods of marriage" to suit a new Christian church and its vastly different sensibility. Procreation and fidelity are preserved (rephrased as "to bring forth fruit" and to "avoid fornication," respectively). But "sacrament" gives way to companionship—something of a revolution in itself. No less significantly, Luther and the Protestants reshuffle the order of value. While Augustine ranked *sacramentum* third, *fides* second, and *proles* first, the Protestants put companionship at the top, followed by procreation, and finally by fidelity. In effect, they move the arbitration of marital morality out of the religious realm (and the grasp of the "filth-preachers") for the first time in fifteen hundred years. In the dominant society to come—middle-class Protestant, or Protestant-influenced—the people themselves become the arbiters of their sex lives.

Soon enough they'll have to choose between the new vision of marriage as a mutually rewarding companionship and the old assumption that wives, as members of the weaker sex, are necessarily subjugated to their husbands; the two elements are incompatible. This can be ignored only as long as expectations of marital happiness remain low. Once they begin to rise, the relationship will have to be reimagined. For starters, women will need to develop their brains so that (a) men can see that women have brains and (b) couples can exchange ideas as well as reproductive fluids.

In the secular West, all of this is still in process, a process that has been neither orderly nor linear. By law and by social consensus, the rule of the husband has gone the way of stoning for adultery. But on the personal level, women are still trying to prove to men (and themselves) that they can think *and* make babies. Men are still trying to prove that they don't need to be called "Doctor" by their wives in public to feel manly. For most of us, marriage is no longer expected to serve as reproductive factory, guarantor of paternal integrity (DNA testing is so much more civilized), land-preservation device, real-estate bonanza, inheritance- insurance policy, cementer of alliances between powerful families, indissoluble bond, or protection against fornication.

Love is the expectation. Romantic, compassionate, erotic, intellectual, emotional, physical—hopefully, and delusionally, all at once and all the time. No surprise that divorce is common, or that hope continues to triumph over experience. The cure for lust is now the cure for loneliness, that cure being love.

Marriage for love: generally feared, denounced, discouraged, marginalized up and down the social ladder (except at the very bottom, where neither side had anything to gain or lose) before the Reformation. By the eighteenth century, it's all the rage. Daniel Defoe writes a screed called *Matrimonial Whoredom*, defining the term as marriage for anything other than love—money, for instance. Defoe is by no means the only writer of his day to trash what was only recently the general rule. He just has the best title.

Of course people still marry for money, among other things, but most won't admit it. The cover story we all at least pay lip service to has changed. Considering how long the old one held the field, it's amazing that the change came about so quickly— amazing that it occurred at all.

Love may not be the answer, but for now, it is the story.

Acknowledgments

T HE support staff required to feed, shelter, calm, cajole, prod, and otherwise sustain an author consumed for thirteen years with a single project—especially a project that induces obsessive talk about medieval castration fantasies and Martin Luther's constipation—is staggering beyond belief, not to mention remembrance. The names mentioned below constitute only a partial list; for everyone else, and you know who you are, please accept my apologies and heartfelt thanks.

Karen Rinaldi came up with the idea for this book. Elaine Pfefferblit suggested me as the writer. I'm grateful to them both, and I can't thank Karen enough for her trust and forbearance. Thanks also to my ever-supportive, never-intrusive agent, Kris Dahl of ICM, for taking care of business with consummate skill and care; to Anna Rosencranz, who provided much-needed research assistance; and to David Smith and Warren Platt of the New York Public Library, for critical intervention at the last minute.

Early on, Ben Cheever provided a thoughtful and ever-witty e-tutorial on the apostles, introduced me to G. K. Chesterton and Dorothy Sayers, and did his best to make me understand the concept of the Trinity; that I still don't get it is not his fault. Later on, my officemates and fellow writers helped out in their own special ways—Andrew Belonsky for submitting gracefully to my weekend quizzes on the ranking of sexual sins, and Jim Traub and Richard

Zacks for producing three books each while I labored over one, without ever lording it over me.

Elene Kolb possesses encyclopedic knowledge of global litera- ture and makes a mean ice-cream cake besides; she fed me both with unfailing generosity. Cynthia Kling provided tea, sympathy, and astute insights and always knew what questions not to ask about my progress.

Judy Hirsch lent me her sanity whenever my own went miss- ing, showered me with attention and affection, and not least, plied me with Dewar's when nothing else would do.

I am indebted to Caroline Miller and Carolyn White for reading portions of this work in draft form and making invaluable suggestions, to Cindy Spiegel for eleventh-hour guidance on a criti- cal chapter, and to Hannah Lehman for sharpening my thinking on the whetstone of her own prodigious brain, for the discerning stream of books, articles, and eye cream, and most important, for her object-constant faith.

Despite having a book of her own to research, another to pro- mote, and two erupting adolescents underfoot, Marilyn Johnson put her life on hold to read the manuscript, more than once and under pressure. She tweaked what needed to be tweaked ever so delicately, improving the book in ways large and small, while her unflagging enthusiasm gave me energy and confidence during the harrowing finale.

Nick Trautwein applied just the right combination of acute editorial skill, shrewd psychology, and when absolutely necessary, brute force. Somehow he managed the monster in me, and I hope that one day he'll tell me the secret.

Getting through the last thirteen years, especially the last two, would be unthinkable without the Plum to my Nancy, Rebecca Guenther, the best sister ever to walk (or in her case, run) the earth. Even better, she's the resident genius at the Library of Congress, capable of tracking down all kinds of arcane sources within seconds of my asking.

Thanks to David Squire for spurring me on in this and every

endeavor, whether he knows it or not; to Pat Squire for being a one-woman lending library and a source of emotional rescue; to Alan and Anexora Skvirsky, hosts extraordinaire; to David Weltman for services beyond the call of avuncular duty, and for marrying Andy; to Helen and Aaron Spiegel for always being there; and to Max Hirshey, for always being himself.

Fortunately I wasn't a wife during the centuries I've written about here. I'd never have gotten away with neglecting my husband the way my husband has let me get away with neglecting him, especially toward the end. For that alone, David Hirshey is the man of my dreams. My daughter, Emily, was similarly neglected, yet she was and is my biggest cheerleader. Unbelievably, she spent her first vacation as a college student doing my personal laundry while I was in Book Hell. I guess you could say they're the family of my dreams.

Notes

PROLOGUE

1. That the connection is not self-evident was famously demonstrated by Bronislaw
    Malinowski in *The Sexual Life of Savages* (1929), a field report on the clueless na-
    tives of the Trobriand Islands near New Guinea. Their sexual creed is un-savage,
    garden-variety monogamy: one man and one woman, living under one roof. But
    while the Trobrianders have developed a social concept of paternity—the man
    is recognized as the "father" of any children born into the household by virtue of
    his cohabitation with the mother—the biological fact of paternity is unknown to
    them. See Reay Tannahill's *Sex in History*, which persuasively argues that general
    ignorance may have persisted as late as 9000 BCE; Donald Symons, *The Evolution
    of Human Sexuality*; Robert Briffault, *The Mothers*.
2. Jewish tradition and current standards of political correctness demand that the
    religiously neutral terms BCE (Before the Common Era) and CE (Common Era)
    be substituted for BC (Before Christ) and AD (Anno Domini).
3. The prehistoric scenario described in this section is necessarily presumptive.
    See Tannahill, *Sex in History*; Symons, *Evolution of Human Sexuality*; Jared
    Diamond, *Guns, Germs, and Steel*; Lionel Tiger, *Men in Groups*; Matt Ridley,
    The Red Queen; H.G. Wells, *The Outline of History*, vol. 1.
4. Theorizing about the evolutionary markers of human sexual relations, intellec-
    tually moot without the concept of evolution already in place, went from zero to
    a million mph after Charles Darwin's mind-blowing *Origin of Species* was
    published in 1859. (The explosive field of primate-behavior studies has pushed
    the speedometer to a gazillion in the last thirty years.) Iterations of the
    idea of group, aka communal, marriage have been as innumerable as its propo-
    nents, starting with Lewis Henry Morgan, who inspired the work that Marx
    began, completed after his death by Engels. See, for instance, Morgan's *An-
    cient Society*; Engels's *The Origin of the Family*; Briffault's *Mothers*, and more
    recently Sarah Blaffer Hrdy's *The Woman That Never Evolved*. The mere sug-
    gestion that humans could ever be anything other than monogamous horrified
    many middle-brow academics in the vehemently pro-monogamy (and privately

pro-prostitution and -pornography) Victorian world of the late nineteenth century. Some of them set out to "prove" the existence of an innate "monogamous instinct" that would have prevented humanity from indulging in a promiscuous practice like group marriage. Leading the pack was Edward Westermarck, whose *History of Human Marriage* (1903) presented highly dubious evidence backing this hopeful idea. Nonetheless, it became the standard text on the subject until Robert Briffault, a Scottish-born surgeon and social anthropologist, successfully discredited it with *The Mothers*. Both sides are still out there, playing what can only be a guessing game, with some guesses more informed than others. But the majority of social anthropologists, evolutionary psychologists, sociobiologists et al. (the field grows ever more specialized, with ever more name tags) concur that some loosely organized, nonexclusive mating system within the group or tribe would have been most likely until late in prehistory—possibly in coexistence with, or succeeded by, "pair-bonding." That's the other big idea, which presumes that the odds of species survival increase if a pregnant woman and her sexual partner(s) stick together until their offspring survives infancy— and further presumes that the wiring for paternal "attachment" was in place long before the relationship between sex and conception was known. The term "pair-bond" was codified by David Barash's 1977 *Sociology and Behavior*; also see Helen Fisher's *Anatomy of Love*, Hrdy's *Woman That Never Evolved* and *Mother Nature*, Barash and Judith Eve Lipton's *The Myth of Monogamy*, and Symons's *Evolution of Human Sexuality*.

5. John Humphrey Noyes, one of the movement's stars, coined the term "complex marriage" to describe the system of glorified mate-swapping he devised—and in which he participated enthusiastically—within the Oneida community in upstate New York. See Raymond Muncy, *Sex and Marriage in Utopian Communities*; Everett Webber, *Escape to Utopia*; Robert S. Fogarty, *Desire and Duty at Oneida*; Sidney Ditzion, *Marriage, Morals, and Sex in America*.

6. *The Civilizing Process* is the revised title of Norbert Elias's seminal work, first published in 1939 as *The History of Manners*.

7. On the human effects of the end of the last Ice Age, see Tannahill, *Sex in History*, and Diamond, *Guns, Germs, and Steel*.

8. James Strong, *The New Strong's Exhaustive Concordance of the Bible*.

9. Eva C. Keuls, *The Reign of the Phallus*.

10. Steven Ozment, *When Fathers Ruled*, 1; Barbara Ehrenreich and Deirdre English, *For Her Own Good*, 35; Merry Wiesner, *Women and Gender in Early Modern Europe*, 265.

11. Adam Jukes, *Why Men Hate Women*, xiv.

12. Geoffrey Chaucer, "The Miller's Prologue," *Canterbury Tales*.

CHAPTER I

1. Unless otherwise noted, biblical quotations in this chapter come from *The Torah: A Modern Commentary*.

2. David Friedman, *A Mind of Its Own*, 7.

3. Genesis 2:18. In order of citation: King James Version; Revised English Bible, Oxford Study Edition; New Revised Standard Version, *HarperCollins Study Bible*.

4. *Torah*, 30n.
5. "Polygyny" specifies many wives, while the more generic "polygamy" refers to "many spouses," implying that the privilege extends to wives—clearly not the case here. To get really technical, the standard form of marriage in ancient Israel combined polygyny with monoandry: multiple wives for the man, one husband for the woman. Bowing to the dominant Christian culture, European (Ashkenazic) Jewry banned polygyny in 1000 CE. Sephardic Jews, living in Islamic territory and feeling no such pressure, maintained the tradition for centuries—in Yemen and Ethiopia, to this day. (Monogamy is the rule in modern Israel, which nonetheless makes an exception for men who arrive as émigrés from other lands with more than one wife in tow; they're permitted to keep the wives they already have, but not to add to their harems once in Israel.) Needless to say, polyandry (many husbands) has thus far been virtually unknown in the male-focused, civilized West. But never say never: the fetching Carla Bruni, now the first lady of France, is an avowed fan of the practice. With Mrs. Nicolas Sarkozy behind it, who's to say that polyandry won't be having a moment of its own?
6. *Torah*, 35n.
7. Norman F. Cantor, *The Medieval Reader*, 191.
8. St. Ambrose, reprinted in The *Human Couple in the Fathers*, 219, 221.
9. Tertullian, "On the Apparel of Women," in *The Ante-Nicene Fathers*, vol. 4, 14.
10. John Calvin, "Sermon on the Epistle of Saint Paul to the Ephesians," in Kate Aughterson (ed.), *Renaissance Woman*, 17.
11. 1 Corinthians 14:34, 1 Timothy 2:11, 2:12.

CHAPTER 2

1. 1 Kings 11:3. Oddly, or maybe not so oddly, the Hebrew word for "concubine," referring to household slaves or servants who sleep with the master, and the Hebrew word for "wife" are one and the same.
2. *Torah*, 111n.
3. Ibid.
4. Ibid.
5. Deuteronomy 25:11; 23:2. The assumption is that the man willfully undergoes surgery for this purpose; *Torah*, 1495n.
6. Deuteronomy 5:18.
7. Lawrence Stone, *The Family, Sex, and Marriage*, 35; Samuel Menefee, *Wives for Sale*, 2. A drunken husband sells his wife in the opening chapter of Thomas Hardy's *The Mayor of Casterbridge* (1886), much to the astonishment of contemporary critics. Oblivious to the informal, unlawful marriage and divorce customs of their less literate brethren ("wife-sale" dates back to c. 1073), they could not imagine such a thing happening on British soil in the nineteenth century, even though popular broadsides depicting the practice (one of which illustrates the cover of Menefee's book) were still being produced and widely circulated during that same century.
8. The matrilineal tradition begins c. 200 C.E.
9. 2 Samuel 11.
10. Numbers 5:12–31; 1052n. Trial by ordeal, usually involving fire or water (ingesting poison and walking over hot coals are among the less common alternatives), has a long, colorful, and nauseating cross-cultural history rooted in faith—pagan

faith in magic or religious faith in God, which often came down to the same thing. Use of the ordeal to determine guilt or innocence became less common in the late medieval period, thanks to the development of even more nauseating, if ingenious, forms of torture, but the tradition continued into the sixteenth century. See Henry Lea, *Superstition and Force*; Jeffrey Russell, *Witchcraft in the Middle Ages*; Robert Bartlett, *Trial by Fire and Water*.

11. Deuteronomy 24:1–4.
12. *Torah*, 1498n.
13. The sequence on adultery begins with Deuteronomy 22:13.
14. Deuteronomy 21:15–17.
15. Deuteronomy 25: 5–10.
16. Wayne A. Meeks, ed., *HarperCollins Study Bible*, 307n.
17. The Onan-Judah-Tamar narrative starts with Genesis 38:9.
18. Genesis 19:31–38.
19. Deuteronomy 24:5.
20. Deuteronomy 21:10–14.
21. Deuteronomy 7:1–14.
22. Samson's tale of woe begins with Judges 16; on Solomon, see 1 Kings 11:11.
23. Jezebel first appears on the stage of 1 Kings 16:31; after 21:29 she takes a long break, not to return until 2 Kings 9:30; text cited from *HarperCollins Study Bible*.
24. Proverbs 31: 10–13. The famous parsing is the English original from the King James version; more modern translations pale by comparison. But those "haveths" and "feareths" can get old fast, so aside from the three verses cited here, all quotes come from the New Revised Standard Version, *HarperCollins Study Bible*.
25. Cited in Steven Ozment, *When Fathers Ruled*, 68.

CHAPTER 3

1. See Cynthia B. Patterson, *The Family in Greek History*, for a contrarian view on the seclusion of wives.
2. Sarah Pomeroy, *Goddesses, Whores, Wives, and Slaves*, 57; Keuls, *Reign of the Phallus*, 5; Tannahill, *Sex in History*, 92, 104.
3. Translation from Floyd Dell, *Love in the Machine Age*, 57.
4. For a detailed discussion on vase paintings, see Keuls, *Reign of the Phallus*.
5. Thomas R. Martin, *Ancient Greece*, 135; Pomeroy, *Goddesses, Whores*, 63.
6. Aristotle, *The Politics*, 293.
7. Quoted by Katharine M. Rogers, *The Troublesome Helpmate*, 28n.
8. Quotes taken from Xenophon, *Oeconomicus*.
9. Henry George Liddell and Robert Scott, *A Greek–English Lexicon*, 368.
10. Keuls, *Reign of the Phallus*, 6.
11. Ibid.
12. Aristotle, *Generation of Animals*, 100n (editor's note).
13. Quotes taken from Aristotle, *Generation of Animals*.
14. Thomas Laqueur, *Making Sex*, 4–5.
15. Pomeroy, *Goddesses, Whores*, chapter 1.
16. On the castration mystery, see Keuls, *Reign of the Phallus*, 30–32.
17. Cited in Pomeroy, *Goddesses, Whores*, 6.

18. Ibid., p. 2.
19. The obscurity and antiquity of Hesiod and the fragmentary nature of his text make many of the legends ambiguous, Pandora's among them. Centuries' worth of questionable translations, from archaic Greek into later Latin and still later into vernacular languages, don't help; the mistranslation of *pithos* (jar) into *pixis* (box), attributed to Erasmus's sixteenth-century Latin version, is just one example. Hesiod, "Works and Days," Tufts University website.
20. Philippe Ariès, "Love in Married Life," in *Western Sexuality*, 132.
21. Robert Crosse, quoted in Lawrence Stone, *The Family, Sex and Marriage*, 102.
22. Euripides, *Iphigenia at Aulis*; the line is spoken by Iphigenia herself.
23. Quoted in David Cherry, *The Roman World: A Sourcebook*, 52, 54.

CHAPTER 4
1. Jo-Ann Shelton, *As the Romans Did*, 299.
2. Cato's analogy of woman and animal, specifically (or so "the reins" would suggest) a horse, makes him an early contributor to what will become a bulging literary archive. Tolstoy covers similarly equine territory: "You mustn't allow them any freedom from the word go. Never trust a horse in the paddock or a wife in the home." (*The Kreutzer Sonata*, 1889.) Jonathan Swift considers the female "a sort of species hardly a degree above a monkey," Nietzsche dismisses all women as "birds of prey," Freud compares them to cats, and so it goes.
3. J. P. V. D. Balsdon, *Roman Women*, 32–37.
4. Ibid., 217.
5. Archaeologists have established that Rome was indeed settled in the mid-eighth century BCE, but what stands as early Roman history must be swallowed with several grains of salt. We're supposed to believe that Romulus and his twin, Remus (already the victim of fratricide in a struggle for power), descend through their mother from none other than the Homeric hero Aeneas, much idolized by Romans in Livy's time; that their mother, a vestal virgin, conceives them after being raped by a god; that they've barely emerged from her womb when she's hauled off to be buried alive (standard punishment for no-longer-virginal vestals, regardless of the circumstances), and that the twins are thrown into the Tiber to die, but are instead rescued—by a she-wolf, who personally suckles the newborns and raises them to healthy young manhood.
6. Livy (Titus Livius), *The History of Rome*, 1.9.
7. Of the many sources on this primitive sexual rite, see William J. Fielding, *Strange Customs of Courtship and Marriage*, chapter 13; George Ryley Scott, *Curious Customs of Sex and Marriage*, chapter 5.
8. Balsdon, *Roman Women*, 181–85.
9. Livy, *History of Rome*, 1.57.
10. The first four centuries of Livy's "history," which he produces nearly eight hundred years after Romulus, or whoever, settles the land, are source-free, unless the literary narratives of Homer and Hesiod can double as nonfiction. Any records that may have existed were destroyed in the sacking of Rome by the Gauls in 390 BCE. When Livy says that Rome began as a monarchy and converted to a republic because a noblewoman was raped by a prince, there's nothing to contradict him. Still, some history is better than none.

11. Plutarch, another moral conservative in the Livy mold, will put his own touches on the Roman history tutorial in the next century. See John T. Noonan, *Contraception*, 41.
12. Balsdon, *Roman Women*, 47–48.
13. On the shifting forms of Roman marriage, see Balsdon, *Roman Women*; Mary R. Lefkowitz and Maureen B. Fant, *Women's Life in Greece and Rome*; Vern Bullough et al., *The Subordinated Sex*; Georges Duby and Michelle Perrot, eds., *A History of Women in the West*, vol. 1.
14. Balsdon, *Roman Women*, 179–80.
15. Ibid., 282.
16. Ibid., 76.
17. Juvenal, "Satire VI" in *The Sixteen Satires*.
18. Balsdon, *Roman Women*, 36.
19. Tannahill, *Sex in History*, 121.
20. On the Augustan marriage reforms, see Balsdon, *Roman Women*; Noonan, *Contraception*.
21. Exposure means just what it sounds like: Unwanted infants are simply exposed to the elements, whether that means being thrown into the Tiber to drown, à la Romulus and Remus, or placed on a mountainside to freeze, be eaten by animals, or whatever.
22. Balsdon, *Roman Women*, 202.
23. Cited in Noonan, *Contraception*, 39. P. Cornelius Tacitus, looking back over the prior century, expounds at some length on the failure of the Augustan laws in *The Annals and the Histories*, Book 3.
24. Tannahill, *Sex in History*, chapter 5.
25. On the marital and sexual proclivities of Augustus, see Balsdon, *Roman Women*; Tacitus, *Annals*, Book 1; Tannahill, *Sex in History*, chapter 5.
26. On the marital and sexual proclivities of everyone else, see Paul Veyne's essay in Ariès and Bejin, *Western Sexuality*, chapter 3.
27. Balsdon, *Roman Women*, 77.
28. Balsdon, *Roman Women*, 14, 201, 277.
29. Plutarch, *Moralia* IV.
30. Garry Wills, *Papal Sin*, 109.
31. Juvenal, "Satire VI" in *The Sixteen Satires*.
32. Ibid.

CHAPTER 5

1. Matthew 1:1–17; Luke 1:27; 1:32, 2:4, 3:23–38; Acts 13:17–23. Unless noted, quotations from the New Testament are taken from the New Revised Standard Version, *HarperCollins Study Bible*.
2. Luke 2:41–52.
3. Isaiah, chapters 24–34.
4. On the early church, see Paul Johnson, *A History of Christianity*, parts 1 and 2; John Dominic Crossan, *The Birth of Christianity*, chapters 1–3; Philip Schaff, *History of the Christian Church*, vols. 1–3.
5. Noonan pulls it all together in his invaluable *Contraception*; the title is deceptively minimal.
6. Ibid., 107.

7. Acts 7:58–8:3.
8. The story of Paul's conversion, proselytizing, and martyrdom takes up most of Acts, starting with chapter 9.
9. Acts 23:6.
10. 1 Corinthians 7:7; 7:1.
11. Ibid., 7:9.
12. Ibid., 7:6.
13. Ibid., 7:3–5.
14. Bertrand Russell, *Marriage and Morals*, 26.
15. These comments are contained in 1 Corinthians 7:26–34.
16. Ephesians 5:22–24.
17. Ibid., 5:28–29, 33.
18. 1 Corinthians 14:34–35.
19. *HarperCollins Study Bible*, 2154n.
20. 1 Corinthians 11:7–9.
21. 1 Timothy 2:11–14.
22. 1 Peter 3:3–5, 7.
23. This would surely please Tertullian, but he might feel differently about being a founder of existentialism. As it happens, that profoundly secular, God-denying, twentieth-century philosophy pivots around the notion of the absurd—and the notion of the absurd originates with none other than Father Tertullian. On the question of why God would assume a man's form to suffer for humanity on earth, Tertullian says that because there is no reasonable answer, because the whole idea is entirely nonsensical, it has to be true: *Creo quia absurdum est*. "I believe because it is absurd." Kierkegaard's insistence that accepting Jesus as Christ, savior of mankind, necessitates a "leap of faith" derives from Tertullian; the existentialists take it from there, straight out of the realm of religion.
24. 1 Corinthians 7:39.
25. Matthew 1:18–25.
26. The references include, but are not limited to, Matthew 13:55, Mark 3:31, Luke 8:19, John 2:12, Acts 1:14, Galatians 1:19, and 1 Corinthians 9:5.
27. Mark 6:3.
28. St. Jerome, "Against Jovinianus," in *The Nicene and Post-Nicene Fathers*, vol. 6, 386.
29. "A husband who is so immoderately in love with his wife and takes his pleasure of her so heatedly that, were she not his wife, he would like her as his mistress, is a sinner," warns the French theologian Jean Benedicti in the late sixteenth century, and the theme preoccupies lay writers as well. Montaigne, for one, allows that "the love we bear to our wives is very lawful," but a husband must "bridle and restrain" that love lest he be transported "beyond the bounds of reason." (Both quotes taken from Jean-Louis Flandrin's essay, "Sex in Married Life in the Early Middle Ages," in Ariès and Bejin, *Western Sexuality*, 122.)
30. St. Jerome, "The Perpetual Virginity of Blessed Mary," in *Nicene and Post-Nicene Fathers*, vol. 6, 334ff.

CHAPTER 6
1. Key sources for this chapter, aside from Augustine's own writing, include Peter Brown, *Augustine of Hippo*, and *The Body and Society*, chapter 19; Elaine Pagels,

Adam, Eve, and the Serpent, chapter 5; Henry Chadwick, *Augustine;* Noonan, *Contraception,* chapter 4.

2. Quotes from Augustine on Augustine are taken from Garry Wills's translation of *The Confessions.*

3. Augustine unfurls his vision of the prequel and aftermath of original sin in *City of God,* Book 14, chapters 10–26.

4. Even the most rabid proponents of the perpetual virginity idea—above all, Augustine's mentor, Ambrose, who joins Jerome in the assault on Helvidius for disputing it—don't suggest that Mary's parents produced her by means other than sexual intercourse. Yet they call hers the "Immaculate Conception." Mary has to be exempt from original sin so that Jesus doesn't spend nine months of gestation soaking up the fumes, or something like that.

5. St. Augustine, "The Good of Marriage," reprinted in *Marriage in the Early Church,* 114.

6. St. Augustine, "To the Married," reprinted in *The Human Couple in the Fathers,* 275.

7. St. Augustine, "Good of Marriage."

8. Noonan, *Contraception,* 405–6.

CHAPTER 7

1. For a fuller sense of just how open—and fertile—that field was, see Charles Freeman, *The Closing of the Western Mind;* Chris Wickham, *Framing the Early Middle Ages;* and Tannahill, *Sex in History,* 136–38.

2. For a more expansive view of the new literature of lust, not to mention the erotic tastes of early medieval Europe, try Pierre J. Payer, *Sex and the Penitentials;* John T. McNeill and Helena M. Gamer, *Medieval Handbooks of Penance.*

3. Noonan, *Contraception,* 206–7.

4. James A. Brundage, *Law, Sex, and Christian Society in Medieval Europe,* 103; Michael M. Sheehan, *Marriage, Family, and Law in Medieval Europe,* 299.

5. Noonan provides a handy comparative chart; *Contraception,* 204.

6. Popular belief in magic, and the perception—surely based in reality—that women are the ones who practice it, will only grow stronger over the centuries, leading directly to the witch hunts of the Inquisition. On the situation during the Dark Ages, see Aron Gurevich, *Medieval Popular Culture,* and Noonan, *Contraception.*

7. Tannahill, *Sex in History,* 152; Noonan, *Contraception,* 199.

8. Oral sex, specifically fellatio, seems to evoke disgust and fascination in equal measure among the laity as well as the clergy in the Middle Ages, although this is nothing new; the Greek and Roman writers were similarly obsessed with the subject. See Ariès and Bejin, *Western Sexuality,* 30–31, 121.

9. Jacqueline Murray, *Love, Marriage, and Family in the Middle Ages,* 44–50.

10. On Burchard: Georges Duby, *The Knight, the Lady, and the Priest,* 59–74; Gurevich, *Medieval Popular Culture,* 84–89; Noonan, *Contraception,* 207–210.

11. Pierre Payer, *The Bridling of Desire,* 76–77.

12. Noonan, *Contraception,* 290.

13. Duby, *Knight, the Lady,* 65–74; Brundage, *Law, Sex, and Christian Society,* 154–65; Pierre Payer, *Sex and the Penitentials,* 24–28.

14. Jack Goody, *The Development of the Family and Marriage in Europe*, 190n.
15. Duby, *Knight, the Lady*, 67.
16. Sheehan, *Marriage, Family, and Law*, 298.
17. Bullough and Brundage, *Sexual Practices and the Medieval Church*, 23.

CHAPTER 8
1. Louise Collis, *Memoirs of a Medieval Woman*, 23.
2. Caroline Walker Bynum, *Holy Feast and Holy Fast*, 215.

CHAPTER 9
1. Duby, *Knight, the Lady*, 71.
2. Catherine Rider, *Magic and Impotence in the Middle Ages*, 24–25.
3. And speaking of the insatiable female: It seems that since the 1920s, "the proportion of wives who consider marital intercourse to be 'too frequent' has steadily fallen and the proportion who consider it to be 'too infrequent' has steadily risen." That's the report of the American social anthropologist Donald Symons, see his *Evolution of Human Sexuality*.
4. John DuVal, *Fabliaux Fair & Foul*, 55–59.
5. R. Howard Bloch, *Medieval Misogyny*, 123–24.
6. The Protestant emphasis on the husband's benevolent lordship seems to have influenced Shakespeare in the writing of *The Taming of the Shrew*. His source was an anonymous English ballad dating back about fifty years, called "A Merry Jest of a Shrewd and Curst Wife Lapped in Morel's Skin for Her Good Behavior." While Shakespeare's character, Petruchio, uses psychological manipulation, his prototype goes the old-fashioned route. He beats his harridan until she faints, bleeding profusely. Then he wraps her in the skin of Morel, a plowhorse killed, flayed, and salted for just this purpose. The salt seeps into the wife's open wounds, causing pain that jerks her awake. Once she vows eternal obedience to her tormentor, Morel's skin comes off, and the natural order is restored. We can assume that both couples live happily ever after.
7. Bullough and Brundage, *Sexual Practices*, 170–71.
8. Bullough and Brundage, *Sexual Practices*, 164.
9. Alison Sinclair, *The Deceived Husband*, 32–33.
10. Natalie Zemon Davis, *Society and Culture in Early Modern France*, 97–105, 140. For the psychoanalytic perspective, see Sinclair, *Deceived Husbands*, 58–63.
11. The Ravenna reference is explained in an editor's note; Giovanni Boccaccio, *The Decameron*, 819.
12. The line appears in "The Miller's Prologue."
13. "The Wife of Bath's Prologue and Tale," in Alfred David, ed., *Norton Anthology of English Literature* (*Middle Ages*), 253–81. Chaucer's depiction of this earthy, lascivious, five-times-married character seems to be his way of thumbing his nose at the "auctoritee" of the Church, specifically its anti-matrimonial platform from way back, embodied by Jerome's paeans to virginity.
14. Eileen Power, trans., *The Goodman of Paris*.
15. The Renaissance has more or less arrived by Chaucer's time, during which Christine de Pizan, Margery Kempe, and Heloise each say their piece. But their

respective backgrounds make them doubly exceptional. Pizan is a professional court writer, reportedly the first of her kind, and a widow to boot; otherwise, she'd be a homemaker. Kempe is illiterate, and Heloise is unmarried.

16. "The Wife's Lament," in David, ed., *Norton Anthology*, 102. An editor's note explains the obscure origins of this text, seeming to take it on faith that the author's gender is as advertised. A mystery unlikely to be solved.

CHAPTER 10

1. The seminal work of lit-crit on courtly love is C. S. Lewis's *Allegory of Love*, but it's getting long in the tooth; try Irving Singer, *The Nature of Love*, vol. 2, and Denis de Rougemont, *Love in the Western World*.

2. See R. Howard Bloch, *Medieval Misogyny*, chapter 7, on courtly love as an escape from the unhappy reality of courtly marriage

3. Brundage, *Law, Sex, and Christian Society*, 140–141, 191–195, 200–201, 203, 238, 243, 288, 355–357, 454.

4. Bloch, *Medieval Misogyny*, 156–61.

5. Maurice Keen, *Chivalry*, 30.

6. Bloch, *Medieval Misogyny*, 158.

7. Alison Weir, *Eleanor of Aquitaine*; Georges Duby, *Knight, the Lady*, chapter 10.

8. Duby, *Knight, the Lady*, 224–25.

9. Jacqueline Murray, *Love, Marriage and Family*, 322.

CHAPTER 11

1. On the course of the Black Death: David Herlihy, *The Black Death and the Transformation of the West*, 24–25; Robert S. Gottfried, *The Black Death*.

2. Philippe Ariès and Georges Duby, ed., *A History of Private Life*, vol. 2.

3. Herlihy, *Black Death*, 73–79.

4. Lotario Dei Segni (Pope Innocent III), *De Miseria Condicionis Humane*, 94, 96, 100.

5. R. Howard Bloch, *Medieval Misogyny*, 212.

6. The Protestant reformers destroy the singular authority of the Church (along with the linguistic existence of "the Church" unmodified by the word "Catholic") and reinforce the husband's at the same time. Their emphasis on family-centered worship positions the household as mini-church, allowing the male head of household to step into the power vacuum left by pope and priest; since they consider the Bible the only relevant source of doctrine on marriage (and everything else), Paul's insistence that wives should be subject to their husbands becomes the Protestant mantra. Only when democracy puts an end to the rule of kings will the rule of husbands slide.

CHAPTER 12

1. Eileen Power, trans., *The Goodman of Paris (Le Ménagier de Paris): A Treatise on Moral and Domestic Economy by a Bourgeois of Paris* (c. 1393).

2. It's no longer kosher—at least not in the West—for a husband to kill his wife (or a father his daughter) for infidelity—whether voluntary or not, so there's been progress. Still, the link seems to be holding. Not so long ago, a former pro-football coach named Bill McCartney told *Sports Illustrated*

(January 16, 1995), "Nothing tells you more about a man than what you see in his wife."

3. Geoffroy de la Tour Landry, *The Book of the Knight of la Tour Landry*, editor's note, ix. All quotes taken from this text.

4. Leon Battista Alberti, *The Family in Renaissance Florence*, Book 3. *Della Famiglia*. All quotes taken from this text.

CHAPTER 13

1. The writer is the Christian humanist Albrecht von Eyb, trilling away in 1472; quoted in Steven Ozment, *When Fathers Ruled*, 7.

2. Quoted in Wills, *Papal Sin*, p. 109–10.

3. Ozment, *When Fathers Ruled*, 1.

4. Montague Summers, trans., *The Malleus Maleficarum of Heinrich Kramer and James Sprenger*, Dover edition, 1971. All quotes from this demented text—which, by the way, was banned by the Church a few years after publication, but it remained the standard for witch hunters and prosecutors throughout Europe until the late seventeenth century.

CHAPTER 14

1. Martin Luther, "Exhortation to the Knights," in *The Christian in Society* II, 144.

2. This charming practice is known as simony, after Simon Magus, a New Testament character who tries to buy spiritual powers from the apostle Peter. (Acts 8:9–24). The account of Leo and Albert's sleazy deal, Tetzel's role in it, and the aftermath comes from Roland H. Bainton, *Here I Stand: A Life of Martin Luther*.

3. Luther's most colorful rants, and there's an embarrassment of riches, are arguably "An Appeal to the Ruling Class . . ." and "The Pagan Servitude of the Church" (more widely known as "The Babylonian Captivity"). John Dillenberger, ed., *Martin Luther: Selections from His Writings*.

4. Bainton, *Here I Stand*, 56.

5. Martin Luther, *Table Talk*, 121.

6. Martin Luther, "Estate of Marriage," in *Christian in Society* II, 18.

7. Ibid.

8. Luther is quoting from Matthew 19:12.

9. Luther, *Table Talk*, 3777.

10. This quote, and those in the following two paragraphs, are from Luther, "Estate of Marriage."

CHAPTER 15

1. The story of the nuns' breakout is told by Steven Ozment in *When Fathers Ruled*, 16–17.

2. Bainton, *Here I Stand*, reveals the mechanics of Luther's surrender to the inevitable, 224–25.

3. Luther, *Table Talk* 3178a.

4. Ibid., 49.

5. Ibid., 1607.

6. Bainton, *Here I Stand*, gives an exhaustive account of Katy's exhausting life, although maybe living it is less exhausting than reading about it.
7. Luther, *Table Talk*, 5537.
8. Luther, "Estate of Marriage," part 3.
9. Ibid.
10. Bainton, *Here I Stand*, 234–35.
11. Luther, *Table Talk*, 4625.
12. Ibid., 2807b.
13. Ibid.
14. Steven Ozment, *Ancestors*, 37.
15. Luther, *Table Talk*, 2980b.
16. Ibid., 4081.
17. Ibid., 1658.
18. Ibid., 55.
19. Ibid., 4105.
20. Ibid., 5578.
21. Ibid., 5524.
22. Ibid.

Bibliography

Aberth, John. *The Black Death*. Boston: Bedford/St. Martin's, 2005.

Agrippa, Henricus Cornelius. *Declamation on the Nobility and Preeminence of the Female Sex*. Trans. Albert Rabil. Chicago: University of Chicago Press, 1996.

Alberti, Leon Battista. *The Family in Renaissance Florence*. Book 3. Trans. Renée Neu Watkins. Prospect Heights, IL: Waveland Press, 1994.

Alvarez, A. *Life after Marriage: Love in an Age of Divorce*. New York: Simon & Schuster, 1981.

Amussen, Susan Dwyer. *An Ordered Society: Gender and Class in Early Modern England*. New York: Columbia University Press, 1988.

Ariès, Philippe. *Centuries of Childhood: A Social History of Family Life*. Trans. Robert Baldick. New York: Vintage Books, 1962.

Ariès, Philippe, and André Béjin. *Western Sexuality: Practice and Precept in Past and Present Times*. Trans. Anthony Forster. Oxford: Basil Blackwell, 1985.

Ariès, Philippe, and Georges Duby, eds. *A History of Private Life*. Vol. 1, *From Pagan Rome to Byzantium*. Cambridge, MA: Harvard University Press, 1987.

———. *A History of Private Life*. Vol. 2, *Revelations of the Medieval World*. Cambridge, MA: Harvard University Press, 1988.

———. *A History of Private Life*. Vol. 3, *Passions of the Renaissance*. Cambridge, MA: Harvard University Press, 1989.

Aristophanes. *Lysistrata*. Trans. Douglass Parker. New York: Mentor Books, 1964.

Aristotle. *Ethics*. Translated by J. A. K. Thomson. Baltimore: Penguin Books, 1956.

———. *Generation of Animals*. Trans. A. L. Peck. Cambridge, MA: Harvard University Press, 1942.

———. *The Politics*. Trans. T. A. Sinclair. Baltimore: Penguin Books, 1962.

Arnold, John H. *Belief and Unbelief in Medieval Europe*. New York: Hodder Arnold, 2005.

Aughterson, Kate. *The English Renaissance: An Anthology of Sources and Documents*. New York: Routledge, 2001.

Bainton, Roland H. *Here I Stand: A Life of Martin Luther*. New York: Meridian, 1995.

Bainton, Ronald H. *The Reformation of the Sixteenth Century*. Boston: Beacon Press, 1952.

Balsdon, J. P. V. D. *Roman Women: Their History and Habits*. London: Cox & Wyman, 1962.

Barash, David P. *Sociology and Behavior*. New York: Elsevier, 1977.

Barash, David P., and Judith Eve Lipton. *The Myth of Monogamy: Fidelity and Infidelity in Animals and People*. New York: W. H. Freeman, 2001.

Bartlett, Robert. *Trial by Fire and Water: The Medieval Judicial Ordeal*. Oxford: Oxford University Press, 1986.

Bataille, Georges. *Erotism: Death & Sensuality*. Trans. Mary Dalwood. San Francisco: City Lights Books, 1986.

Bernard, Jessie. *The Future of Marriage*. New Haven, CT: Yale University Press, 1982.

Bitel, Lisa M. *Women in Early Medieval Europe, 400–1100*. Cambridge, UK: Cambridge University Press, 2002.

Blackstone, William. *Commentaries on the Laws of England*. Vol. 1. Chicago: University of Chicago Press, 1979.

———. *Commentaries on the Laws of England*. Vol. 3. Chicago: University of Chicago Press, 1979.

———. *Commentaries on the Laws of England*. Vol. 4. Boston: Beacon Press, 1962.

Blamires, Alcuin, ed. *Woman Defamed and Woman Defended: An Anthology of Medieval Texts*. Oxford: Clarendon Press, 1992.

Bloch, R. Howard. *Medieval Misogyny and the Invention of Western Romantic Love*. Chicago: University of Chicago Press, 1991.

Boccaccio, Giovanni. *The Decameron*. Trans. G. H. McWilliam. New York: Penguin Books, 1972.

Bloom, Harold. *The Western Canon: The Books and School of the Ages*. New York: Harcourt Brace, 1994.

Bowman, Henry A. *Marriage for Moderns*. New York: McGraw-Hill, 1942.

Braden, Gordon. *Petrarchan Love and the Continental Renaissance*. New Haven, CT: Yale University Press, 1999.

Breitenberg, Mark. *Anxious Masculinity in Early Modern England*. Cambridge, UK: Cambridge University Press, 1996.

Briffault, Robert. *The Mothers*. New York: Atheneum, 1977.

———. *Sin and Sex*. New York: Macaulay Co., 1931.

Briffault, Robert, and Bronislaw Malinowski. *Marriage: Past and Present*. Boston: Porter Sargent, 1956.

Brooke, Christopher. *The Medieval Idea of Marriage*. Oxford: Oxford University Press, 1989.

Brown, Peter. *Augustine of Hippo: A Biography*. Berkeley: University of California Press, 1967.

———. *The Body and Society: Men, Women, and Sexual Renunciation in Early Christianity*. New York: Columbia University Press, 1988.

Brundage, James A. *Law, Sex, and Christian Society in Medieval Europe*. Chicago: University of Chicago Press, 1987.

———. *Medieval Canon Law*. London: Longman, 1995.

Bumke, Joachim. *Courtly Culture: Literature and Society in the High Middle Ages*. Woodstock, NY: Overlook Press, 2000.

Bullough, Vern L. *Sex, Society, and History*. New York: Science History Publications, 1976.

Bullough, Vern L., and James Brundage. *Sexual Practices and the Medieval Church*. Buffalo, NY: Prometheus Books, 1994.

Bullough, Vern L., Brenda Shelton, and Sarah Slavin. *The Subordinated Sex: A History of Attitudes Toward Women*. Rev. ed. Athens: University of Georgia Press, 1988.

Burford, E. J. *The Bishop's Brothels*. London: Robert Hale, 1976.

Burgess, Glyn S., and Keith Busby, trans. *The Lais of Marie de France*. New York: Penguin Books, 1986.

Burke, Peter. *Popular Culture in Early Modern Europe*. Rev. reprint. Aldershot: Ashgate, 1999.

Bynum, Caroline Walker. *Holy Feast and Holy Fast*. Berkeley: University of California Press, 1987.

Cantor, Norman F. *The Last Knight: The Twilight of the Middle Ages and the Birth of the Modern Era*. New York: Harper Perennial, 2005.

———. *The Medieval Reader*. New York: HarperCollins, 1994.

Capellanus, Andreas. *The Art of Courtly Love*. New York: Columbia University Press, 1960.

Castiglione, Baldesar. *The Book of the Courtier*. Trans. George Bull. New York: Penguin Books, 1967.

Chadwick, Henry. *Augustine*. Oxford: Oxford University Press, 1986.

———. *The Early Church*. New York: Penguin Books, 1990.

Chapman, George. *The Widow's Tears*. Ed. Ethel M. Smeak. Lincoln: University of Nebraska Press, 1966.

Chaucer, Geoffrey. *The Canterbury Tales*. Ed. A. C. Cawley. New York: Alfred A. Knopf, 1992.

Cherry, David. *The Roman World: A Sourcebook*. Malden, MA: Blackwell Publishing, 2001.

Cohen, Jeremy. *"Be Fertile and Increase, Fill the Earth and Master It": The Ancient and Medieval Career of a Biblical Text*. Ithaca, NY: Cornell University Press, 1989.

Collis, Louise. *Memoirs of a Medieval Woman: The Life and Times of Margery Kempe*. New York: HarperCollins, 1983.

Coulton, G. G. *Chaucer and His England*. London: Methuen, 1963.

Cowell, F. R. *Cicero and the Roman Republic*. London: Sir Isaac Pitman and Sons, 1948.

Crossan, John Dominic. *The Birth of Christianity*. San Francisco: HarperSanFrancisco, 1998.

David, Alfred, ed. *The Norton Anthology of English Literature: The Middle Ages*. Vol. 1A. New York: W. W. Norton, 2000.

Davies, R. T., ed. *Medieval English Lyrics: A Critical Anthology*. Evanston, IL: Northwestern University Press, 1964.

Davis, Natalie Zemon. *Society and Culture in Early Modern France*. Stanford, CA: Stanford University Press, 1975.

Davis, Natalie Zemon, and Arlette Farge, eds. *A History of Women: Renaissance and Enlightenment Paradoxes*. Vol. 3. Cambridge, MA: Harvard University Press, 1993.

Dei Segni, Lotario. *De Miseria Condicionis Humane.* Ed. Robert E. Lewis. Athens, GA: University of Georgia Press, 1978.

De Lafayette, Madame. *The Princesse de Clèves.* Trans. Robin Buss. New York: Penguin Books, 1978.

De Lorris, Guillaume, and Jean de Meun. *The Romance of the Rose.* Trans. Charles Dahlberg. 3rd ed. Princeton, NJ: Princeton University Press, 1995.

Dell, Floyd. *Love in the Machine Age.* New York: Octagon Books, 1973.

De Pizan, Christine. *The Book of the City of Ladies.* Trans. Jeffrey Richards. New York: Persea Books, 1998.

De Rougemont, Denis. *Love in the Western World.* Trans. Montgomery Belgion. Princeton, NJ: Princeton University Press, 1983.

Diamond, Jared. *Guns, Germs, and Steel: The Fates of Human Societies.* New York: W. W. Norton, 1999.

Dillenberger, John, ed. *Martin Luther: Selections from His Writings.* Garden City, NY: Doubleday, 1961.

Ditzion, Sidney. *Marriage, Morals, and Sex in America: A History of Ideas.* New York: W. W. Norton, 1969.

Dorlan, Frances E. *Dangerous Familiars.* Ithaca, NY: Cornell University Press, 1994.

Duby, Georges. *The Knight, the Lady, and the Priest: The Making of Modern Marriage in Medieval France.* Chicago: University of Chicago Press, 1993.

———. *Love and Marriage in the Middle Ages.* Chicago: University of Chicago Press, 1994.

———. *The Three Orders: Feudal Society Imagined.* Trans. Arthur Goldhammer. Chicago: Chicago University Press, 1980.

———. *Women of the Twelfth Century.* Vol. 2, *Remembering the Dead.* Chicago: University of Chicago Press, 1997.

Duby, Georges, and Michelle Perrot, eds. *A History of Women in the West.* Vol. 1, *From Ancient Goddesses to Christian Saints.* Cambridge, MA: Harvard University Press, 1992.

Du Val, John. *Fabliaux Fair & Foul.* Asheville, NC: Pegasus Press, 1999.

Ehrenreich, Barbara, and Deirdre English. *For Her Own Good.* New York: Anchor Books, 1979.

Elias, Norbert. *The Civilizing Process,* Trans. Edmund Jephcott. Oxford: Blackwell, 1994.

Elliott, Dyan. *Spiritual Marriage: Sexual Abstinence in Medieval Wedlock.* Princeton, NJ: Princeton University Press, 1993.

Emerton, Ephraim, trans. *The Correspondence of Pope Gregory VII.* New York: Columbia University Press, 1990.

Engels, Frederick. *The Origin of the Family, Private Property, and the State.* New York: International Publishers, 1942.

Erasmus. *Ten Colloquies.* Trans. Craig R. Thompson. New York: Macmillan, 1986.

Erikson, Erik H. *Young Man Luther: A Study in Psychoanalysis and History.* New York: W. W. Norton, 1958.

Euripides. *Alcestis and Other Plays.* Trans. John Davie. New York: Penguin Books, 1996.

Fielding, William J. *Strange Customs of Courtship and Marriage*. Philadelphia: Blakiston Co., 1942.

Findlay, Alison. *A Feminist Perspective on Renaissance Drama*. Malden, MA: Blackwell, 1999.

Fisher, Helen. *Anatomy of Love*. New York: Fawcett Columbine, 1992.

Flandrin, Jean-Louis. *Families in Former Times: Kinship, Household, and Sexuality in Early Modern France*. Cambridge, UK: Cambridge University Press, 1979.

Fletcher, Anthony. *Gender, Sex, and Subordination in England, 1500–1800*. New Haven, CT: Yale University Press, 1995.

Fletcher, Anthony, and John Stevenson, eds. *Order and Disorder in Early Modern England*. Cambridge, UK: Cambridge University Press, 1985.

Fletcher, Richard. *The Barbarian Conversion: From Paganism to Christianity*. New York: Henry Holt, 1997.

Fogarty, Robert S., ed. *Desire and Duty at Oneida*. Bloomington: Indiana University Press, 2000.

Fonte, Moderata (Modesta Pozzo). *The Worth of Women*. Trans. Virginia Cox. Chicago: University of Chicago Press, 1997.

Fredriksen, Paula. *Jesus of Nazareth, King of the Jews*. New York: Vintage Books, 1999.

Freeman, Charles. *The Closing of the Western Mind: The Rise of Faith and the Fall of Reason*. New York: Vintage Books, 2005.

Freud, Sigmund. *Sexuality and the Psychology of Love*. New York: Collier Books, 1963.

Friedan, Betty. *The Feminine Mystique*. New York: Dell, 1963.

Friedman, David M. *A Mind of Its Own: A Cultural History of the Penis*. New York: Penguin Books, 2001.

Gasparro, Giulia Sfameni, Cesare Magazzu, and Concetta Aloe Spada. *The Human Couple in the Fathers*. Boston: Pauline Books and Media, 1999.

Gassner, John, ed. *Elizabethan Drama*. New York: Bantam Books, 1967.

Gay, Peter. *The Bourgeois Experience: Victoria to Freud*. Vol. 2, *The Tender Passion*. Oxford: Oxford University Press, 1986.

Gies, Frances, and Joseph Gies. *Marriage and the Family in the Middle Ages*. New York: Harper & Row, 1987.

Goldsmith, Oliver. *The Vicar of Wakefield*. 3rd ed. New York: Penguin Books, 1986.

Goody, Jack. *The Development of the Family and Marriage in Europe*. Cambridge, UK: Cambridge University Press, 1983.

———. *The European Family*. Oxford: Blackwell, 2000.

Gottfried, Robert S. *The Black Death: Natural and Human Disaster in Medieval Europe*. New York: Free Press, 1983.

Gottlieb, Beatrice. *The Family in the Western World*. Oxford: Oxford University Press, 1993.

Groves, Ernest R. *Marriage*. New York: Henry Holt, 1933.

Grubbs, Judith Evans. *Law and Family in Late Antiquity*. Oxford: Oxford University Press, 1999.

Gurevich, Aron. *Medieval Popular Culture: Problems of Belief and Perception*. Cambridge, UK: Cambridge University Press, 1988.

Hale, J. R. *Renaissance Europe*. Berkeley: University of California Press, 1977.

Hamilton, G. V. *A Research in Marriage.* New York: Medical Research Press, 1929.

Hanawalt, Barbara A. *"Of Good and Ill Repute": Gender and Social Control in Medieval England.* New York: Oxford University Press, 1998.

————. *The Ties That Bound: Peasant Families in Medieval England.* New York: Oxford University Press, 1986.

Harbage, Alfred, ed. *William Shakespeare: The Complete Works.* Baltimore: Penguin Books, 1969.

Henderson, Katherine Usher, and Barbara F. McManus. *Half Humankind.* Urbana: University of Illinois Press, 1985.

Hensley, Jeannine, ed. *The Works of Anne Bradstreet.* Cambridge, MA: Harvard University Press, 1967.

Herlihy, David. *The Black Death and the Transformation of the West.* Cambridge, MA: Harvard University Press, 1997.

Herlihy, David, ed. *Medieval Culture and Society.* New York: Harper Torchbooks, 1968.

Hinkle, Beatrice M. "Marriage in the New World," in *The Book of Marriage.* Ed. Hermann Keyserling. New York: Harcourt, Brace & Co., 1926.

Hofstadter, Richard. *Social Darwinism in American Thought.* Boston: Beacon Press, 1955.

Howe, Quincy, ed. *Selected Sermons of St. Augustine.* New York: Holt, Rinehart and Winston, 1966.

Hrdy, Sarah Blaffer. *Mother Nature: A History of Mothers, Infants, and Natural Selection.* New York: Pantheon Books, 1999.

————. *The Woman That Never Evolved.* Rev. ed. Cambridge, MA: Harvard University Press, 1999.

Hufton, Owlen. *The Prospect Before Her: A History of Women in Western Europe, 1500–1800.* New York: Vintage Books, 1995.

Huizinga, Johan. *The Autumn of the Middle Ages.* Trans. Rodney J. Payton and Ulrich Mammitzsch. Chicago: University of Chicago Press, 1996.

————. *Erasmus and the Age of Reformation.* New York: Harper Torchbooks, 1957.

Hull, Suzanne W. *Chaste, Silent, and Obedient.* San Marino, CA: Huntington Library, 1982.

————. *Women According to Men.* Walnut Creek, CA: AltaMira Press, 1996.

Hunter, David G., ed. *Marriage in the Early Church.* Minneapolis: Fortress Press, 1992.

Jacquart, Danielle, and Claude Thomasset. *Sexuality and Medicine in the Middle Ages.* Princeton, NJ: Princeton University Press, 1985.

James, Henry. *The Golden Bowl.* Oxford: Oxford University Press, 1983.

Johnson, Paul. *A History of Christianity.* New York: Touchstone, 1976.

Jukes, Adam. *Why Men Hate Women.* London: Free Association Books, 1993.

Juvenal. *The Sixteen Satires.* Trans. Peter Green. New York: Penguin Books, 1967.

Key, Ellen. *Love and Marriage.* New York: Knickerbocker Press, 1912.

Kazin, Alfred, ed. *The Portable Blake.* New York: Viking Press, 1968.

Keen, Maurice. *Chivalry.* New Haven, CT: Yale University Press, 1984.

Kelly, John. *The Great Mortality.* New York: HarperCollins, 2005.

Ker, W. P. *Epic and Romance: Essays on Medieval Literature.* New York: Dover Publications, 1957.

Keuls, Eva C. *The Reign of the Phallus: Sexual Politics in Ancient Athens*. Berkeley: University of California Press, 1985.

King, Margaret L. *Women of the Renaissance*. Chicago: University of Chicago Press, 1991.

Kirshner, Julius, and Suzanne F. Wemple, eds. *Women of the Medieval World*. Oxford: Basil Blackwell, 1987.

Laqueur, Thomas. *Making Sex: Body and Gender from the Greeks to Freud*. Cambridge, MA: Harvard University Press, 1990.

Lasch, Christopher. *Haven in a Heartless World: The Family Besieged*. New York: W. W. Norton, 1977.

———. *Women and the Common Life: Love, Marriage, and Feminism*. New York: W. W. Norton, 1997.

Laslett, Peter. *Family Life and Illicit Love in Earlier Generations*. Cambridge, UK: Cambridge University Press, 1977.

La Tour-Landry, Geoffroy de. *The Book of the Knight of La Tour Landry*. Ed. G. S. Taylor. London: John Hamilton Ltd., 1906.

Lea, Henry. *Superstition and Force*. New York: Barnes & Noble, 1996.

Lecky, W. E. H. *History of European Morals*. New York: George Braziller, 1955.

Lefkowitz, Mary R., and Maureen B. Fant. *Women's Life in Greece and Rome*. 2nd ed. Baltimore: Johns Hopkins University Press, 1992.

Leites, Edmund. *The Puritan Conscience and Modern Sexuality*. New Haven, CT: Yale University Press, 1986.

Lemay, Helen Rodnite, trans. *Women's Secrets: A Translation of Pseudo-Albertus Magnus's* De Secretis Mulierum *with Commentaries*. Albany: State University of New York Press, 1992.

Lewis, C. S. *The Allegory of Love*. New York: Oxford University Press, 1958.

Liddell, Henry George and Robert Scott. *A Greek–English Lexicon*. Oxford: Clarendon Press, 1968.

Lovejoy, Arthur O. *The Great Chain of Being: A Study of the History of an Idea*. New York: Harper Torchbooks, 1960.

Lucas, Angela M. *Women in the Middle Ages: Religion, Marriage and Letters*. New York: St. Martin's, 1983.

Luhmann, Niklas. *Love as Passion: The Codification of Intimacy*. Trans. Jeremy Gaines and Doris L. Jones. Stanford, CA: Stanford University Press, 1982.

Luther, Martin. *Luther's Works*. Vol. 45, *The Christian in Society II*. Ed. Walther I. Brandt. Philadelphia: Fortress Press, 1962.

———. *Luther's Works*. Vol. 54, *Table Talk*. Trans. Theodore G. Tappert. Philadelphia: Fortress Press, 1967.

Mackenzie, Henry. *The Man of Feeling*. New York: W. W. Norton, 1958.

Malinowski, Bronislaw. *The Sexual Life of Savages in North-Western Melanesia*. New York: Eugenics Publishing Co., 1929.

Marcus, Steven. *The Other Victorians*. New York: Basic Books, 1966.

Marinella, Lucrezia. *The Nobility and Excellence of Women and the Defects and Vices of Men*. Trans. Anne Dunhill. Chicago: University of Chicago Press, 1999.

Martin, Thomas R. *Ancient Greece*. New Haven: Yale University Press, 1996.

Maus, Katharine Eisaman. *Four Revenge Tragedies*. Oxford: Oxford University Press, 1995.

243

McManners, John, ed. *The Oxford History of Christianity.* Oxford: Oxford
    University Press, 1993.
McNeill, John T., and Helena M. Gamer. *Medieval Handbooks of Penance.* New
    York: Columbia University Press, 1990.
Meeks, Wayne A., ed. *The HarperCollins Study Bible: New Revised Standard
    Version.* New York: HarperCollins, 1993.
Menefee, Samuel Pyeatt. *Wives for Sale: An Ethnographic Study of British Popular
    Divorce.* Oxford: Basil Blackwell, 1981.
Milton, John. *Paradise Lost* and *Paradise Regained.* Ed. Christopher Ricks. New
    York: New American Library, 1968.
Mitchell, Stephen. *The Gospel According to Jesus.* New York: HarperPerennial, 1993.
Montaigne. *The Complete Essays.* Trans. Donald M. Frame. Stanford, CA:
    Stanford University Press, 1965.
Morgan, Lewis Henry. *Ancient Society.* Tucson: University of Arizona Press, 1995.
Muncy, Raymond Lee. *Sex and Marriage in Utopian Communities:
    Nineteenth-Century America.* Baltimore: Penguin Books, 1974.
Murray, Jacqueline, ed. *Love, Marriage, and Family in the Middle Ages.* Toronto:
    Broadview Press, 2001.
Newman, Barbara. *From Virile Woman to WomanChrist.* Philadelphia: University of
    Pennsylvania Press, 1995.
Nohl, Johannes. *The Black Death: A Chronicle of the Plague.* Trans. C. H. Clarke.
    Yardley, PA: Westholme Publishing, 2006.
Noonan, John T. *Contraception.* New York: Mentor-Omega Books, 1967.
Okin, Susan Moller. *Women in Western Political Thought.* Princeton, NJ: Princeton
    University Press, 1979.
O'Neill, Nena, and George O'Neill. *Open Marriage.* New York: Avon Books, 1972.
Orlin, Lena Cowen. *Private Matters and Public Culture in Post-Reformation
    England.* Ithaca, NY: Cornell University Press, 1994.
Ovid. *The Art of Love and Other Poems.* Trans. J. H. Mozley. 2nd ed. Cambridge,
    MA: Harvard University Press, 1979.
Ozment, Steven. *The Age of Reform, 1250–1550.* New Haven, CT: Yale University
    Press, 1980.
———. *Ancestors: The Loving Family in Old Europe.* Cambridge, MA: Harvard
    University Press, 2001.
———. *The Bürgermeister's Daughter.* New York: HarperPerennial, 1996.
———. *Flesh and Spirit.* New York: Viking, 1999.
———. *Magdalena and Balthasar.* New Haven, CT: Yale University Press, 1986.
———. *When Fathers Ruled: Family Life in Reformation Europe.* Cambridge, MA:
    Harvard University Press, 1983.
Pagels, Elaine. *Adam, Eve, and the Serpent.* New York: Vintage Books, 1989.
———. *The Origin of Satan.* New York: Vintage Books, 1995.
Patterson, Cynthia B. *The Family in Greek History.* Cambridge, MA: Harvard
    University Press, 1998.
Payer, Pierre J. *The Bridling of Desire: Views of Sex in the Later Middle Ages.* Toronto:
    University of Toronto Press, 1993.
———. *Sex and the Penitentials.* Toronto: University of Toronto Press, 1984.
Plato. *Dialogues.* Ed. J. D. Kaplan. New York: Pocket Books, 1950.

Plutarch. *Moralia* IV. Trans. Frank Cole Babbitt. Cambridge, MA: Harvard University Press, 1936.

————. *Essays*. London: Penguin Books, 1992.

Pomeroy, Sarah B. *Goddesses, Whores, Wives, and Slaves*. New York: Pantheon, 1995.

Power, Eileen. *Medieval People*. London: University Paperbacks, 1963.

Power, Eileen, trans. *The Goodman of Paris*. London: George Routledge & Sons, 1928.

Quasten, Johannes et al., eds. *Ancient Christian Writers: St. Augustine*. Trans. John Hammond Taylor. New York: Newman Press, 1982.

Quasten, Johannes, and Walter J. Burghardt, eds. *Ancient Christian Writers: St. Jerome*. Trans. Charles Christopher Mierow. New York: Newman Press, 1963.

Quasten, Johannes, and Joseph C. Plumpe, eds. *Ancient Christian Writers: Tertullian*. Trans. William P. Le Saint. New York: Newman Press, 1951.

Ramsey, Lee C. *Chivalric Romances*. Bloomington: Indiana University Press, 1983.

Reay, Barry. *Popular Cultures in England, 1550–1750*. London: Longman, 1998.

Rider, Catherine. *Magic and Impotence in the Middle Ages*. Oxford: Oxford University Press, 2006.

Ridley, Matt. *The Red Queen: Sex and the Evolution of Human Nature*. New York: HarperPerennial, 2003.

Robinson, Jane. *Women Out of Bounds*. New York: Carroll & Graf, 2002.

Rogers, Katharine M. *The Troublesome Helpmate: A History of Misogyny in Literature*. Seattle: University of Washington Press, 1966.

Ruggiero, Guido. *Binding Passions: Tales of Magic, Marriage, and Power at the End of the Renaissance*. Oxford: Oxford University Press, 1993.

Rummel, Erika, ed. *Erasmus on Women*. Toronto: University of Toronto Press, 1996.

Russell, Bertrand. *Marriage and Morals*. New York: Liveright, 1970.

Russell, Jeffrey Burton. *Witchcraft in the Middle Ages*. Ithaca, NY: Cornell University Press, 1972.

Rybczynski, Witold. *Home: A Short History of an Idea*. New York: Penguin Books, 1986.

St. Ambrose. "The Relationship Between Adam and Eve," in *The Human Couple in the Fathers*, trans. Thomas Halton. New York: Pauline Books & Media, 1999.

St. Augustine. *Concerning the City of God against the Pagans*. Trans. Henry Bettenson. New York: Penguin Books, 1972.

————. *Confessions*. Trans. Garry Wills. New York: Penguin Books, 2006.

————. *On Free Choice of the Will*. Trans. Anna S. Benjamin. New York: Library of Liberal Arts, 1964.

————. "The Good of Marriage," in *Marriage in the Early Church*. Ed. David G. Hunter. Minneapolis: Fortress Press, 1992.

————. Saint Augustine. "Different Roles and Equal Zeal in Conjugal Chastity," in *The Human Couple in the Fathers*, trans. Thomas Halton. New York: Pauline Books & Media, 1999.

St. Jerome. *The Nicene & Post-Nicene Fathers*. Vol. 6. Grand Rapids, MI: Wm. B. Eerdmans, 1996.

————. Letters of St. Jerome, Vol. 1. *Ancient Christian Writers 33*. New York: Newman Press, 1963.

Salisbury, Joyce, ed. *Sex in the Middle Ages*. New York: Garland, 1991.

Sanders, E. P. *The Historical Figure of Jesus*. New York: Penguin Books, 1995.

Scott, George Ryley. *Curious Customs of Sex and Marriage.* London: Senate, 1995.

Shakespeare, William. *The Complete Works.* Baltimore, MD: Penguin Books, 1969.

Shelton, Jo-Ann. *As the Romans Did: A Sourcebook in Roman Social History.* New York: Oxford University Press, 1988.

Shepherd, Simon, ed. *The Women's Sharp Revenge.* New York: St. Martin's Press, 1985.

Shorter, Edward. *The Making of the Modern Family.* New York: Basic Books, 1975.

Sinclair, Alison. *The Deceived Husband.* Oxford: Clarendon Press, 1993.

Singer, Irving. *The Nature of Love.* Vol. 1, *Plato to Luther.* 2nd ed. Chicago: University of Chicago Press, 1984.

———. *The Nature of Love.* Vol. 2, *Courtly and Romantic.* Chicago: University of Chicago Press, 1966.

———. *The Nature of Love.* Vol. 3, *The Modern World.* Chicago: University of Chicago Press, 1987.

Spenser, Edmund. *Poetical Works.* Ed. J. C. Smith and E. De Selincourt. Oxford: Oxford University Press, 1970.

Stone, Lawrence. *The Family, Sex, and Marriage in England, 1500–1800.* Abridged ed. New York: Harper Torchbooks, 1977.

Stopes, Marie C. *Married Love.* New York: Eugenics Publishing Co., 1931.

Strong, James, *New Strong's Exhaustive Concordance of the Bible: King James Version.* Nashville: T. Nelson, 1995.

Summers, Montague, trans. *The Malleus Maleficarum of Henrich Kramer and James Sprenger.* New York: Dover Publications, 1971.

Suggs, M. Jack et al., eds. *The Oxford Study Bible.* New York: Oxford University Press, 1992.

Symons, Donald. *The Evolution of Human Sexuality.* Oxford: Oxford University Press, 1979.

Tacitus, P. Cornelius. *The Annals and the Histories.* Trans. Alfred John Church and William Jackson Brodribb. New York: Barnes & Noble, 2005.

Tannahill, Reay. *Sex in History.* Rev. and updated ed. Chelsea, MI: Scarborough House, 1992.

Taylor, G. Rattray. *Sex in History.* New York: Harper Torchbooks, 1970.

Tertullian. *The Ante-Nicene Fathers,* 4. Grand Rapids, MI: Wm. B. Eerdmans, 1994.

———. *Ancient Christian Writers* 13. New York: Newman Press, 1951.

The Bible: Authorized King James Version. Oxford: Oxford University Press, 1998.

The Torah: A Modern Commentary. Ed. W. Gunther Plaut. New York: Union of American Hebrew Congregations, 1981.

Tiger, Lionel. *Men in Groups.* New York: Vintage Books, 1970.

Ulrich, Laurel Thatcher. *Good Wives: Image and Reality in the Lives of Women in Northern New England, 1650–1750.* New York: Vintage Books, 1980.

Vives, Juan Luis. *The Education of a Christian Woman.* Trans. Charles Fantazzi. Chicago: University of Chicago Press, 2000.

Von Campenhausen, Hans. *The Fathers of the Latin Church.* Trans. Manfred Hoffman. Stanford, CA: Stanford University Press, 1964.

Waller, Willard. *The Old Love and the New: Divorce and Readjustment.* Carbondale: Southern Illinois University Press, 1967.

———. *The Family: A Dynamic Interpretation.* New York: Holt, Rinehart and Winston, 1938.

Walster, Elaine, and G. William Walster. *A New Look at Love*. Reading, MA: Addison-Wesley, 1978.

Webber, Everett. *Escape to Utopia: The Communal Movement in America*. New York: Hastings House, 1959.

Weinstein, Donald, and Rudolph M. Bell. *Saints and Society*. Chicago: University of Chicago Press, 1982.

Weir, Alison. *Eleanor of Aquitaine: A Life*. New York: Ballantine, 2001.

Wells, H. G. *The Outline of History*. Vol. 1, *Prehistory to the Roman Republic*. Garden City, NY: Garden City Books, 1920.

———. *The Outline of History*. Vol. 2. *The Roman Empire to the Great War*. Garden City, NY: Garden City Books, 1920.

Westermarck, Edward. *The History of Human Marriage*. London: Macmillan and Co., 1903.

Wickham, Chris. *Framing the Early Middle Ages*. Oxford: Oxford University Press, 2005.

Wiesner, Merry E. *Women and Gender in Early Modern Europe*. 2nd ed. Cambridge, UK: Cambridge University Press, 2000.

Wilcox, Donald J. *In Search of God and Self: Renaissance and Reformation Thought*. Prospect Heights, IL: Waveland Press, 1987.

Wills, Garry. *Papal Sin: Structures of Deceit*. New York: Doubleday, 2000.

———. *Saint Augustine*. New York: Viking, 1999.

Williams, Marty, and Anne Echols. *Between Pit and Pedestal: Women in the Middle Ages*. Princeton, NJ: Markus Wiener Publishers, 1994.

Xenophon. IV. *Oeconomicus*. E. C. Marchart, O. J. Todd. Loeb Classical Library. London: Harvard University Press, 1997.

Zacks, Richard. *History Laid Bare: Love, Sex, and Perversity from the Ancient Etruscans to Warren G. Harding*. New York: HarperCollins, 1994.

Zeldin, Theodore. *An Intimate History of Humanity*. New York: HarperPerennial, 1994.

WEB SITES

Euripides. *Iphigenia at Aulis*. Trans. Edward P. Coleridge. http://etext.library. adelaide.edu.au/e/euripides/ip_aulis/. January 14, 2008.

Hesoid. "Works and Days." Tufts University web site. http://www.perseus.tufts.edu/cgi-bin/ptext?lookup=Hes.+WD+1. January 14, 2008.

Livy. "History of Rome, Book 1: The Earliest Legends." University of Virginia web site. http://etext.virginia.edu/etcbin/toccernew2?id=Liv1His.sgm&images= images/modeng&da. January 14, 2008.

Schaff, Philip. *History of the Christian Church*. The Electronic Bible Society. http://www.ccel.org/print/schaff/hcc1/titlepage. January 21, 2008.

Index

PHOTOGRAPH BY FRANS DE WAAL, AUTHOR OF *OUR INNER APE*

This photograph of two copulating bonobos was taken by Frans de Waal. Bonobos and chimpanzees, which are related to each other, are our closest primate relatives. They are also known as the "make love, not war" primates, as they show very little violence and lots of sex. It used to be thought that face-to-face sex was uniquely human.